Networked News, Racial Divides

Against conventional wisdom, pervasive Black-White disparities pair with vitriolic public conversation in politically progressive communities throughout America. *Networked News, Racial Divides* examines obstacles to public dialogues about racial inequality and opportunities for better discourse in mid-sized, liberal cities. The book narrates the challenges faced when talking about race through stories about communities struggling with K–12 education achievement gaps. Media expert Sue Robinson applies Bourdieusian field theory to understand media ecologies and analyze whose voices get heard and whose get left out. She explores how privilege shapes discourse and how identity politics can interfere with deliberation. Drawing on network analysis of community dialogues, interviews with journalists, politicians, activists and citizens, and deep case study of five cities, this reflexive and occasionally narrative book chronicles the institutional, cultural, and other problematic realities of amplifying voices of all people, while also recommending strategies to move forward and build trust.

Sue Robinson holds the Helen Franklin Firstbrook Professor of Journalism research chair in the School of Journalism and Mass Communication at University of Wisconsin-Madison, where she teaches and researches digital technologies and information authority in journalism studies. Robinson is widely published, has won many grants and awards – including the Krieghbaum Under-40 Award – and consults for newsrooms, school districts, and other organizations. She worked as a reporter for thirteen years before entering academia.

T0384715

Communication, Society and Politics

Editors

W. Lance Bennett, University of Washington
Robert M. Entman, The George Washington University

Politics and relations among individuals in societies across the world are being transformed by new technologies for targeting individuals and sophisticated methods for shaping personalized messages. The new technologies challenge boundaries of many kinds – between news, information, entertainment, and advertising; between media, with the arrival of the World Wide Web; and even between nations. Communication, Society and Politics probes the political and social impacts of these new communication systems in national, comparative, and global perspective.

Other Books in the Series

(continued after the Index)

Networked News, Racial Divides

*How Power and Privilege Shape Public Discourse
in Progressive Communities*

SUE ROBINSON

University of Wisconsin-Madison

CAMBRIDGE
UNIVERSITY PRESS

CAMBRIDGE
UNIVERSITY PRESS

University Printing House, Cambridge CB2 8BS, United Kingdom

One Liberty Plaza, 20th Floor, New York, NY 10006, USA

477 Williamstown Road, Port Melbourne, VIC 3207, Australia

314–321, 3rd Floor, Plot 3, Splendor Forum, Jasola District Centre, New Delhi – 110025, India

79 Anson Road, #06–04/06, Singapore 079906

Cambridge University Press is part of the University of Cambridge.

It furthers the University's mission by disseminating knowledge in the pursuit of education, learning, and research at the highest international levels of excellence.

www.cambridge.org
Information on this title: www.cambridge.org/9781108419895
DOI: 10.1017/9781108304405

© Sue Robinson 2018

This publication is in copyright. Subject to statutory exception and to the provisions of relevant collective licensing agreements, no reproduction of any part may take place without the written permission of Cambridge University Press.

First published 2018

Printed in the United States of America by Sheridan Books, Inc.

A catalogue record for this publication is available from the British Library.

ISBN 978-1-108-41989-5 Hardback
ISBN 978-1-108-41232-2 Paperback

Cambridge University Press has no responsibility for the persistence or accuracy of URLs for external or third-party internet websites referred to in this publication and does not guarantee that any content on such websites is, or will remain, accurate or appropriate.

This book is dedicated to my mother and best friend,
Gloria P. Robinson,
whose incredible strength and resourcefulness
have been my inspiration.

Contents

Figures

Tables

Boxes

Acknowledgments

First and foremost, I want to thank Cambridge University Press, editors Sara Doskow, Claudia Bona-Cohen, and Julie Hrischeva, as well as the series editors, Lance Bennett and Robert Entman, the board, copy editor Brian Black, and anonymous reviewers for their suggestions and for helping to make this book as good as it could be.

Next, I want to give a shout-out to the nonprofit, nonpartisan Kettering Foundation and its members, whom I met in 2014. The Foundation is a research organization interested in enabling citizens to participate more fully in solving communities' problems. Being connected with them meant an immediate real-world application to all of this. It is not an understatement that I would not have been able to finish this book in a timely manner without their partnership. In particular, I'd like to thank Paloma Dallas, Paula Lynn Ellis, Alice Diebel, David Holwerk, and Maura Casey for their high-level feedback and general kindness. In addition, I'd like to thank the group of reporters and engaged citizens via Martin Reynolds at the Maynard Institute for Journalism who helped me revise the recommendations that we are sending to newsrooms across the country. Also, Kettering Foundation served as a collaborator in the research for a section in Chapter 2 as seen in the table on roles in the emergent media ecology.

I used parts of an article published in Taylor & Francis' *Journalism Studies* journal for Chapter 5 on legitimation strategies. That 2015 article is titled "Legitimation Strategies in Journalism: Public Storytelling about Racial Disparities." I thank *Journalism Studies* for allowing us to republish some of that article here.

The amazing art on the book cover was done by artist and graphic designer Claire Michelle Miller of Madison, Wisc., whom I met through the Simpson Street Free Press, a nonprofit youth organization that trains kids to be researchers and journalists and seeks to resolve K–12 achievement disparities.

In other acknowledgments: The Minority Student Achievement Network, run by Madeline Hafner, became my partner in understanding these racial achievement disparities as well as identifying cities across the country that met my criteria. I am happy to call Madeline my friend. In addition, I'd like to give a shout-out to all the superintendents in MSAN to whom we talked; they were all so forthcoming in the important work they are doing in these districts. The Graduate School at University of Wisconsin-Madison gave me some resources to fund different phases of the project, and the School of Journalism and Mass Communication supported this project in myriad ways as well. In addition, more than 120 citizens (parents, journalists, bloggers, Facebook commenters, activists, community leaders, superintendents, school officials, city politicians, administrators, teachers, and others) took the time to sit down with me and chat about race – never an easy topic to talk about. The fact that I am a White academic made these conversations awkward sometimes. These people gave their trust, and I feel honored that they talked to me. Kaleem Caire, TJ Mertz, John Matthews, Matt DeFour, Dr. Rev. Alex Gee, Rev. Everett Mitchell, John Odom, Derrell Connor, Ananda Mirilli, Jennifer Cheatham, and Shakil Choudhury in particular spent time making sure the information in here is accurate. A special shout-out to Jonathan Gramling, Paul Fanlund, Katie Dean, Zoe Sullivan, Nathan Comp, John Smalley, Pat Schneider, Matthew DeFour, Judy Davidoff, Karen Lincoln Michel, Brennan Nardi, Pat Dillon, and all the other journalists I met who were committed to "staying in the room." During Spring 2016, 14 UW-Madison students took a chance on a new service-learning class that was the result of the findings from this book. They were very forthcoming in their feedback, and I thank them for participating.

Someone had to read parts of this manuscript besides me (and my research team) and that dubious honor fell to Lucas Graves, Rachelle Winkle-Wagner, Seth Lewis, Wilson Lowrey, Nikki Usher, Matthew Powers, Chris Anderson, and Matthew Carlson. Rodney Benson read the entire thing – and parts of it twice – and gave me amazing feedback, and Lewis and Carlson were huge supporters from conception to completion. My gratitude extends to my colleagues within the University of Wisconsin-Madison who helped with various parts of the conceptualization or publication as well: Robert Asen, Shawnika Hull,

Hemant Shah, Lewis Friedland, Kathleen Culver, Dhavan Shah, Doug McLeod, Hernando Rojas, Chris Wells, Kathy Cramer, Julie Petrokubi, Karyn Riddle, Lindsay Palmer, Michael Wagner, Young Mie Kim, and the late James Baughman. Thanks to Janet Buechner, Lisa Aarli, and Rowan Calyx in the front office of SJMC for helping me with the logistics of grants, reimbursements, and graduate students on the project. Beth Horstmeier transcribed interviews on deadline and with incredible accuracy given how some of them were done in noisy coffee shops.

A long list of UW graduate students contributed to the data collection in some way – from the first phase documenting Madison's whole media ecology to literature reviews to interviews: Jordan Foley, Mark Mederson, Michael Mirer, Cathy DeShano, Emily Eggleston, Mitchell Bard, Linda Pfeiffer, Ashley Hinck, Cara Lombardo, German Alvarez, Mitchael Schwartz, and Mary Sussman. I add to this list two of the most competent undergraduates I have ever had the pleasure to work with: Tyriek Mack and Alexa Grunwaldt. I fully expect them both to do great things. Ho Young Yoon, who was a graduate student at the time of data collection, was instrumental in helping me design and execute the network analysis portion of the project. Plus, he was extremely patient with me, helping me to learn a number of software programs and then coding thousands of pieces of copy (along with Mitchael Schwartz) and drawing the maps and tables in Chapters 2 and 3. Proofreader extraordinaire (and SJMC graduate student) Catasha Davis copyedited with a very critical eye. Graduate student K. C. Councilor helped me turn the data into the service-learning class I mention in the conclusion. And last but definitely not least, I'd like to thank the "Dream Team" comprising Meredith Metzler and Caitlin Cieslik-Miskimen who worked with me for two years on this project. In addition to the copious amount of data collection, in-depth interviews, and analyses we did during Summer 2015, they gave me professional-level editing of the book. They are amazing scholars.

So many of my friends have had to listen to me throughout this process – some every day – and a whole slew of people brainstormed titles. I can't list everyone but you know who you are. Thank you, friends.

A very special dedication goes to Dr. Shawnika Hull, now of George Washington University, who pushed me on my journey to understand my own White privilege. She also stepped in to facilitate two focus groups for me so that conversation could be open and less awkward for parents. She is a wonderful friend and brilliant colleague.

Finally, I dedicated this book to my amazing mother but I want to give a shout-out to my dad, Samuel Robinson, as well. I've rarely met an individual so talented in so many areas, and I have tried to emulate his work ethic in my life. My love and husband, Dr. Robert Asen, is that rare partner who both understands and appreciates not only academic life but also communication theory in particular. His support both professionally as a colleague at the University of Wisconsin-Madison and personally at home have been essential to the completion of this book. My smart and insightful stepdaughter Simone helped brainstorm possible titles for the book. Finally, I acknowledge my little one, Zachary, who is my joy and gets me through every day.

PART I

I

Introduction

A Plea for Progressives to "Stay in the Room"

When Kaleem Caire arrived back to his hometown of Madison, Wisc., in 2010 after working for President Obama on the Race to the Top education plan, he found a community little changed from the one he'd left years prior – at least in terms of the opportunities available to people of color.[1] He, his wife, and his five children – two girls and three boys – were African American. Yet, there in that midsized, college-dominated city, the achievement disparities between White, Black, and Brown people were some of the worst in the United States. African American and Latino students trailed their White counterparts at all education levels in areas such as reading test scores. One in every two Black males in Madison were failing to graduate high school in four years – compared to a graduation rate of 88 percent for their White counterparts. The situation seemed to get worse every year as more and more African Americans, Hispanics and other minorities enrolled in the local schools; minority groups comprised a majority of the Madison schools' population. The thought of raising his kids in that environment dismayed the new head of the Urban League of

---

[1] A note about terminology: I have elected to use the more inclusive "people of color" as well as "Black," "White," "Brown" people in addition to more specific labels such as "African American" or "Hispanic" and "Latino" throughout this book (even as I honor that all of these terms encompass lots of different ethnicities and heritages). I am capitalizing these labels as a way to draw attention to race delineation. Please also note that this book focuses explicitly on Black-White (and sometimes Brown) relations, leaving out the many other racial dynamics in the cities to have more room to dive more deeply into what is happening. (In truth, this book is written for White people primarily.) As a White person still on her own racial journey, I am sure I've made a lot of mistakes and perhaps even offended people here and there. I am open to hearing about it so that I may continue my own awareness.

Greater Madison and he was ready to effect change in a real way. While he was away, people had been working on the problem; committees had been formed, reports had been written. But political stalemate, financial uncertainty, inertia, and an unwillingness to redirect resources away from other student groups for 20 percent of the student population stymied any major solutions from being implemented. Caire rolled up his sleeves and set to work.

In September 2011, Kaleem Caire won a planning grant to develop a publicly funded charter school called Madison Preparatory Academy that would educate Black and Latino boys in grades 6–12. After much research, Caire had landed on what he considered to be the best alternative to the public schools. Madison Prep was modeled after Chicago Preparatory Academy and a variety of other charter schools across the country that seemed to be meeting the needs of Black children where public schools were failing. His first proposal (which changed several times over the year) at first excluded girls in order to focus on Wisconsin's Black boys, who ended up in prison more frequently than in any other state. The students would wear uniforms, attend school for longer hours, and participate in summer learning activities. It would cost the district an additional $4 million over the course of five years.[2] It wasn't perfect, but Caire thought it was a stab at something, an experiment in a place that seemed to him to be badly in need of new ideas.

Caire needed the approval of the 2011 Madison Metropolitan School District's seven-member Board of Education (BOE), made up of White, older progressives with the exception of one Black male. The BOE represented Madison voters (mostly White), not Madison kids (now a majority minority) and had historically had strong connections to the local teachers' union. He also knew he needed the community of Madison behind him. The capital city of nearly 250,000 skewed liberal – indeed, it liked to brag about itself as the birthplace of the Progressive Party. Madison regularly appeared on "Best City" lists for its friendly community, livable environment, world-class education, bike paths, dog parks, and many other metrics. Its White citizens imagined themselves to be community oriented, volunteered in their kids' schools, and donated to charity. If White people did not encounter many people of color during their commute to the university or their law office at the Capitol, they enjoyed hearing several

---

[2] This number would get pared down after a private donation and other changes came about to about $2.7 million over the course of five years (the exact figure varies depending on the source).

languages spoken and many considered themselves color-blind. And these White residents were well off, with an average household income of $61,000 and ranked as having the highest concentration of PhDs in the country.

Yet Madison, like many places in the world, harbored implicit biases and enacted institutionally racist policies. Cops picked up Black teens at a rate six times that of White teens. Employers passed over Black applicants such that the unemployment rate for Black people was 25.2 percent compared to just 4.8 percent for White people in 2011. Even the schools were disciplining Black children more harshly and frequently than the White kids, with a suspension ratio of 15 to 1.[3] And though many White people in town would bristle at the idea that such an intellectually progressive place could harbor such racial problems, the Black people I talked to for this book – without exception – described a segregated city where hostile environments were the norm for people of color.[4] Caire knew he had an uphill battle, not only in behind-the-scenes negotiating with school officials, but also in the public realm. He knew he'd encounter resistance and suspicion and defensiveness: He just wanted people to "stay in the room" to hear him out.

The proposal immediately generated controversy and a raging public debate ensued – borne out in local news outlets, education blogs, Facebook, and other social media. The Urban League of Greater Madison appealed for public support in YouTube videos, showing charts filled with achievement gap metrics. Local activists debated it in popular blogs with one linking to dozens of reports full of research evidence. Reporters covering the proposal wrote articles full of meeting logistics and he-said/she-said "evidence." Hundreds of Madison citizens commented on Facebook posts and news articles, railing against Madison Prep or persuading BOE members to give the charter school a try, relaying personal stories, quoting experts, or citing blog posts. Caire spent much of his time posting upcoming hearings or newly released reports on charter schools on his Facebook page, emailing out messages that were picked up by blogs or local media, and answering phone calls from reporters.

On one level this book documents the story of Caire, Madison Prep, and the aftermath as it unfolded in the public sphere. As a White, liberal

---

[3] These statistics were compiled in a dramatic report by the Wisconsin Council on Children and Families released in 2013: Erica Nelson and Lawrence Torry Winn, "Race to Equity: A Project to Reduce Racial Disparities in Dane County" (Wisconsin Council on Children and Families, 2013), http://racetoequity.net/.

[4] Check out Madison365 for more context on how Black and Brown people in Madison feel and fare, http://madison365.com/.

professor at the University of Wisconsin-Madison as this narrative took shape, I had a front row seat to the onslaught of vitriolic commentary and stilted debate that occurred in the news media, on Facebook, on Twitter, and in the blogosphere. I read all of Caire's public Facebook, Twitter, and blog posts and the intense discussions that followed. I watched the hearings where parent after parent talked about the marginalization of their children in the school systems and then I saw these same parents' experiences discounted by other speakers. I noted the meeting-driven, he-said/she-said coverage in the local media. And overall, I became intrigued at the ineffective communicative patterns I saw, especially how important voices in the discussion about the achievement gap were ignored, suppressed, or completely absent. I began documenting how community information circulated on the issue via different media – social, traditional, and other. I was particularly interested in the quality of the material that was flowing so quickly, so voluminously, and wondered: how can public content about significant racial issues reflect inclusive, credible, meaningful information that could create healthier deliberation?

I began looking at other similar suburban-microcosms like Madison – Cambridge, Mass., Chapel Hill, N.C., Ann Arbor, Mich., and Evanston, Ill. – all of which were close to major universities, suffered under noxious racial achievement disparities, and were committed to resolving them. And all of them were hyperliberal, even progressive, and yet still had difficulty navigating the tricky discourse around race. In all of them, I and my research team found intense, ongoing public dialogues about the gaps between White people and Black and Brown people, combined with frustration and confusion about why things have not improved much, a lot of defensiveness, and a keen desire to "do better." In all of them, we found excellent, well-meaning journalists whose coverage of disparities consistently failed to meet the expectations and hopes of many in and those supporting marginalized communities. In all of them, we found community leaders, activists, and would-be politicians writing in blogs and Facebook, to bypass media in posts that often ignited healthy debate even as they also advanced political careers for those ensconced in the dominant White progressive hegemony, shifted power networks, and helped amplify conversations that had once been private. This book explores how we can improve public dialogues about race in liberal cities that should be better at such conversations.

On a deeper level, this book portrays a grand theoretical view of what's happening with evolving media ecologies and the public information exchange at the local community level during the digital age. The conversation about how new technologies network our social, political, economic, and other lives is well underway. Despite the optimism that digital networks will diffuse power through entrenched structures, scholarly evidence has shown how online networks act as echo chambers for the powerful. In these spaces, offline inequalities not only persist but are exacerbated in digital spaces.[5] This book joins that dialogue and takes up where those studies leave us, grappling with how new social-media tools are reconstituting these networks and how power flows through these information-exchange structures. Using case studies from across the nation, my main goal is to examine whether journalists and other content producers can adapt reconstituted networks for new conversations, in keen consideration of the existing infrastructure governed as it is by dominant power constructs, embedded hegemony, and long-established institutions. To do this, I document the emerging media ecology for Madison, Wisc., and the roles taking shape within it. I will use field theory (from sociologist Pierre Bourdieu) to help me explain the power structures within that ecology via the overlapping fields of information-exchange (journalism, education). And I will use some light network analysis as a methodology to help me visualize the ecology.

In this work I reveal meaningful connections, identify key influencers, and uncover the ways in which the scaffolding of the information structure can be manipulated to incorporate marginalized voices. I argue that entrenched identity constructs in these liberal cities prevent the healthy heeding and other necessary components of trust building for true deliberation. Those seeking to promote an alternative message use social-media networks to bypass mainstream journalists in order to spread their messages, build trust, and gain social and political capital. But, they can be stymied by their own isolation in the network or come up against mainstream ideological forces. In these progressive or highly liberal places in particular, the political landscape served to hamper rather than ameliorate conditions for discussions. This is ironic, given that one of the stalwart tenets of a progressive ideology is a commitment to freedom of the press and to the free flow of ideas in civil society. Healthy community and vibrant democracy, progressives believe, depend upon open communication. Yet many White people who thought of themselves as social-justice advocates

---

[5] boyd, *It's Complicated: The Social Lives of Networked Teens* (New Haven: Yale University Press, 2014); Matthew Hindman, *The Myth of Digital Democracy* (Princeton: Princeton University Press, 2008); Manuel Castells, *Communication Power* (Oxford: Oxford University Press, 2013).

Box 1.1 An interlude: The timeline of Madison Prep and its aftermath

- Summer 2010: Kaleem Caire works with the Urban League of Greater Madison on a proposal for an all-boys charter school run by the Madison Metropolitan School District (MMSD) for high school. In August, *The Capital Times* newspaper writes an article about the plan.
- Fall 2010: Caire hosts a large kickoff planning meeting for the school, asking for input from nearly three dozen community members on the details of the proposal. Several task forces are created to work on different aspects of the proposal.
- December 2010: The MMSD Board of Education (BOE) hears the initial proposal. It would be all-boys, they would wear uniforms, classes would be all day and through the summer.
- January 2011: The MMSD BOE asks follow-up questions of Caire on the proposal.
- February 2011: Madison Prep gets sponsorship from two BOE members, including the Black president of the board at the time, James Howard, to move Madison Prep forward into a more detailed plan. Caire begins work on a federal planning grant application. During this same time period, protests erupt at the state Capitol as hundreds of thousands of people turn out to condemn Gov. Scott Walker's assault on public unions, including school teachers. The Madison Teachers' Union is dealt a devastating blow as Act 10 takes away its collective bargaining power.
- March 2011: The MMSD BOE voted 6 to 1 to approve that $225,000 grant application. Caire puts together a team of leaders for the school, embarking on numerous meetings to persuade key influencers in the city of Madison Prep's merits.
- Summer 2011: Caire changes his proposal multiple times in response to critique from the Madison Teachers' Union and BOE members. For example, the school went from being all-boys to co-ed, and he relents on demanding that all teachers be nonunion (holding strong on the mandate that the school's counselors and social workers be of color).
- September 2011: Caire wins the planning grant. He closes a meeting to discuss Madison's achievement disparities to media

Box 1.1 (cont.)

and receives much pushback from local progressives and journalists.

- December 19, 2011: The BOE hears public input for several hours before voting no to Madison Prep, 5 to 2. A follow-up motion to extend discussion of Madison Prep gets rejected as well. Caire vows to try to open it as a private school.
- March 2012: Superintendent Dan Nerad announces he will step down and leave Madison.
- April 2012: Arlene Silveira, who had opposed Madison Prep, wins reelection to the BOE, but Trek Bicycle Inc. executive Mary Burke (who was going to give Madison Prep $2.5 million to offset per-pupil expenditures and make the school more palatable to the BOE) won a seat. Two years later Burke ran against Wisconsin Gov. Scott Walker for governor (and lost).
- June: 2012: Nerad's $12.4 million plan to address Madison's achievement disparities gets chopped. The BOE passes a $4.4 million in initiatives (most of which merely enhanced those already in place).
- January 2013: A primary race to replace BOE member Maya Cole becomes intense as a Latina, Ananda Mirilli, challenges two long-time White progressive activists in the city – Sarah Manski (whose husband was a leader in Progressive Dane) and TJ Mertz, a blogger and education history professor (also a member of Progressive Dane).
- February 2013: Manski announces the day after she won the primary, with Mertz coming in second, that she was actually moving to California. People in the city cry foul with some hinting that the announcement was purposefully delayed until after the vote as an orchestrated move to keep a person of color who supported Madison Prep off the board.
- March 31, 2013: The BOE election is held with Mertz uncontested on the ballot. Despite a write-in campaign for Mirilli, Mertz wins.
- Spring 2013: BOE hires Jennifer Cheatham, a new superintendent who comes from Chicago with a major initiative to resolve K–12 racial gaps.

Box 1.1 (cont.)

- October 2013: The Wisconsin Council on Children and Families release the "Race to Equity: A Baseline Report on the State of Racial Disparities in Dane County" that shows Madison's county to be among the worst in the nation on many metrics, including employment, education, and criminal justice.
- December 2013: *The Capital Times* invites African American Rev. Alexander Gee to write a front-page column about his experiences as a Black man in Madison. This column is followed by another one by African American Michael Johnson. Also, a White BOE member who had voted against Madison Prep wrote a mea culpa, describing himself as "swimming in the water of White privilege."
- February 2014: The first meeting of what would become a movement called "Justified Anger" is held with eight hundred people coming together to talk about race in Madison. The next few years followed dozens of forums, training initiatives for White people in social justice, and other initiatives in the community. The Evjue Foundation, which owns half of *The Capital Times*, donates Justified Anger $20,000 in May 2014. The media organization joins with Wisconsin Public Radio to hold another forum on race in Madison, moderated by award-winning journalist Keith Woods from National Public Radio.
- April 2014: *The Capital Times* announces a dedicated website called "Together Apart" to aggregate stories about race. It includes a history of African Americans in Madison.
- September 2014: Superintendent Cheatham implements a new discipline policy in the schools, replacing a zero-tolerance program that disproportionately affected students of color.
- March 2015: An 18-year-old biracial man named Tony Robinson who is unarmed is killed by a White Madison cop. Protests erupt.
- June 2015: The Evjue Foundation awards another $150,000 to Justified Anger.
- Summer 2015: The founders of Madison 365 begin fundraising for a news site about communities of color and issues of race. A Kickstarter campaign nets $10,000 and they go online in August 2015.

became defensive and hostile when forced to confront how White privilege had informed liberal policies, such as in the public schools, and led to exacerbated disparities. Though rich, deliberative conversations were happening on digital platforms in public spaces in most of these cities, many of them existed in isolated silos of talk away from the eyes and ears of major policymakers – and this effect is exacerbated in cities with decreasing media coverage. Essentially I am arguing that progressive ideologies become doxic (in field theory language) in the information-exchange fields. And those who practice progressivism in these places are governed so closely by this doxic mentality that they fail to see how exclusive the politics can be when exercised according to established norms of a place. That is, the thought leaders in these cities have accumulated so much political and civic capital through their networks that they can dictate what information circulates – and how it gets circulated. In the conclusion, however, rather than advocating for radical revolution, I consider how a careful recommitment to the ideal of progressivism with digital tools like social media and an understanding of networked, mediated ecologies can build the necessary social capital to shift these problematic dynamics.

Here, it may be useful to unpack the term "progressive" politics as it is employed in this book. In Wisconsin, almost 20 percent of its residents identified as "progressive," and it still had a small organization (called Progressive Dane) that ran campaigns. The label "progressive" emerged in all of my datasets in all the other cities as well. Conceptually, progressivism stems from the early-1900s Progressive Era of American politics. The excesses of capitalism, which emphasized individual economic success, were reined in by reforms that emphasized collective democratic governance and the revitalization of middle-class workers.[6] The foundation of this concept was that "Progressives were not revolutionists, it was also an attempt to work out a strategy for orderly social change."[7] Progressivism focuses on "improving the lives of others" and presumes that "human beings were decent by nature, but that people's and society's problems lay in the structure of institutions."[8] Social stratification and inequality were not predetermined by biology, history, or some other ontological

---

[6] Richard Hofstadter, *The Progressive Movement, 1900–1915* (Englewood Cliffs, N.J.: Prentice-Hall, 1963); Lynn D. Gordon, *Gender and Higher Education in the Progressive Era* (New Haven: Yale University Press, 1990).

[7] Hofstadter, *The Progressive Movement, 1900–1915*, 3.

[8] Aldridge D. P., "Of Victorianism, Civilizationism, and Progressivism: The Educational Ideas of Anna Julia Cooper and W.E.B. Du Bois, 1892–1940," *History of Education Quarterly* 47(4)(2007): 443, doi.org/10.1111/j.1748-5959.2007.00108.x.

category, but were historically contingent circumstances that could be remedied by the appropriate political reforms within the existing framework of socio-political action. In the midst of these political reforms, schooling practices took center stage as the site of social, political, and economic change. To many progressive educators, traditional educational models that presumed students to be passive recipients of information were wrongheaded approaches that didn't prepare students for successfully navigating civic life.[9] What followed was a child-centered pedagogy that emphasized equipping children with the democratic tools to become active participants in the learning process and in their communities.[10]

The problem with this model has been that these child-centered pedagogical practices were carried out in the midst of deep racial segregation. Leading progressive thinkers in education at the time made little to no mention of the Black experience in America and presumed that their colorblind approaches were sufficient.[11] This emphasis on shifting away from an individual student focus to a more communitarian educational paradigm meant that predominantly White communities would focus on predominantly White problems. The works of Black scholars like Carter Woodson and W. E. B. Du Bois made such failures more salient, emphasizing the unique social location of Black children in predominantly White spaces. In this progressive model of education, Black students were being "prepared to 'begin the life of a White man'," yet were "completely unprepared to face the harsh realities of a segregated labor market and a society saturated with prejudice and discrimination. Black students who wanted to pursue journalism, for instance, were trained how to edit a paper like *The New York Times*, 'which would scarcely hire a Negro as a janitor'."[12] Furthermore, the colorblind approach of progressivism preaches tolerance, but largely eschews proactive forms of racial reconciliation in the development of educational policies, as scholars have seen in

---

[9] John Dewey, *Democracy and Education* (Simon & Brown, 1916); Jeffrey Aaron Snyder, "Progressive Education in Black and White: Rereading Carter G. Woodson's Miseducation of the Negro," *History of Education Quarterly* 55(3)(August 1, 2015): 273–93, doi:10.1111/hoeq.12122.

[10] Jeffrey Mirel, "Old Educational Ideas, New American Schools: Progressivism and the Rhetoric of Educational Revolution," *Paedagogica Historica* 39(4)(2003): 477.

[11] Aldridge, "Of Victorianism, Civilizationism, and Progressivism: The Educational Ideas of Anna Julia Cooper and W. E. B. Du Bois, 1892–1940"; Snyder, "Progressive Education in Black and White."

[12] Snyder, "Progressive Education in Black and White," 280–281, citing Carter G. Woodson's *Miseducation of the Negro*.

Houston,[13] Raleigh-Durham,[14] and New Orleans.[15] These dynamics become all too clear in the story of Caire and Madison Prep, as well as the other racially segregated, liberal hubs examined in this book. For those who practice this kind of politics, this exercise transcends votes and signs, and achieves paradigm status, a way of life, and an identity; in field theory terms, we would call this governing belief system a kind of "doxa,"[16] which I will define more comprehensively shortly. And for those who wish to challenge the status quo in these places, the question becomes what is the best way to counter all of this and strive for change? Leverage networks and various kinds of capital to work within the progressive doxa or call for a revolution? All of this is important to think about as we move through the cases and the public's discussion of K–12 achievement disparities.

As a progressive liberal myself, I believe in funding our public schools, paying teachers more, increasing government safety nets such as welfare programs, social security, and other programs, and reforming institutions to making them more democratic with more engaged citizens. I've long considered myself "racially aware" and knew enough to know we were not in the "postracial" America so many championed after President Obama's election in 2008. However, as a White person who grew up in a tiny, seacoast town in a northeastern state with very few people of color, I had had little experience talking about race until college, and I interacted with very few people whose skin looked different than mine. Until I embarked on this book, my White privilege occupied all of me with nary an awareness of its presence. This venture parallels my own racial journey, as I moved beyond the recognition of my White privilege and sank into what my racial stake means for my research. Peppered with personal memoir, the book at hand relates my uncomfortable experiences during interviews as reflective of the paths these progressive cities will have to take to better facilitate community conversations about race. From the

[13] Karen Benjamin, "Progressivism Meets Jim Crow: Curriculum Revision and Development in Houston, Texas, 1924–1929," *Paedagogica Historica* 39(4)(2003): 457.

[14] Karen Benjamin, "Suburbanizing Jim Crow The Impact of School Policy on Residential Segregation in Raleigh," *Journal of Urban History* 38(2)(2012): 225–246 doi:10.1177/0096144211427114.

[15] Adrienne D. Dixson, Kristen L. Buras, and Elizabeth K. Jeffers, "The Color of Reform Race, Education Reform, and Charter Schools in Post-Katrina New Orleans," *Qualitative Inquiry* 21(3)(2015): 288–299, doi:10.1177/1077800414557826.

[16] See for example this exploration of identity in political action: Katherine J. Cramer, *The Politics of Resentment: Rural Consciousness in Wisconsin and the Rise of Scott Walker* (Chicago; London: University of Chicago Press, 2016).

first awkward conversations where I was called out for failing to build trust with the parents whom I wanted to participate in my focus groups, to the final interviews when my connection with informants merely highlighted how long my own journey will be, a strong reflexivity informs this work. I contended with my stubborn conceptions regarding proper engagement in an interview, for example, and the dominating role of researchers in focus groups. Even as I interviewed Caire and others about the charter school, I also felt conflicted about the idea of such a venture and was sympathetic (but not convinced) to the arguments in opposition. I struggled, in other words, with the very power dynamics and identity confliction I uncover and interrogate in these communities.

Next I am going to explain the concept of media ecology, as I am using it, and talk about how I found the framework important in the documentation of how social media was changing the manner in which information flowed. Media ecology privileges different media and their production actors as well as helps to isolate information flows – making it very useful to snapshot how digital technologies might be creating new roles and transforming mediated relationships. However, media ecologists do not seem to be in the forefront of power dynamics that dictate how and why those mediated relationships play out in the ways that they do. For this, I turned to another conceptual framework – Pierre Bourdieu's field theory – which helps explain the particular structuring of these ecologies in these mid-sized, progressive communities. I explain the field contribution to this book after the next section on ecology.

EMERGENT MEDIA ECOLOGIES AND THE NETWORKED FIELDS WITHIN THEM

A Media Ecology

In early 2010, Kaleem Caire was still in Washington D.C. working on President Barack Obama's Race to the Top school reform initiative. But he and his wife Lisa Peyton Caire were contemplating a move back to the Midwest with their kids. Caire had grown up on Madison's south side and graduated from the University of Wisconsin-Madison in 2000. It was home and family beckoned. At the time, I was looking around for a new project and after spending a lot of time studying how newsrooms worked and citizens acted given digital technologies, I was keen to understand the more macro structures at work in those organizational and individual productions. I formed a research team and we started taking an accounting of all the media players in our community of Madison, Wisc., to see how it was being reconstituted by digital platforms in information exchange. I wanted to somehow show its media ecology – which I define as the constellation of news organizations, blogs, social media, and other mediated content platforms that connect us in local community. It quickly became clear that we had to focus our efforts around a particular topical area such as politics or education because so many niche-oriented websites and blogs, hashtags, and Facebook group pages had emerged. Choosing education as our niche, we finished this in early 2011 – just as protests broke out at the Capital because of Gov. Scott Walker's assault on teacher and other public unions. By that time Caire had come back, become head of the Urban League, and introduced his proposal for the Madison Prep charter school. Though I had never researched race specifically, I knew racial achievement disparities in the K–12 schools would help us narrow in on an ecology and also reveal important moments of power differentials between those ideologically dominant and more marginalized groups of citizens. Plus the timing of K–12 racial disparities were right because Caire was just proposing Madison Prep. So my team recorded all the mainstream publications online and offline as well as the blogs, hashtags, public Facebook Group pages, and websites that produced anything at all on racial disparities, especially Madison Prep. And before we knew it, we had documented a media ecology. But what did that mean exactly?

The ecological argument builds on a biological metaphor (in terms of structure, evolution, and systems), and over nearly a century in sociology it has been applied to everything from urban settings to professions. For groundbreaking theorists such as Odum,[17] the metaphor forces an examination of the whole, especially at a time when academics were studying the phenomena piecemeal. At first, medium theorists Marshall McLuhan (of "medium is the message" fame) and, later, Neil Postman, postulated about the "study of media as environments."[18] Postman first formally[19] adapted the metaphor to communication systems in thinking about how

---

[17] Eugene Odum, "The New Ecology," *BioScience* 17(7)(1964): 14–16.

[18] Neil Postman, "The Reformed English Curriculum," in *High School 1980: The Shape of the Future in American Secondary Education*, by Alvin Eurich (New York: Pittman Publishing, 1970), www.media-ecology.org/media_ecology/.

[19] Postman acknowledged that Marshall McLuhan first thought about the metaphor for media in a letter McLuhan wrote to Clare Booth Luce in which he remarked "that it may be necessary for a culture to limit its use of some medium in the interests of promoting a balance in the media ecology." See: Neil Postman, "The Humanism of Media Ecology," *Proceedings of the Media Ecology Association* 1(2000): 13.

language, imagery, and other material ways of relating to each other constituted its own media ecology. In this school of thought about media ecology, the theoretical focus centered on the technologies of communication – in other words, the technical constructs of information.

But I am also interested in how sociologists co-opted the metaphor to understand how people and media were interconnected, using each other to create and recreate systems and structures in ecology-like ways. James Carey emphasized the ecological linking of citizens to each other as well as to an imagined national (and, ultimately, international) community through media.[20] As in biological ecologies, new communication technologies evolved the media ecology to be more fragmented as groups became more connected to their competitors, Carey wrote: "For example, each ethnic group had to define itself which meant each had to know, understand, compete, name, and struggle against other ethnic groups inhabiting contested physical and symbolic space."[21] In *Media Ecologies*, Fuller argued that media comprise the environment, but they do not make up a static scaffolding. I am using the two approaches together: not only does the interplay between media continually reshape the ecological environment (a Postman[22] postulation) but also the interactions between media and humans have the potential to express power relationships, create patterns of inequities, and subvert.[23]

For my purposes in trying to capture Madison's media ecology, I had to remember that all ecologies, therefore, are fluid and continually in flux – growing, pulsing, contracting in places, birthing new appendages, etc. Ecologies in general, though, are more concerned with a collective "species" (such as journalists but also all the other content producers working in relationships with the information flowing) than with individuals such as a single reporter. Media ecologists examine actors in relation to one another, as well as their role in the collective. Media ecology is about one's movement in a space as part of a complex system that entails networks of networks, linked within an amorphous system without discrete borders.[24]

---

[20] James W. Carey, "The Internet and the End of the National Communication System: Uncertain Predictions of an Uncertain Future," *Journalism & Mass Communication Quarterly* 75(1)(1998): 28–34.

[21] Ibid., 32.

[22] Carlos A. Scolari, "Media Ecology: Exploring the Metaphor to Expand the Theory," *Communication Theory* 22(2012): 204–225.

[23] Matthew Fuller, *Media Ecologies: Materialist Energies in Art and Technoculture* (Cambridge, Mass.; London: The MIT Press, 2007).

[24] Andrew Abbott, "Linked Ecologies: States and Universities as Environments for Professions," *Sociological Theory* 23(3)(2005): 245–374.

As open systems that depend on outside environments, ecologies evolve constantly and the actors within work together in synergetic ways but also in constant competition for resources. So looking at the information ecology we had laid out for Madison, Wisc., around education issues at a certain point in time during 2011–2012 I could see groupings of mainstream journalists, progressive bloggers, and education and other activists as regular Facebook posters. I could see from our documentation how new individual actors such as Caire, newly arrived from D.C., and others were creating new kinds of actor groups and changing the very nature of the ecology and how information was flowing through it. Even emails, memos, and other private correspondence that prior to social platforms never would have been widely distributed were now becoming of some consequence for the ecology.

But as I watched the story of Caire and Madison Prep unfold, I became intrigued at the other things that were happening. Veiled (and not-so-veiled) racism tainted, obscured, and dominated the flows of information and mediated bits of content. Internal fighting and past personal conflicts also seemed to influence postings, even news accounts. An individual's digital savvy propelled his or her commentary to prominence in the community dialogue. But even someone who seemed to be well positioned in the ecology in terms of relationships and resources didn't act or achieve in ways that we might expect, given that positionality. Why? The particular problem of the media ecology we had documented – that of K–12 racial achievement disparities – and my desire to also investigate these power relationships at work meant I needed a similarly robust theoretical framework to explain what was happening within the ecology. While media ecology provides a powerful metaphor for capturing information flows, it has somewhat less to say about the power dynamics that shape those flows. I landed on the conceptualization of journalism as a "field" – that is, a system made up of actors that is networked according to power relationships and social positions.

How Fields Structure Ecology

When Caire began the public discussion in Madison about the charter school for Black boys, he entered a media ecology with nesting information-exchange fields that included not only journalism but also content-producing influencers in the school system and in education in general. Two century-old media organizations, an alternative weekly, television networks, radio talk shows, ethnic news organizations, and a dozen or so blogs characterized journalism in this city. The field of education included the school-district administration and board of education, filled with progressives who were prolific as bloggers and Facebook commenters as well as adept at working large networks that encompassed social, professional, and civic spheres in the town. Spread across both of these interlocking fields were progressive politicians intent on keeping the status quo intact and activists aiming to dismantle it. Together they made up a large, complex information-exchange field that operated according to certain rules and helped maintain the status quo within a macro media ecology.

But let's step back a minute and just wrap our heads around the idea of fields within a media ecology. Stemming originally from the physical sciences, the sociological approach to field theory arose as a way to observe and analyze how political institutions work, control their environments, effect change, deal with interlopers, and evolve in society on a large scale.[25] Although several core threads of field theory exist, this book is most concerned with the work of French sociologist and philosopher Pierre Bourdieu, who thought of the field as comprising relational actors with strategic goals competing for dominance within a hierarchal structure.[26] Using Bourdieu as one main source, Neil Fligstein and Doug McAdam defined "strategic action fields" as "mesolevel social orders as the basic structural building block of modern political/organizational life in the economy, civil society, and the state."[27] In other words, action fields comprise the media ecology.

Fligstein and McAdam advanced Bourdieu's work into a more comprehensive offering that incorporated how actors' individual conceptualization of identity and construction of meaning direct their actions with a field. This idea of identity construction within a complex system of power relationships, organizational/institutional realities, and networks of producers and audiences fit with what I wanted to capture. In a significant application of field theory to immigration coverage in American and

---

[25] Neil Fligstein and Doug McAdam, *A Theory of Fields* (New York: Oxford University Press, 2012); John Levi Martin, "What Is Field Theory?" *American Journal of Sociology* 109(1)(2003): 1–49, doi:10.1086/375201.

[26] Pierre Bourdieu, "Intellectual Field and Creative Project," *Social Science Information* 8 (1969): 189–219; Pierre Bourdieu, *Distinction: A Social Critique of the Judgment of Taste* (Cambridge, Mass.: Harvard University Press, 1984); Pierre Bourdieu, *The Field of Cultural Production: Essays on Art and Literature* (New York: Columbia University Press, 1993); Pierre Bourdieu, "The Political Field, the Social Science Field and the Journalistic Field," in *Bourdieu and the Journalistic Field*, by Rodney Benson and Erik Neveu (Cambridge: Polity, 1995), 29–47; Pierre Bourdieu, *On Television* (New York: New Press, 1999).

[27] Fligstein and McAdam, *A Theory of Fields*, 3.

French news, Rodney Benson heralded the theory as a framework for understanding power relations in journalism.[28] He wrote that field theory

is crucially concerned with how media often serve to reinforce dominant systems of power. Yet compared to hegemony, the field framework offers the advantage of paying closer attention to distinctions in forms of power, how these may vary both within a society and cross-nationally, and how they might be mobilized for democratic purposes.[29]

Key concepts of field theory – the ones I will be most engaging with in this book – are doxa, habitus, path dependency, and capital. As I mentioned above, I think of doxa as one's paradigm from which one operates through life as a set of beliefs and "determines the stability of the objective social structures."[30] Habitus enacts doxa; that is, that which exercises one's way of seeing the world and enacts the relationships one has with it.[31] If doxa are the rules of the game, habitus is the practice.[32] Path dependency is essentially how what actions that were taken previously will help determine the direction of any new path. The successful utilization of these – doxa, habitus, and path dependency – can yield capital for an actor in the field. Capital can be social, political, economic, and also informational, which Bourdieu might consider "cultural" or "symbolic." And sometimes it can be all of these things at once. It is in essence a kind of currency used in a system of exchanges between parties. Furthermore, those in positions of power tend to wield forms of capital more and better than those who are not.[33] I am looking at only the public information-exchange world here, thinking about how one can gain or lose the ability to influence people through what they say in the media, post in a blog, or write in a Facebook status update. In this book, progressive ideology structured people's actions as actors – both those dominant and established as well as those challenging the status quo – spent and attained capital through their content production in public spaces.

[28] Rodney Benson, *Shaping Immigration News: A French-American Comparison* (Cambridge University Press, 2013).

[29] Ibid., 195.

[30] Cecile Deer, "Doxa," in *Pierre Bourdieu: Key Concepts*, by Michael Grenfell (Durham, UK: Acumen, 2008), 119–130.

[31] Karl Maton, "Habitus," in *Pierre Bourdieu: Key Concepts*, by Michael Grenfell (Durham, UK: Acumen, 2008), 49–65; Pierre Bourdieu and L. Wacquaint, *An Invitation to Reflexive Sociology* (Cambridge: Polity, 1992).

[32] This is paraphrased from Maton, 2008, p. 57.

[33] Robert Moore, "Capital," in *Pierre Bourdieu: Key Concepts*, by Michael Grenfell (Durham, UK: Polity, 2008), 101–117.

For the purposes of this book, my overarching media ecology is determined by the overlapping information-exchange fields of journalism and education:

Journalism: Bourdieu defined the field as being made up of reporters, officials, and activists (and other sources) and audience members, who act and react constantly as *agents* within an industry constrained by a series of organizational, institutional, political, social, and other forces. A combination of political, economic, cultural, and symbolic capital ensures a journalistic agent of its position in the field, which shifts constantly on the whims of everything from power plays to audience tastes to rising platforms to economic realities.[34] "Journalists are caught up in structural processes which exert constraints on them such that their choices are totally pre-constrained."[35] Their actions in the field tend to be "path dependent," which is the idea that previous actions will shape any new path. Once these paths are established, it is difficult to diverge from them, at least according to the neo-institutionalists.[36] Many press scholars have investigated the forces at work in the institution that shape reporters' habitus. For example, we know that in power indexing of sourcing, journalists are trained to reach out to experts and officials for stories. They fail to be inclusive.[37] Journalists as agents tend to define the parameters of any social problem via the "right" sources.[38] One could

---

[34] Several scholars have looked at how the press acts as part of a field, including: Monika Krause, "Reporting and the Transformations of the Journalistic Field: US News Media, 1890–2000," *Media, Culture & Society* 33(1) (January 2011): 89–104, doi:10.1177/0163443710385502; Bourdieu, "The Political Field, the Social Science Field and the Journalistic Field"; Rodney Benson, "News Media as a 'Journalistic Field': What Bourdieu Adds to New Institutionalism, and Vice Versa," *Political Communication* 23(2)(2006): 187–202, doi:10.1080/10584600600629802; Benson, *Shaping Immigration News.*

[35] Bourdieu, "The Political Field, the Social Science Field and the Journalistic Field," 45.

[36] Walter W. Powell, "Expanding the Scope of Institutional Analysis," in *The New Institutionalism in Organizational Analysis,* by Walter W. Powell and P. J. DiMaggio (Chicago: University of Chicago Press, 1991), 183–203; Benson, *Shaping Immigration News.*

[37] Stuart Allan, *Citizen Witnessing: Revisioning Journalism in Times of Crisis* (Polity, 2013); W. Lance Bennett, Regina G. Lawrence, and Steven Livingston, *When the Press Fails: Political Power and the News Media from Iraq to Katrina* (Chicago, Ill.; Bristol: University of Chicago Press, 2008); Harvey Molotch and Marilyn Lester, "News as Purposive Behavior: On the Strategic Use of Routine Events, Accidents and Scandals," *American Sociological Review* 9(1974): 107.

[38] Eric Darras, "Media Consecration of the Political Order," in *Bourdieu and the Journalistic Field,* by Rodney Benson and Erik Neveu (Cambridge: Polity, 2005), 156–173; Dominique Marchetti, "Subfields of Specialized Journalism," in *Bourdieu and the Journalistic Field,* by Rodney Benson and Erik Neveu (Cambridge: Polity, 2005), 64–82.

conceptualize this as a path-dependent phenomenon of habitus: that is, reporters have a hard time choosing different sources because of the practices established previously, the expectations that have developed in the newsroom, and the information capital that had been gained in the past by such behavior. The more built legitimacy, authority, and social capital a source, reporter, or news organization has accumulated according to the "rules" of the field, the more influential in terms of being quoted, getting something published, and receiving attention in the overall media ecology.

Education: Scholars have applied Bourdieu's conceptualizations such as habitus and social capital to school systems.[39] This field includes school officials and administrators, youth-oriented nonprofits, academic education experts, teachers, students, and parents, among others. Actors within the education field use information exchange to vie for position in the field and influence education policy.[40] Performance improvement can be achieved by tapping into relationships that generate rich social capital and offer access to the resources necessary to achieve success.[41] But field position can also be a major reason for academic disparities, according to some research. For example, Bourdieu and Passeron argued that students bring disparate levels of cultural capital to school from their home, where different economic and cultural conditions prepare kids unevenly for their position in the field.

Bourdieusian fields are hierarchal at their core, meaning the actors within them occupy certain positions according to their class, race, professional title, social networks, etc., and these fields in my progressive cities

[39] To name just a few: Pierre Bourdieu and Jean-Claude Passeron, *Reproduction in Education, Society, and Culture* (Beverly Hills, CA: SAGE, 1972); James G. Ladwig, "For Whom This Reform?: Outlining Educational Policy as a Social Field," *British Journal of Sociology of Education* 15(3)(1994): 341–363, doi:10.1080/0142569940150303; Annette Lareau, "Social Class Differences in Family-School Relationships: The Importance of Cultural Capital," *Sociology of Education* 60(2) (April 1987): 73–85; Wellington Samkange, "Decentralization of Education: Participation and Involvement of Parents in School Governance: An Attempt to Explain Limited-Involvement Using Bourdieu's Theory of Social Practice," *International Journal of Social Sciences & Education* 3(4)(2013): 1156–1169.

[40] Alan Daly and Kara Finnigan, "A Bridge between Worlds: Understanding Network Structure to Understand Change Strategy," *Journal of Educational Change* 11(2) (May 2010): 111–38, doi:10.1007/s10833-009-9102-5; Meredith I. Honig and Cynthia Coburn, "Evidence-Based Decision Making in School District Central Offices: Toward a Policy Research Agenda," *Educational Policy* 22(4) (2008): 578–608.

[41] Ricardo D. Stanton-Salazar, "A Social Capital Framework for the Study of Institutional Agents and Their Role in the Empowerment of Low-Status Students and Youth," *Youth & Society* 43(3)(2011): 1066–1109, doi:10.1177/0044118X10382877.

reflected these traits. In my case studies, some people wielded much more influence – such as being cited by others in public content – than others in terms of the public information available about the gap, whereas others worked more behind the scenes but their names rarely appeared in print. Still others used digital technologies to connect with niche publics, not caring whether their words echoed beyond that community, while several prominent bloggers in different cities each parlayed their writings into political candidacies that ultimately won them election to the school board or city council. Each individual occupied positions in the field according to his or her social, professional, and civic networks as well as how much decision-making power he or she held in the system. And most importantly for this book, journalists performed their jobs according to long-established field norms and routines that perpetuated the White-dominated, progressive-directed status quo.

This discussion evokes the dominant themes that run throughout this book. In order to appreciate how these fields work within a media ecology in a digital age, I will examine how authority, privilege, power, and trust are being exercised and used to promote and share information. Additionally, I analyze the way these forces work to persuade, influence, and inform various acting citizens in the public. In this book, I track these specific dimensions of the field, thinking about them as conceptual agents whose presence (and absence) manipulate the information flow within the overarching ecology. While field theory doesn't have much to say about "technologies" or information platforms per se, media ecology does. And while media ecology allows a broader capturing of who and what are determining information flows, field theory can help understand the why and how around the central power questions we have. Close scrutiny of the dynamics that shape how people communicate about issues of race in public, mediated spaces highlight how old roles of production such as journalists are adapting and how new roles such as bloggers and social-media posters are making an impact. More importantly, an understanding of these processes within these two nested frameworks can help us to overcome obstacles and employ strategies toward improving dialogue in the future.

AUTHORITY, PRIVILEGE, POWER, AND TRUST IN LOCAL MEDIA ECOLOGY

Years after the Madison Prep vote, Kaleem Caire was invited to talk about leadership at a Madison downtown event sponsored by the local progressive news organization, *The Capital Times*. In his remarks at the public library during a chilly November night in 2016, he touched on authority, privilege, power, and trust as he reminisced about the community dialogue around the charter school. He told the story of another local community leader, a White man named Steve Goldberg (executive director of CUNA Mutual Foundation and a well-known activist in the city) who addressed the large crowd at the December 19, 2011 hearing when the school board voted on the charter school. Caire said:

> I'll never forget it. He was very brief. He told the Board of Education, he said, "you know, you guys, sometimes to gain power and to gain respect, you have to be willing to give up power and give respect." And so I say to people who are asking how do we get more leaders of color into positions of power: "Even I. Even I have got to be willing to give up my authority so that someone else's authority can emerge. I've got to be willing to give respect to other leaders so that I can also gain respect but so that that respect that that other person can share with the rest of the world can show too."

For Caire, it is only when privilege, authority, and power are wielded in consideration of what the entire community needs that community trust can develop and thrive. Yet, authority, privilege, power, and trust manifest via doxa, social capital, and habitus; they are how an actor such as a journalist retains status in a field, moves position, and influences other actors. I could write four books each on authority, privilege, power, and trust, but that's not my aim. Instead, I wanted to think about them in play together within the grand case study of Madison, Wisc., and a series of micro case studies in other cities – Ann Arbor, Mich., Cambridge, Mass., Chapel Hill, N.C., and Evanston, Ill. By observing the interactions of authority, privilege, power, and trust, we can begin to understand how important their presence (and absence) are for public talk as well as to highlight how digital technological agents might help diffuse power structures in this information-exchange world.

Bourdieu[42] equated "authority" to symbolic capital because its possession depended on the social recognition that comes with political, economic, and other kinds of power. In press scholarship, authority is defined as "the power possessed by journalists and journalistic organizations that allow them to present their interpretations of reality as accurate, truthful, and of political importance."[43] Like Furedi, Foucault, and others,

---

[42] Pierre Bourdieu, "Social Space and Symbolic Power," *Sociological Theory* 7(1)(1989): 14–25.
[43] Anderson C.W., "Journalism: Expertise, Authority and Power," in *The Media & Social Theory*, by David Hesmondhalgh and Jason Toynbee (New York: Routledge, 2008), 250.

Matthew Carlson argues authority must be thought of as a relational concept such that it must be granted and accepted. In addition, he notes that authority depends upon its exclusion of others' articulations of knowledge.[44] He draws on Bourdieu's understanding of fields as existing in conjunction – embedded and overlapping, but also in competition and in synergy – with other fields, and suggests authority plays a central part in how actors in those fields relate to one another. Journalistic authority, writes Carlson, is something constantly negotiated with every new project, every new interaction between media organization and sources or audiences – especially as interactivity restructures the traditional hierarchy of influence among all the players of information flow.[45]

In education, authority discussions tend to revolve around the moral authority of a teacher or the authority a parent might have over her kids' schooling.[46] But I am interested in how might education researchers conceptualize authority as it relates to the schools' relationship with the community, particularly as it manifests in public spaces. Education has its own institutional dynamics and hierarchies that affect what gets said in the public sphere. Like journalism, education is facing its own authoritative challenges – and has since the time of philosopher and education theorist John Dewey, who wrote in 1936:

> We need an authority that, unlike the older forms in which it operated, is capable of directing and utilizing change and we need a kind of individual freedom unlike that which the unrestrained economic liberty of individual has produced and justified; we need, that is, a kind of individual freedom that is general and shared and that has the backing and guidance of socially organized intelligent control.[47]

This is such an appropriate statement for this work at hand, isn't it? But the question remains: how is this "individual freedom" playing out in a local community, especially in terms of authority? This will be a major engagement throughout this work.

[44] Matt Carlson and Seth C. Lewis, *Boundaries of Journalism* (New York: Routledge, 2015); Matt Carlson, *Journalistic Authority: A Relational Approach* (New York: Columbia University Press, 2017).

[45] This comes from Shoemaker and Reese. Pamela J. Shoemaker and Stephen D. Reese, *Mediating the Message: Theories of Influences on Mass Media Content* (White Plains, N.Y.: Longman, 1996).

[46] Bryan Warnick, "Parental Authority over Education and the Right to Invite," *Harvard Educational Review* 84(1)(2014): 53–71; Miriam Amit and Michael M. Fried, "Authority and Authority Relations in Mathematics Education: A View from an 8th Grade Classroom," *Educational Studies in Mathematics* 58(2)(2005): 145–168.

[47] John Dewey, "Authority and Social Change," in *John Dewey: The Later Works*, by Jo Ann Boydston, vol. 11 (Carbondale: Southern Illinois University Press, 1987), 137.

For Black people, authority is not as benevolent a topic as it might be for White journalists or educators, especially if we are talking about the authority that exists in institutions (like the schools and the press) that have historically marginalized them. Institutional racism abounds in both the schools and the press, which has been well documented. How would people of color, then, appreciate such authority? Many, many scholars have looked at the differences with which middle-class White people can approach an authoritative institution like the schools compared to someone whose skin is somewhat darker or whose economic class is somewhat lesser. One reason for the achievement gap might be the way in which families of different classes feel comfortable engaging with authorities. And communities of color have long been suspicious of mainstream information outlets where they rarely find positive representations of themselves. They themselves do not feel authoritative in these spaces, with these actors. Merely suggesting that people of color become active, show up in mainstream public spaces, and let their voice be heard does not account for the power dynamics at work that have created generations of intense distrust. This is in part because if authority is indeed a form of symbolic capital that derives from political or other kinds of capital, then people who do not have a ton of money, power, or influence historically in the progressive networks that govern information-exchange fields might find it elusive.

I want to spend some time talking about the role of trust in authority, privilege, and power. A complex concept, trust "is a psychological state comprising the intention to accept vulnerability based upon positive expectations of the intentions or behavior of another."[48] For my purposes, trust represents an essential element for the positionality of professional journalists in any local community information flow as well as an instrumental technique to attaining authority. Trust must be attained, like capital, and is something that can be gained and lost fluidly. Örnebring theorized the profession of reportage is authoritative because of its "trustworthiness," which is in turn a result of its autonomy and independence from faction.[49] Journalists answer a higher call than an individual operating as a single actor and take part in a collective movement regarding

---

[48] Denise M. Rousseau et al., "Introduction to Special Topic Forum: Not So Different After All: A Cross-Discipline View of Trust," *The Academy of Management Review* 23(3) (1998): 395.

[49] Henrik Örnebring, "Anything You Can Do, I Can Do Better? Professional Journalists on Citizen Journalism in Six European Countries," *International Communication Gazette* 75(1)(2013): 35–53.

community information, reporters from around the world told Örnebring. It is this sense of *societal* duty that engenders a kind of trust: "The straw-man citizen journalist is outside this collective, outside the system of shared knowledge and controls."[50] But this is basically a kind of institutional trust.

In public forums, trust takes on an additional role, a more social role.[51] Robert Asen examined school boards in Wisconsin to understand the components of healthy deliberation as it yields good decisions in public. His major point is that trust is essential to deliberation but must be done as part of a relationship and as a form of engagement between *individuals*. Without interaction between two actors, trust will not emerge. He writes:

When interlocutors craft a trusting relationship, they may address district issues efficaciously in making decisions about policy that may not thrill all stakeholders but nevertheless constitute reasonable decisions that holdouts can understand. When interlocutors do not enact trusting relationships, their deliberations break down, divisions harden, and recriminations abound. In especially troubling cases, the failure to build trusting relationships threatens the very possibility of deliberation itself.[52]

Asen holds a similar idea of trust as Carlson does of authority: Trust is a relational construct – something enacted through practice by individuals, something that can ebb and flow with new actors, new procedures, new relationship dynamics and over time (and I would add, dependent upon place or platform as well). Asen and other scholars have noted the following qualities as necessary in building trust for good dialogue: From Asen, flexibility, forthrightness, engagement, and heedfulness; from Byrk and Schneider, respect, competence, personal regard for others, and integrity;[53] and from Mayor, Davis and Schoorman, ability, benevolence, and integrity as well.[54] As with authority, others must perceive an individual as being trustworthy. And it develops and exists over time, offering not only a template from past interactions but also the opportunity for future relationship work. Hauser and Benoit-Barne write that trust is "a

[50] Ibid., 48.
[51] Robert D. Putnam, *Bowling Alone: The Collapse and Revival of American Community*, 1st edition (New York: Touchstone Books by Simon & Schuster, 2001).
[52] Asen, *Democracy, Deliberation & Trust*, 144.
[53] Anthony S. Bryk and Barbara Scheider, *Trust in Schools: A Core Resource for Improvement* (New York: Russell Sage Foundation, 2002).
[54] Roger C. Mayer, James H. David, and F. David Schoorman, "An Integrative Model of Organizational Trust," *Academy of Management Review* 20(1995): 709–734.

process that relies on the familiar in order to anticipate the unfamiliar."[55] This can be problematic if the past relationship eschewed trust or operated according to a paradigm of distrust, as we will see in my cases.

It is at this point we see how trust as a relational practice is inevitably caught up in issues of power and privilege. When two people come together to discuss publicly a racially charged issue such as an achievement gap, differing positions of vulnerability can inhibit a smooth exchange of information. I saw this over and over in the examples given from our participants for this book. We would have a working Black parent articulate a personal experience, afraid to be too specific lest her complaint become public and the school retaliate against her school-aged son. She didn't trust that the officials would allow her to be forthright without repercussions. She told of experiences in the schools or with the press where promises were made and broken. She spoke of distrust specifically and refused to speak to reporters or to attend hearings. This parent existed in the same space as one of our elected school board members with a popular blog, friends in high positions, and kids who did fine in the system – in other words, lots of political, civic, social, and symbolic capital. The school board member trusted the institution because the system had proven beneficial for him and his family. These different positions contain different levels of intimidation and risk for the actors. As Asen articulated, "explicit and implicit discursive norms may place uneven burdens on participants to justify their positions." Patti Lenard notes that "extending trust expresses a willingness to put oneself in a position of vulnerability" but "when one comes to feel vulnerable more globally, extending trust (and thereby exacerbating one's vulnerable condition) becomes more difficult and less likely."[56] This vulnerability stymies reciprocity in the trusting relationship. It also forestalls the willingness of someone in a risky position (or even a *perceived* risky position) to participate – especially in the public realm. Asen optimistically suggested that practicing the dimensions of trust he laid out – flexibility in a stance, forthrightness in dialogue, engagement with individuals and a heeding of ideology – in context and in conjunction would surely bolster overall trust and foster good deliberation. But my data suggest that even if an individual practices these qualities of trust, if the partners at the

[55] Gerard A. Hauser and Chantal Benoit-Barne, "Reflections on Rhetoric, Deliberative Democracy, Civil Society, and Trust," *Rhetoric and Public Affairs* 5(2002): 270.
[56] Patti T. Lenard, "Rebuilding Trust in an Era of Widening Wealth Inequality," *Journal of Social Philosophy* 41(2010): 81.

hearing or in the commenting sections hold a perception of their own vulnerability, no engagement will happen at all. This advances Asen's notion that trust is as much about the interaction as it is about any individual actions or perceptions.

Thus, we might hypothesize that even those marginalized must not only acknowledge their lack of trust and their feelings of vulnerability, but also attempt to overcome these feelings. Engage despite feeling vulnerable. Participate even in consideration of past injustice from the same parties. Is this a reasonable statement and expectation? In theory, perhaps, but in practice we are faced with an intractable problem – at least on the face of it. I suggest that making this statement results in what Nancy Fraser would call "status bracketing," which means moving forward with deliberation as if all the players were of the same social class, gender, race, distinction, etc.[57] Asen, Fraser, and Young all place the burden on those in positions of power to facilitate an open space for discussion.[58] Indeed, it is one of my contentions in this book that journalists in particular are in a unique position to develop neutral places for this kind of engagement to happen. News spaces online are a place to start the trust-building process. Yet, first the immense distrust that reigns between journalists and their communities must be overcome. And this can only be done through individuals – like superintendents or reporters – and not in the name of the institution or organization they represent, necessarily. In the stories we were told for this book, *individuals* were trustworthy; *institutions* were almost always not.

During my data collection, I witnessed journalists engaged in this "status bracketing" too (that is, assuming all of their sources operate under the same mantle of communication or information privilege), which brings me to my point and a major purpose of this book: how can journalistic spaces be used to build (and restore) trusting relationships? The story of one reporter's sourcing decisions exemplifies the problems that status bracketing can create in coverage of education issues. The news organization wrote a piece about the zero-tolerance policy of the school system for kids who make mistakes such as bringing alcohol onto school property. The reporter profiled a White middle-class honors student rather than a student of color to highlight how unreasonable the district's discipline policy was. Many in the Madison community believed this

[57] Nancy Fraser, "Rethinking the Public Sphere: A Contribution to the Critique of Actually Existing Democracy," *Social Text* 25/26(1990): 63.

[58] Iris Marion Young, *Inclusion and Democracy* (Oxford: Oxford University Press, 2000).

coverage spurred action on the part of the school board to revise the discipline policy for the district. The uneven school discipline implementation had existed for some time among Black students, and many in town described the reporter's choice of a White student to tell the story as somewhat racist: why not have done the piece using a Black student and highlighting the persistent disparities and systemic racism at work in the district's policies?[59] The reporter wrote in a special column how she couldn't get any students of color to go on the record but that the White student and her family offered both to be named and welcomed the coverage:

I would have happily written about either – and I'm pretty sure most reporters who know a good story would have also jumped at the chance. But you can't write an in-depth human-interest piece on the effect of school policy on minors without the buy-in of a minor and her family. ... There are lots of important stories that unfortunately get away because they need to be told from the inside out.[60]

Here, framing her decision in the color-blind cloak of *institutional* journalistic values (such as needing named sources), the reporter absolves herself of any responsibility to create a safer space for a family that would have had much more to lose in speaking up than the family that offered to speak. Furthermore, she discounts how much easier it is for a middle-class White family accustomed to advocating for themselves to advance their cause within a system run by people who look and operate like them. Even in childhood, White, middle-class people are encouraged to speak out, and know that the public sphere belongs to them.[61] Compare this to a family who has reason to distrust an innately biased system, one that offers their son a 50-percent chance of graduating on time, one that has long discounted and disadvantaged their children. Many people – particularly those of lower economic status – feel little empowerment to question authoritative institutions like the schools or the

---

[59] In fact, the superintendent told me that policy change had been well under way before the incident and ensuing coverage.

[60] Judith Davidoff, "Madland: Why Isthmus Wrote about the Expulsion of a 'White, Middle-Class Honors Student'," *Isthmus*, April 8, 2014, www.thedailypage.com/daily/article.php?article=42458.

[61] This too is documented in research. For example, sociologist Annette Lareau followed several families of different races and income around, documenting how those with more money tended to raise children better prepared to compete in a White, capitalist society because parents encouraged kids' engagement with coaches, doctors, and teachers, among other reasons. An excellent read: Annette Lareau, *Unequal Childhoods: Class, Race, and Family Life* (Berkeley, Calif.: University of California Press, 2011).

press. Should the reporter here have dealt with these authority, privilege, power, and trust realities in some way? Offering anonymity perhaps or creating a different kind of forum for that side of the story to come out? Of course!, you might argue. The issue, however, is complicated: this is a traditional reporter who abides strictly by norms that had been set in the field long before she took up pen and paper. She is merely reinforcing her position in the field and doing what any other reporter would have done. As someone who herself spent more than a decade in newsrooms as a traditional print reporter, I can tell you how entrenched reportorial protocols are, how conceptualizations of what constitutes credibility and truth are innate to the very identity of journalists, and how one's job security depended upon the reporter's exercising these essentially codified routines toward building authority. To break from the institution and act as an *individual* would counter her instincts for job security. My goal is to document the process of local-community information exchange in the digital age. That includes detailing the ways in which power structures shape that exchange, how field challenges are poking the establishment seeking change, and the constant field-domain boundary struggles over local-community knowledge.

DOCUMENTING FIELDS WITHIN ECOLOGIES

Documenting fields within a media ecology is tricky. Typical techniques by themselves would not begin to reach the three levels of analyses (micro-meso-macro) that I would need. I detail everything I did for this project in the appendix, but the gist involves a fairly new method called network ethnography, which combines quantitative network mapping with qualitative community ethnography, rich textual analysis, and in-depth interviews. "Network ethnography" is used as a way to observe a community in action by thinking about that community as a network and combining some light network analysis with qualitative techniques such as in-depth interviewing and textual analysis. Coined by Philip Howard in 2002, network ethnography offers a way to study a community that is also steeped in what Howard called "hypermedia organization" online, a way to consider in context not only what one is observing in the physical world but also what occurs virtually.[62] The method served as an effective

---

[62] Philip N. Howard, "Network Ethnography and the Hypermedia Organization: New Media, New Organizations, New Methods," *New Media & Society* 4(4)(December 1, 2002): 550–574, doi:10.1177/146144402321466813.

analytic device for C. W. Anderson's diagramming of the Philadelphia media world.[63] He employed some brief network analysis to determine who and what to study in the overarching ecology of his site – with great success. Similarly, in Madison, I was able to conduct some limited network analysis to demonstrate how the information-exchange relationships were becoming networked in the public realm. I used this information, which visually showed me the information flow (and which I will demonstrate in Chapters 2 and 3) and its major influencers, to direct me in the next phase of the study – in-depth interviews, community observation of hearings and meetings, and both content and textual analyses. In five case studies, I and various research teams conducted more than 120 interviews of major information players – journalists, bloggers, activists, and commenters – in addition to analyzing more than four thousand news articles, blog posts, Facebook updates, and their comments. I supplemented this data with three focus groups totaling 15 citizens from both Black and Brown communities to provide a unique perspective on those voices not in this public content stream as well as ten interviews with international leaders in communication about race.[64] All of the network maps depict Madison; the four other cities of Chapel Hill, Evanston, Ann Arbor, and Cambridge represent micro-case studies meant to corroborate and substantiate the Madison themes. In sum, I used network ethnography as a methodological technique to document an emergent media ecology and its information flow as well as how that ecology was structured hierarchically with action fields in a deep dive that is rarely performed in media studies.[65]

This method allowed me to tell the full story of one progressive city in the Midwest struggling with talking and writing about racial disparities in public mediated spaces. I tracked how its communicative ecology evolved over a period of 4–5 years by analyzing the fields within it. It is a story of distress, no doubt, as we learn of the seemingly inevitable obstacles that line the path toward improved racial justice dialogue and note how people's information-exchange strategies reflect domineering habits of ideology and history that make up the place's doxa. But it is also a

---

[63] Anderson C.W., *Rebuilding the News: Metropolitan Journalism in the Digital Age* (Philadelphia: Temple University Press, 2013).

[64] A complete description of what was done in terms of data collection and analysis appears in this book's Appendix.

[65] Frankly, because of the significant resources such an enterprise requires. This project consumed six years, the time of 18 student assistants, and a high methodological learning curve. More specifics can be found in the Acknowledgments and Appendix.

narrative meant to inspire as we witness the communicative changes in this city from the beginning anecdotes in 2011 to the 2015 disruptions that came with the brand new, provocative Madison365 website, significant new money from traditional institutions for a social movement, proactive hires of journalists of color, the thriving Black Lives Matter work, and other actions that in aggregate offer a much different environment for public talk and networked voices than had existed just a few years prior.

OUTCOMES AND OPPORTUNITIES WITHIN A MEDIA ECOLOGY

At its core, this book is concerned with how the journalistic field and its boundaries of performance can *change* at a meso level by looking at micro actions on the part of individual actors in relation to internal structural developments. By 2016, the information-exchange field in Madison, Wisc., looked very different from the one Caire entered in 2011, as a result of the communicative efforts of Caire and others around this issue. The interactive capabilities of the Internet – that is, the abilities of non-professional journalists, activists, citizen bloggers, and others to produce content and relay evidence alongside reporters – are innately changing the dynamics of our fields. Bourdieu argued that when a new actor performs in new ways within a field (i.e., assumes a new position), the entire field shifts to accommodate the new activity. Those previously dominant may become "outmoded."[66] He wrote: "As Einsteinian physics tells us, the more energy a body has, the more it distorts the space around it, and a very powerful agent within a field can distort the whole space, cause the whole space to be organized in relation to itself."[67]

New public spaces enabled by technologies within the overall media ecology abound – commenting spaces, forums, Facebook posts, blogs, Twitter, and other social-media platforms – and these spaces for information flow also represent opportunities for movement within these fields. Many scholars have expounded on how social-media platforms such as Twitter and Facebook are creating a networked culture in which informational authority is waning and new patterns of knowledge flow are emerging.[68] Shirky argued the "new ease of assembly" of information has meant

---

[66] Bourdieu, *The Field of Cultural Production*, 32.
[67] Bourdieu, "The Political Field, the Social Science Field and the Journalistic Field," 43.
[68] Yochai Benkler, *The Wealth of Networks: How Social Production Transforms Markets and Freedom* (Yale University Press, 2006); Manuel Castells, *The Rise of the Network Society: The Information Age: Economy, Society, and Culture Volume 1* (Chichester, West Sussex; Malden, Mass.: Wiley-Blackwell, 2009); Sue Robinson, "Journalism as

a new "ability to share, to cooperate with one another, and to take collective action, all outside the framework of traditional institutions and organisations."[69] This empowerment, posited Tapscott and Williams,[70] results in a more horizontal power distribution of information and could mean a mass collaboration of information production and exchange that leads to a more fruitful, efficient, and knowledgeable democratic society. People of color in particular have taken to digital outlets for expression, dialogue, the creation of counterpublics, and other connections, networking, and sharing. In her book characterizing the relationship between Black people and the media, Squires wrote:

The research and observations collected here suggest that people of African descent have launched internet initiatives in great numbers, and, perhaps, may be on the verge of having more control as individuals and as groups over this medium than any other since the use of paper and ink dominated mass public communications.[71]

Ideally, social-media platforms such as Facebook and Twitter could be used to change the power dynamics in any field, particularly for the field positions of marginalized groups. As Heinrich stated: "This is a sphere where hierarchies – at least in theory – do not exist."[72] It's not a giant leap to consider the minorities' growing use of social-media platforms might offer an opportunity for change. I am arguing that these new places of public commentary alongside journalism – sometimes disguised as journalism – offer opportunities for bridging communities, social action, and field change.

Of course, there are several problems with this assumption, not least of which is the digital divide that continues to plague cities such as those in our sample. Only half the Black and Brown parents in the Madison Metropolitan School District in my Wisconsin case study give the school an email that they check regularly. Some research has suggested subordinated cultures give up (or adapt) and rebuild their own field on the edges,

Process: The Labor Implications of Participatory Content in News Organization," *Journalism & Communication Monographs* 13(3)(2011): 138–210.

[69] Clay Shirky, *Here Comes Everybody: The Power of Organizing Without Organizations* (New York: Penguin Books, 2009), 20.

[70] Don Tapscott and Anthony D. Williams, *Wikinomics: How Mass Collaboration Changes Everything* (New York: Portfolio, 2010).

[71] Catherine Squires, *African Americans and the Media* (Cambridge England; Malden, Mass.: Polity, 2009), 277.

[72] Ansgard Heinrich, "What Is 'Network Journalism'?" *Media International Australia* 144 (1)(2012): 64.

away from the mainstream.[73] Another reality is the ways in which these communities' relate to technologies according to their position in their field, level of social and cultural capital, and "habitus." These factors limit the benefits of technology. For example, one study reinforced Bourdieu's contention that one's poor economic circumstances, inability to increase social and cultural capitals, and demoralizing habitus stymie a person's movement within the field.[74] Furthermore, these fields – journalism and education – operate according to a White majority paradigm whose systemic policies and insular professional and social networks tend to benefit majorities and reinforce marginalization.[75] In general, some scholars have offered a cautionary note to all the idealized rhetoric about the utopian world digital technologies may bring. For example, Beckett and Mansell point out that even with new spaces of flows engendering the possibility for egalitarian deliberation, the opportunities for rife misunderstanding also exist. "The new forms of journalism that are emerging today will not achieve their potential for enhancing a public service environment if the new opportunities are treated simply as a way to securing 'free' content to compensate for cutbacks." They recommend scholars critically approach research questions and sites of inquiry like the one I have here in Madison and to be particularly concerned with "power, its redistribution, and its consequences for those engaged in the production and consumption of news."[76]

In examining the effectiveness of communicative patterns in discussions about the achievement gap, this book offers insight into the mechanics of public information exchange at the community level in the digital age. It looks at the quality of the discourse and the barriers to good public talk, but also questions how the promises of digital communication are challenged when contentious issues arise. This book is divided into two parts. Part I provides the theoretical framework for the data in the aim of advancing the scholarly conversation around media ecology, field

---

[73] Michael Schwalbe et al., "Generic Processes in the Reproduction of Inequality: An Interactionist Analysis," *Social Forces* 79(2)(2000): 419–452, doi:10.1093/sf/79.2.419.

[74] Bourdieu, *Distinction*.

[75] Eduardo Bonilla-Silva, *Racism without Racists: Color-Blind Racism and the Persistence of Racial Inequality in America* (Lanham, Md.: Rowman & Littlefield, 2006); Gillborn D., "Education Policy as an Act of White Supremacy: Whiteness, Critical Race Theory and Education Reform," *Journal of Education Policy* 20(4) (2005): 485–505; Kinder D and L. Sanders, *Divided by Color* (Chicago: University of Chicago Press, 1996); Squires, *African Americans and the Media*.

[76] Beckett C. and R. Mansell, "Crossing Boundaries: New Media and Networked Journalism," *Communication, Culture & Critique* 1(2008): 92–104.

theory, and journalism. In the first chapter, I lay out how I want to document an emergent media ecology, explaining its structure using field theory, and delving deep into the major themes of information authority, privilege, trust, and power in mediated racial discourse within progressive places. I explain why marginalized voices have difficulty being heard and how those facilitating public discourse on race issues reify existing exclusive structures. In the end, who succeeds in getting their voice heard and their content seen depends upon how much symbolic information capital they have attained, their position in the field, and their choice of a posting platform. Often, the more visible their writing, the more influence they have. But this effect is mitigated by the actor's position in the field as well, and his or her practice of the progressive doxa in these case-study cities. Chapter 2 describes the emerging communicative ecology in Madison, Wisc. specifically. It explains how social media is reconstituting the ecology, who remains marginalized, and how communities and media are networked. It provides network maps of who is producing content in which channels. I argue that new roles are emerging in the reconstituted media ecology, and that each of these roles occupies networked positions of potential power in the fields that make up that ecology. This typology represents the early work we did on documenting the ecology. Also in Chapter 2 I frame out the notion of boundary work, and demonstrate how it throws up obstacles to successful public talk in journalism and other journalistic spaces. Boundary work offers a way to talk about how our community actors are working the public information-exchange field to be heard – or why they may try to become visible but have no luck. Chapter 3 shows how these roles play out in the information flow of Madison during my study period given social media and other kinds of digital production. I found, for example, how prolific blogging and posting for some in these cities built sufficient symbolic capital to lead to election to public office – political power. This chapter argues that how one can achieve information authority expands within these emergent ecologies. These three chapters demonstrate the process of local–community information exchange in the digital age, the ways in which power structures shape that exchange, how field challengers are poking the establishment seeking change, and the constant field-domain boundary struggles over local–community knowledge within a macro-mediated ecology.

For those readers less interested in the esoteric academic speak of ecologies and fields, skip ahead to Part II. These chapters apply my typology to these locales and shows how information moves within and between the journalism and education fields to constitute an overall media ecology. Chapter 4 reveals the boundary struggles of this landscape, both in the public content and in the interviews with the most prolific content-producing actors, including journalists, bloggers, and activists. I look at what inhibited good public discussion in Madison and in the four other liberal cities, specifically the role of White reporters and their institutional practices. For example, objectivity and other boundary struggles are both perceived and explicit obstacles inhibiting not only information exchange itself, but also the influence any information might have. Chapter 5 analyzes the strategies being employed to overcome these hindrances of information exchange and offers insight into what strategies appear to be successful and what makes others fail. I consider how people attempt to build information capital in this conversation. Those challenging dominant discourses call on alternative legitimation techniques such as experiential storytelling but lack the networks for effective amplification. I find three techniques of strategy prevail: repetition across and within platforms, the making of dynamic dialogues, and the taking advantage of the fluidity of public and private networks, particularly in the sense of border crossing. Finally, Chapter 6 explores the ways in which evolving networks of information exchange can substantially alter the way a field is working, and thus reconstitute the umbrella media ecology. It characterizes successful discourse and explores whether social media can alleviate problematic exchange. How might digital technologies be employed in the building of symbolic capital for individuals? While Chapter 6 is the most optimistic in the book, I also confront the themes of information authority, privilege, power, and trust as they change with new and old agents acting with digital technologies. I argue for a recommitment to progressive ideals as well as foundational tenets of journalism and suggest that reporters, bloggers, activists, and others who want to improve community dialogues tap into digital networks by way of offline connections to create the trusting, heeding kind of spaces necessary for deliberative exchange. This concluding chapter includes a series of recommendations for how those interested in producing content for public information exchange in such cities might approach that dialogue.

CONCLUSION

This book aims to tell a story of one community as it grapples with a constantly changing media environment, constrained by legacy organizations and their active boundary work, and reflective of the uncertain world of social media and blogs pushing new (and also redundant) inter-active content. Four other cities serve to corroborate the themes the macro case study revealed: all of the cities are highly educated but with a growing population of children in poverty, all have a majority White population but have schools made up of increasing diversity, and all have a keen commit-ment to progressive values such as good public schools. See Table 1.1 for a breakdown of these communities' demographics.

And yet all also report deep rifts around the issue of race, using words like "distrust" and "blind spots" and "defensiveness" to describe the communal racial climate. In Chapel Hill, one White politician in town said:

Chapel Hill is largely a liberal, even progressive community politically. So the debates that we had were almost never debates that were broken down along democrat or republican or even liberal or conservative lines. They were almost always between people who consider themselves politically liberal. The Black community certainly is aware of and critical of the ways in which the White liberal community in Chapel Hill can be dismissive of the Black community's concerns . . . The Black community can read between the lines when White readers try to portray something as good for all kids and not really listen to or acknowledge the specific concerns that the Black community had.

We heard versions of this throughout our cities. In Madison, Caire and others who supported Madison Prep jumpstarted [into the mainstream] a conversation that has yet to cease in this Midwestern city. They hoped to prevail, winning over the dialogue as well as positive votes for the charter school. By the end of the year of conversation in 2011, Madison Prep had become a symbol for those in the Black community, an indicator of whether they could trust Madison "to do the right thing." If it didn't pass, some suggested in interviews, if they all came out and told the town what was needed and the town didn't respond, well ... they knew just where they stood. Progressive Madison, indeed, they muttered. They were tired of the paternalistic attitude and wanted action.

Action, though, requires a culmination of forces. For example, it has traditionally required the networks of power to push for change and even give up power as well. As this book will argue, any individual's mobility within fields has been limited by his her historic position. Gender, class, and race in particular often characterize the ability to advance one's interests.[77] Describing gender, class, and race as the "results of processes

---

[77] Tom Meisenhelder, "Toward a Field Theory of Class, Gender, and Race," *Race, Gender & Class* 7(2)(2000): 76–95.

TABLE 1.1 *Case study demographics (2010–2013)*

Metrics	Cambridge	Chapel Hill	Ann Arbor	Evanston	Madison
Population	105,000	57,233	113,934	74,486	233,209
% White	62	69	70	61	76
% of Color	39	31	30	40	25
Major University	Harvard University, Massachusetts Institute of Technology	University of North Carolina– Chapel Hill	University of Michigan	Northwestern University	University of Wisconsin-Madison
Nearby City	Boston	Durham, Raleigh	Detroit	Chicago	Milwaukee, Chicago
School Population	5,955	11,800	16,600	High school: 2,875; elementary school: 6,825	23,600
% Students on Free & Reduced Lunch	44	21	19	HS: 39, ES: 39	44
Per Pupil Spending	27,163	10,734	13,614	HS: $11,817 (instructional), $21,606 (operational); ES: $8,358 (instructional), $14,471 (operational)	14,000

Metrics	Cambridge	Chapel Hill	Ann Arbor	Evanston	Madison
Population	105,000	65,700	117,770	75,658	243,000
% White	66	73	73	66	80
% of Color	34	27	27	34	20
University	Harvard, MIT	University of Chapel Hill	University of Michigan	Northwestern	University of Wisconsin-Madison
% White Students	36	58	57	HS: 48, ES: 44	51
% Students of Color	59	42	34	HS: 52, ES: 56	49
Nearby City	Boston	Durham	Detroit	Chicago	Milwaukee, Chicago
School Population	6,019	12107	17,104	3500 (high school), 5975	27,000
% Students on Free & Reduced Lunch	44	27	22	28	48
Per Pupil Spending	27,163	10,872	11,645	22,100	14,000
% White Students	39	52	55	44	44
% Students of Color	61	48	45	56	56

of field di-visioning and category formations,"[78] Meisenhelder applied Bourdieu's structuring of a field to understand why marginalized groups such as Black people or the poor have a hard time improving their position in the field:

> Domination also means that the dominant group has the symbolic capital and power necessary to produce a misrecognition of their dominance as natural and inevitable so that even the dominated come to think in the categories provided by the ruling principles of field di-visioning. The combination of resource inequality and ideological hegemony means that in ordinary times the structuring of social fields is maintained and reproduced by the social practices that compose the "game" being played in those fields.[79]

We are not in ordinary times. Social media and information-exchange savvy proliferate. The lack of news outlets in some of my cities meant activists took over the platforms for dialogue – and could do so easily with the interactivity of online spaces. Citizens were having rich conversations in public-but-unconnected places. Trolls – online commentators who purposefully start arguments – were taking over entire dialogues in other (often institution-run) sites within these ecologies. The question is: Could these digital platforms be manipulated to bring together the powerful and those marginalized in productive deliberation in concert? Would such spaces be more conducive for those progressives who might otherwise feel defensive to explore community problems? Would Madison's policymakers and journalists "stay in the room," as Caire hoped they might during this Madison Prep debate? What about afterward? Let us begin the documentation of the extraordinary that characterizes local community information exchange today. Caire and the story of Madison Prep await.

---

[78] Ibid., 91.
[79] Ibid.

Networked Media Ecologies

When Thomas J. (TJ) Mertz first arrived in Madison for his PhD program at the University of Wisconsin-Madison's School of Education Policy in the mid-1990s, the media landscape in Madison thrived. The city's-long-simmering achievement disparities between White people and people of color also was being documented. But Mertz, a White progressive who would become a significant player in the Madison Prep controversy, had a new baby and a new curriculum of graduate work at the time and put off community involvement for a decade. In February 2006, he responded to a call for the Madison Metropolitan School District to join an equity task force made up of education experts, nonprofit directors, special education advocates, progressive activists, parents and others – a grassroots collective of Madison's thought leaders on the issue of equity in the schools. By then Mertz had two children in the district schools and was teaching part-time at local Edgewood College. He also was contributing to a local blog called Schoolinfosystem.org and soon, in February 2007, began his own blog, AMPS (Advocating on Madison Public Schools), posting sometimes daily. Posts included long, well-sourced observations of Board of Education meetings and were filled with charts, statistics, and even quotes from officials and others. By early 2011, Mertz found himself marching with hundreds of thousands of others at the Capitol building in the heart of a snowy Wisconsin winter, protesting the budget repair bill called Act 10 that eliminated collective bargaining power for public unions. When he got back to his home, he stowed his signs and sat down to his computer to type out another post urging people to "scream and organize" as he did in a February 20, 2011 entry. "I know I'll be marching in March and probably April, May and beyond," he promised readers. And then he linked to six websites that would have more information on dates and times for marches.[1]

Later in 2011 when he found out about the Madison Prep proposal by the Urban League of Greater Madison, he was intrigued. Mertz wanted nothing more than to address the persistent equity issues he and his 2006 task force had identified. Frustration still lingered that very little ever came of their lengthy report. But Caire was asking Mertz – who was a member (a former co-chair even!) of the Progressive Dane political party – and others to support a charter school at a time when he felt public education was under attack by conservatives. Hadn't they just spent months marching in the cold trying to protect teachers and prevent cuts to schools? The charter school was only going to be able to serve a small fraction of Madison's growing population of color at a cost of some $10 million over five years. It also reeked of resegregation and hadn't they worked in Madison, which bused kids across the city for better integrated schools, for years against that? And he had questions about the proposal itself. Lots of questions. Why was the Urban League going to garner $900,000 in administrative costs? What about the rumor that Caire had ties to the conservative billionaire Koch Brothers and other conservative political players and think tanks? And so he started blogging about these questions. Ultimately Mertz became one of the proposal's biggest and most vocal opponents – writing prolifically on AMPS but also throughout the media ecology in Madison on Facebook, websites, and news articles. Through his writings, he connected with not only his fellow progressives but also teachers, parents, neighbors, and other education experts.

In another era, Mertz would have taught his education history classes, kept his rally signs handy for public-space protesting, and written loads of letters to the editor or newsletters, eventually running for school board with a door-to-door campaign and pamphlets. Indeed, since their founding, media organizations have operated as political, institutional entities, reporting on – and facilitating – a networked public sphere that helped to constitute local communities. As newspapers began proliferating in the American colonies during the 1700s, this printed information channel offered a sense of cohesiveness among geographically distant and diverse populations so that an "imagined" community formed.[2] Communities

---

[1] https://madisonamps.org/2011/02/20/the-other-shoe-or-will-you-be-marching-in-march/.
[2] An "imagined community" is where news and other cultural vehicles (such as the ubiquitous Unknown Soldier tombs) enable people from many different backgrounds to form a common nation under which they could unite, understand each other (even if they did not

developed a media ecology that comprised a layered, fluid bricolage of power elites and other "official" sources, mainstream and other kinds of journalists. Information flows were structured and limited in diversity by the available mediated platforms (e.g., ownership of a printing press) and subverted only by one-to-one interpersonal communication. Up through the mid-1990s, news came from the newspapers, magazines, public radio, 24-hour cable, mail, or from the opinion leaders within their communities and was redisseminated through conversations, which were typically geographically defined. Niche, alternative, and radical sources of public content existed, such as ethnic media and neighborhood newsletters, but they had a limited distribution and audience.

Today's news media ecology looks much different from the structure of the past. And Mertz represents a new production player in this mix. An increasingly complex, digitally networked society has emerged where new technologies restructure information systems and thus reorganize communities.[3] In 2001 Friedland posited that a place-based yet "communicatively integrated" community must exist in order for democracy to thrive. This community should account for and facilitate the current condition of the network-based social and political system. I build on Friedland's idea that "the larger analytical framework of the communicatively integrated community can best be understood and empirically investigated as a communication ecology"[4] in my analysis of the information system that surrounded achievement disparities and Madison Prep in Madison. It struck me as we were analyzing these cities not only how quickly information could flow through the ecology but also how old articles from the past could gain new life in blog posts and columns and how information could seep into new corners of society on social platforms.

As an activist blogger, Mertz fulfills an emergent position in this evolving ecology, and I am calling him a "niche networker" who also acts as a "community bridge" (defined later). His effectiveness in his dual societal roles – as a credentialed scholar (thus an "expert") and his eventual

---

speak the same language), and form an identity as being from one community. See Benedict Anderson, *Imagined Communities: Reflections on the Origin and Spread of Nationalism* (Verso, 2006).

[3] Manuel Castells, *The Rise of the Network Society: The Information Age: Economy, Society, and Culture, Volume I* (Chichester, West Sussex; Malden, MA: Wiley-Blackwell, 2009); Manuel Castells, *Communication Power* (Oxford: Oxford University Press, 2013); Yochai Benkler, *The Wealth of Networks: How Social Production Transforms Markets and Freedom* (Yale University Press, 2006).

[4] Lewis Friedland, "Communication, Community and Democracy: Toward a Theory of the Communicatively Integrated Community," *Communication Research* 28(4)(2001): 361.

election to the Board of Education (BOE) – must be understood in context with his prolific public writings on achievement disparities and his finesse of the city's networked media world among his fellow active, progressive Madisonians. Citizens are producing public content and, in this developing role, are changing the ecology. For example, in the wake of those months of marching in 2011 to demonstrate against Gov. Walker's budget reform bill, many citizens told me the protests had propelled them onto social-media platforms – often for the very first time. And for those we spoke to, this digital consumption and production – on Twitter, Facebook, and blogs – didn't cease once the signs were put away. They talked about having found a communal pool of information that led to new kinds of civic work. Thus, when the Madison Prep proposal emerged just a few months later, citizens were already used to speaking out through a plethora of these digital platforms.

In this chapter, I think through what this new activity in the media ecology meant for the macrostructures of local society in Madison during this time period, taking into account its particular ideological makeup and its complex, communicatively integrated community. First, this chapter uses some limited network analysis to map this emergent news ecology in my major case study of Madison, Wisc. It considers the new players, such as blogger TJ Mertz, in relation to Urban League of Greater Madison's Kaleem Caire from our Chapter 1 as well as the other officials, bloggers, experts, parents, reporters, and citizens who shared, posted, and commented on content about race. I drew from these maps to develop a typology of mediated roles at work in the ecology and to examine the relationship between the individual and his or her information-exchange field at the micro-meso levels, including social, professional, organizational, and communal connections. Through this analysis, I ask: What is the emerging communicative structure of media ecology in local community today? What are the acting roles that exist? How are social-media platforms reconstituting the ecology?

ESTABLISHING WHO'S WHO IN THE MEDIA ECOLOGY

The method by which I established the emerging communicative structures of the media ecology involved some network analysis to visually map a who's who at work in producing or sharing information in Madison at the time of our study. After my team and I had spent all that time in 2010 and 2011 figuring out all of the major news organizations, blogs, websites, and public Facebook groups with content or dialogue about race in the schools as well as where they linked – 6,331 unique data entries – we turned toward understanding how it was all interconnected. Working with two brilliant graduate students,[5] we mapped the whole information-exchange network in Madison using a year's worth of content from the entire ecology according to author (in other words, role) and platform (traditional news outlet or social media). This technical work allowed us to see right away which organizations and people were the most prolific on which platforms, but also who seemed to be more influential in terms of information exchange at least. In all, we documented the (public) information-exchange relationships among some 1,329 people.

In the network map[6] (Figure 2.1), we can see how many different media platforms (i.e., articles, blogs, websites, and Facebook posts) are engaged in the information flow.[7] Each shape represents a different channel. We can note from this map how much social-media restructures the information flow. All the nodes in white are content that are posted only within Facebook, a blog, or some other online platform. Indeed, the digital network of information-exchange was 36 percent larger than the network for mainstream news.

The biggest shapes in the map represent the 10 most prolific authors of content in the entire network, and you can see that they produce on a multitude of platforms. Four of these are journalists (Matthew DeFour of the *Wisconsin State Journal*, Pat Schneider of *The Capital Times*, Chris Rickert of *Wisconsin State Journal*, and Nathan Comp, a freelancer working for *Isthmus*); the remaining six are all activists or active citizens (Kaleem Caire of the Urban League, progressive blogger TJ Mertz, radio host Alan Ruff, freelancer Rebecca Kemble, blogger Jim Zellmer, and progressive activist Jackie Woodruff).[8] Furthermore, these 10 are responsible for 56.5 percent of all the content in the entire information flow. The information stream is directed by a limited number of actors in these networks as only a few held most of the information capital in this community, during this issue topic. In fact, only 22 people

---

[5] Ho Young Yoon and Mitchael Schwartz.

[6] As I mention in the appendix, I am indebted to University of Wisconsin-Madison graduate student Ho Young Yoon for his work on the calculations and network maps.

[7] Although I collected tweets around my issues, I didn't find any significant content exchange happening around this topic in Madison during this time period and so excluded what I did collect. No tweet was retweeted and all of the content was posted in other venues.

[8] I distinguish between professional "activists" who get paid to speak in public about topics of race and/or youth and "active citizens" who are performing acts of civic engagement aside from their day job. Both are important parts of this ecology.

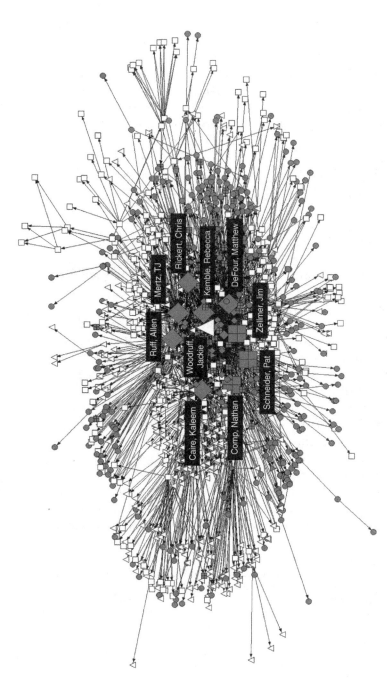

FIGURE 2.1. A Networked media ecology. The map shows the local, networked media ecology of the major case study of Madison, Wisc. The ten major nodes are identified by name and became dominant nodes in the information-exchange field during the Madison Prep controversy. **Legend:** Colors: Gray nodes: People who appeared in mainstream news outlets; White: People who appeared only in social media; Shapes: Circle: Individual posting content only in mainstream news; Single square: Individual posting only in blogs; Upward Triangle: Individual posting only on Facebook; Box of squares: Individual posting both in mainstream news and blogs; Downward triangle: Individual posting both in mainstream news and on Facebook; Circle-in-box: Individual posting both in blogs and on Facebook; Diamond: Individual posting in mainstream news, blogs and Facebook

authored more than 10 posts or articles in total. Yet, this map also is key to showing just how many new voices help comprise the ecology today. The vast majority of these voices tend to be professional activists and community leaders.

A dense cluster of people (in the middle of the network) appear regularly in articles, blogs, and Facebook posts. Cited by both journalists and nonjournalists, these sources were key influencers, such as the school superintendents, school board officials, community leaders like Caire, or locally based experts such as African American Professor Gloria Ladson-Billings of the University of Wisconsin-Madison. From this map we could appreciate core concentrations of "power" – that is, actors (or roles) who were more central to this network than others. In Madison, these tended to be people who occupied leadership positions in the field such as an activist on Facebook, a school board member who blogged, and an education-beat reporter.

We drilled down to understand the direction of this flow by breaking four key influencers out into ego-networks[9] (Figure 2.2), showing only their associations in comparison to the journalists. Our four most prolific content producers in the entire information-exchange realm were two professional reporters (Matthew DeFour of the *Wisconsin State Journal*, who covered K–12 education during the study period, and Pat Schneider, a long-time reporter of local communities and social justice issues for *The Capital Times*) and our two activists (Kaleem Caire, who proposed the Madison Prep charter school and posted frequently to his public Facebook page, and our progressive blogger and education professor TJ Mertz, who began this chapter). Between September 1, 2011 and September 1, 2012, these four people accounted for about 40 percent of all the public content published on the racial achievement gap in Madison in news articles, blogs, Facebook pages, tweets, and commenting forums.

Stunned by this percentage of content, we isolated these four networks into Figure 2.2 to understand their relationships and associations in the information exchange at hand. Here, you can see the four white, large squares who are our four information actors; the top two are the activists and the bottom two the journalists. The agents (all the little gray shapes) connecting to our four main nodes are all of the sources they quoted or mentioned in their public writings on this issue. The small white nodes in the center of the network are those sources that were mentioned by all four

---

[9] An "ego network" is one person's entire network. Here I look at four individual's entire network together.

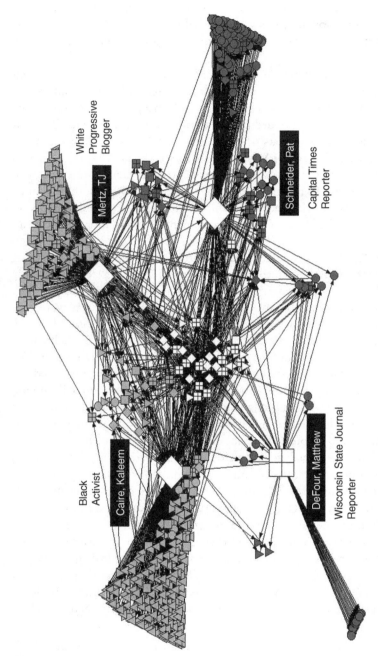

FIGURE 2.2. Four top influencers.

of the actors and included the superintendent, vocal activists, and experts – those people whom everyone turned to for information about Madison Prep or racial disparities in the schools. These nodes are all the key public figures and represent the dense core of our networked ecology. It is important to note that these people were also all the policymakers – those with the decision power around proposals such as Madison Prep. Those dark gray nodes to the right of Pat Schneider and to the bottom left and right of Matthew DeFour were all of the people sourced by the traditional reporters such as state officials and other activists as well as some parents, teachers and other sources – mostly found during public meetings. Then I considered the light gray nodes connected to Mertz and Caire near the top of the map; these were the additional sources brought in by our two activists. These nodes represented many more diverse sources, including White, Brown and Black parents, local religious leaders, alternative press, national activists and political leaders, and local progressive insiders as well as parents and teachers. Immediately we see three things: First, how just these two activists – Caire and Mertz – were able to expand the number of viewpoints and types of evidence being used to build knowledge and consensus on this issue. The lines show the connections between all of these people. For example, if a reporter or a commenter mentioned the superintendent in their post, a line will connect them. Second, we can also see distinct, isolated niches of dialogue happening. We don't see a lot of linking (the lines) between Mertz's community and Caire's community other than the institutional public officials in the middle. All the lines connect to the white nodes in the middle, those policymakers. Third, few of those people in Caire and Mertz's social-media information-exchange networks were in positions of power in Madison's policy sphere.

I was curious about how people were expanding the media ecology using URL links and where those links were taking us. So my research team and I collected and coded the links that each piece of content contained to understand how widespread information sources were being used in the information flow. I wanted to know: Were we just getting the same sources circulating throughout the ecology (that is, a closed system) or, rather, was the media ecology expanding exponentially as some have surmised in the age of information overload? Was social media really amplifying marginalized sources of information? A total of 1,140 unique URLs were represented in this dataset, with an average of 3.56 URLs used in each blog, news article, or social-media post. A review of the URLs from the content (see the long-tail graph in Figure 2.3) showed that a few mainstream

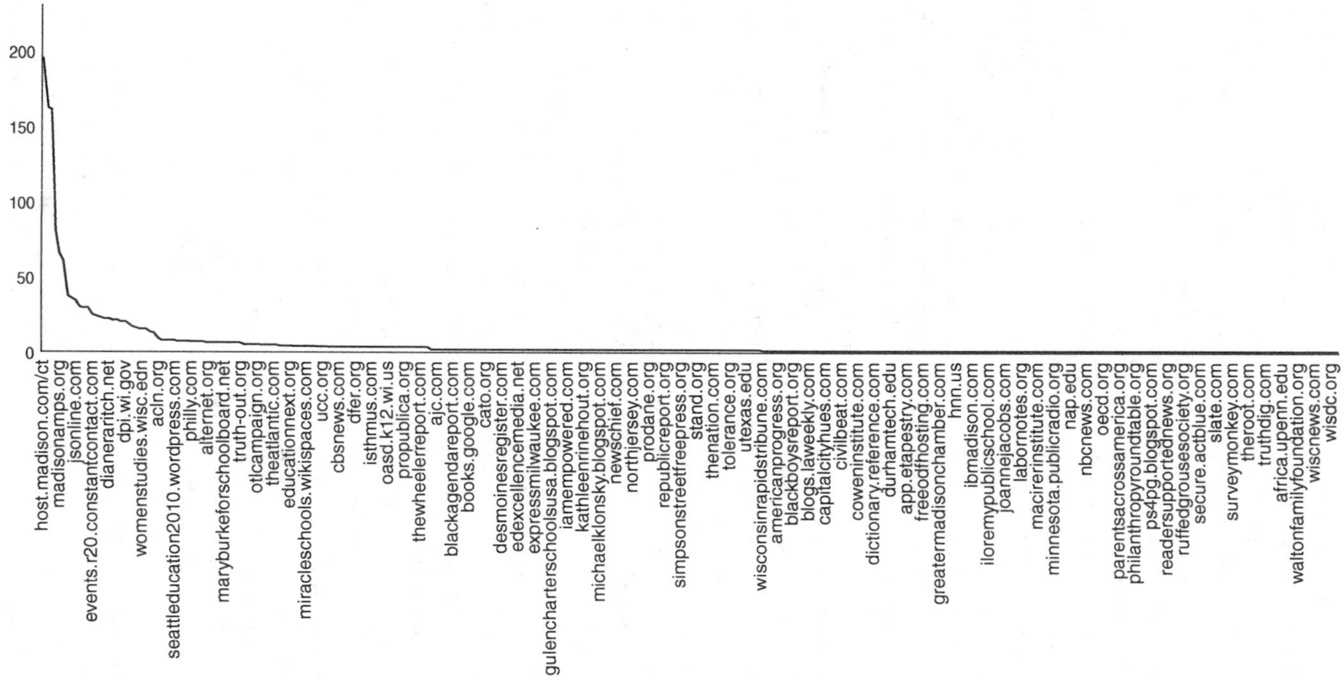

FIGURE 2.3. Long tail of URLs.

wisdc.org
wiscnews.com
waltonfamilyfoundation.org
africa.upenn.edu
truthdig.com
theroot.com
surveymonkey.com
slate.com
secure.actblue.com
ruffedgrousesociety.org
readersupportednews.org
ps4pg.blogspot.com
philanthropyroundtable.org
parentsacrossamerica.org
oecd.org
nbcnews.com
nap.edu
minnesota.publicradio.org
macireninstitute.com
labornotes.org
joannejacobs.com
iloremypublicschool.com
ibmadison.com
nnu.us
greatermadisonchamber.com
freedhosting.com
app.etapestry.com
durhamtech.edu
dictionary.reference.com
coweninstitute.com
civilbeat.com
capitalcityhues.com
blogs.lawweekly.com
blackboysreport.org
americanprogress.org
wisconsinrapidstribune.com
utexas.edu
tolerance.org
thenation.com
stand.org
simpsonstreetfreepress.org
republicreport.org
prodane.org
northjersey.com
newschief.com
michaelkonsky.blogspot.com
kathleennnehout.org
iamempowered.com
gulencharterschoolsusa.blogspot.com
expressmilwaukee.com
edexcellencemedia.net
desmoinesregister.com
cato.org
books.google.com
blackagendareport.com
ajc.com
thewheelerreport.com
propublica.org
oasd.k12.wi.us
isthmus.com
dfer.org
cbsnews.com
ucc.org
miracleschools.wikispaces.com
educationext.org
theatlantic.com
oticampaign.org
truth-out.org
maryburkeforschoolboard.net
alternet.org
philly.com
seattleducation2010.wordpress.com
acln.org
womenstudies.wisc.edu
dpi.wi.gov
dianeratitch.net
events.r20.constantcontact.com
jsonline.com
madisonamps.org
host.madison.com/ct

200
150
100
50
0

news pieces were linked to repeatedly. In addition, a large number and variety of alternative sources also appeared throughout the ecology. Several URLs represented an individual's Facebook post being shared or connected to YouTube channels. About 70 percent of all the blog URLs led to government databases and other reports.

The other two major findings to come from this URL analysis indicated a difference in how reporters and White progressive bloggers linked – and to whom – and the ways in which others, such as "regular" citizens, made statements. Reporters almost always linked to their own work or other journalists, usually within their own publications. Those who were highly influential and active professionally or politically on the issue of school achievement disparities cited more (mainstream) reports and government sources as well as political blogs – usually progressive, but not always.

And of course we wanted to know, for those who were not linking, how were people making their arguments? The vast majority of those citizens posting in Facebook or making comments under news articles eschewed linking to outside sources in favor of personal stories and experiences – often accounts that bore witness about disparities, for example, or the varied attempts to resolve them. These people who did not engage publicly on the achievement disparities as part of their daily job – such as parents with kids in the schools and teachers – relayed anecdotes about incidents in the classroom or quoted from a family dinner conversation. This kind of content resonated with other commenters and should be privileged for those interested in facilitating better public dialogues. I will discuss the connective power of such personal storytelling more in the conclusion of the book.

TJ Mertz, one of our most frequent contributors to this information flow and our activist who began this chapter, believed that URLs equated to authority and credibility for his more than 200 followers. Half a dozen or so people commented on average to each of his blog posts about Madison Prep, which garnered 500–700 hits. And he wrote a lot, as I have mentioned and as the data show. By the end of 2012, he had written 17 blog and 249 Facebook posts about K–12 racial achievement disparities and each typically had half a dozen or more URL links. One post of 2,730 words boasted 17 active links, and he said he did this because:

You want to give people the opportunity to sift through the evidence themselves. It also indicates an intellectual journey you took. It gives you some kind of authority, that "this is not just what TJ says; he has evidence behind it." I don't want them to not take my word for it. I want conversations around it to start.

He was extremely careful about where he linked, sticking to reports from think tanks and academic journals, news organizations, and politically liberal websites (he even took an advanced regression analysis class to help him dissect data better). During this proposal and afterward, people started sending him obscure datapoints that then took up space in this information flow and redirected some dialogue. And Mertz used his public writing to establish relationships with both policymakers and journalists, all of whom reported reading it regularly. In some very directed ways, Mertz' blog AMPS connected people in his social network, such as parents, with school administrators and school board members. Mertz – remember he was a trained researcher who was a PhD candidate in education policy in Madison – purposefully used his blog and other public content production as a way to exercise his civic agency in town, as well as his progressive agenda. The argument I am making in this book is that the largely digital work of Mertz and others in these cities we examined were part of an evolving media ecology whose information flow was being reified, redirected, and reconstituted because of new players in content production taking advantage of interactivity. And as a result, people like Mertz gained political capital and ultimately, an elected office or some other powerful position because of savvy networking done from within the status quo.

THE ROLES IN THE EMERGING ECOLOGY

In identifying these new – and also old – roles in the K–12 achievement disparities information-exchange field existing within the Madison media ecology, I thought about all three layers of the macrostructure: one, the micro-level individual citizens; two, the meso-level groups and organizations; and three, the macro-level media system and institutional-societal systems. I asked what the relationship is between a single individual to the other levels of the overall media ecology? How are organizations and their agents networked with each other and with citizens? How are socially mediated content platforms such as Facebook or blogs reconstituting this ecology and changing these power relationships within the information-exchange field? Because I am analyzing such a complex, multi-level networked ecology – unlike anything Bourdieu wrote about – I found I needed to develop new terms that meshed my framework lexicon to help describe what was going on with the information flow in these cities. Thus, in this section, I will delineate a working typology of information-exchange players in the media ecology for my study sites using Madison as the exemplar case. These position roles represent those people who take action in some manner with public content about racial achievement disparities (See Table 2.1 for the most influential producers). Although I use Madison as my exemplar case, these roles existed in all of my cases. Using this network data from above and drawing from network-analysis thinking, I typologized the key roles for the emergent media ecology in local community as: Institutional Producers, Individual Institutional Producers, Alternative Sites, Network Facilitators, Niche Networkers, Community Bridges, and Issue Amplifiers. I explain each role below.

Institutional Producers: Institutional producers represent established entities operating at the macro-meso level such as a legacy news organization or the school district website. To be an institutional producer, an entity must be a large organization or institution with significant financial backing, staff, and an established protocol for content production. Despite media watchers' persistent claims of the death of traditional news organizations, my evidence demonstrated in most (but not all) of my communities how pivotal these traditional institutional producers remained in the media ecologies. Yet it is also important to note that in all of the communities, these legacy organizations contracted significantly during the study period, until they were no longer present because of shuttering or mergers. In all, fifty-four professional, mainstream journalists wrote at least one story, column, or editorial about the achievement disparities in the city of Madison. All of these journalists were White people.

In Madison, three newspapers and one monthly magazine reigned as the major printed content producers on the achievement disparities during the study period. These three – a strong daily called the *Wisconsin State Journal*, the twice-weekly magazine and web-focused *The Capital Times*, and the alternative weekly *Isthmus* – share a long history of intense competition in Madison but have recently been rattled by industry financial strife, repeated layoffs, and scaled-back community coverage. The *Wisconsin State Journal*, founded in 1839, was owned by the struggling Lee Enterprises and considered the most conservative of the papers.[10] A White moderately conservative man named John Smalley served as executive editor of the paper at the time of this study. About 53 reporters and

---

[10] http://host.madison.com/download-a-media-kit-pdf/pdf_4b15e152-3f20-11e2-98e5-00 19bb2963f4.html.

TABLE 2.1 *Most influential producers*

Rank	Journalists	Betweenness Centrality (BC)	Ratio of Average BC over Entire Network	Rank	Activists, Active Citizens	Betweenness Centrality (BC)	Ratio over Average BC of Network
6	DeFour, Matthew	0.021	73.4	1	Caire,_Kaleem	0.096	335.7
15	Comp,_Nathan J.	0.004	14.0	2	Zellmer, Jim	0.035	122.4
23	Rickert,_Chris	0.003	10.5	3	Mertz,_TJ	0.034	118.9
24	Schneider,_Pat	0.003	10.5	4	Hughes,_Ed	0.027	94.4
25	Troller, Susan	0.003	10.5	5	Nerad,_Dan	0.027	94.4

editors worked in the newsroom during the period of this study, covering state politics and sports as well as the local Madison community.[11] It shared offices, production, marketing, and some administrative resources with *The Capital Times* – a kind of joint operating agreement dating back to 1934. They have distinct editorial structures. Begun in 1917 by William Evjue to support progressive politician "Fighting Bob" LaFollette, *The Capital Times* remains committed to its progressive mission with a staff of just 20 reporters and editors, a circulation of 95,000 in 2013 after the 2007 downsizing to a twice-weekly print edition, with a beefed-up online presence. In 2013 the executive editor and self-proclaimed Evjue-progressive Paul Fanlund announced a renewed mission to report on race, creating a website called TogetherApart as an aggregator of its race-related coverage. Finally, the *Isthmus*[12] came to be in 1976 as a "hip, smartass" alternative to the other papers with a median readership of age 40, more than 75 percent with a college degree, and incomes in the $70,000 range. With a circulation of 43,000 "local adults," Isthmus was bought by a group of Madison businessmen in 2014 – the first turnover of ownership in its entire history.[13] The paper had also slowly decreased its staff through attrition and as of my study period had no beat reporter dedicated to K–12 education, though freelancers and the occasional editor wrote pieces about Madison Prep and other achievement gap issues. (Nathan Comp wrote frequently on this topic during this time period.) The local papers together boast about an 85 percent penetration into the community of South Central Wisconsin where Madison is located.

In addition, the 35-year-old *Madison Magazine* reached some 216,000 city residents, reporting on arts and culture, business, and health.[14] The publisher and editors of *Madison Magazine* identified race relations as important to the community with several of the leadership sitting on local nonprofit boards. During our study, the longtime editor – a White woman named Brennan Nardi – handed over the reins to Karen Lincoln Michel of the Ho-Chunk Nation in Wisconsin. The magazine frequently produced video editorials on the topic of achievement disparities, as well as regular columns and cover stories featuring African Americans and Latinos in the city. Columnist John Roach, a White man who was a top producer of

---

[11] This is 60 percent fewer than when the new millennium began.

[12] Technically *Isthmus* would consider itself an "alternative" publication. But for the purposes of this study, it operated as mainstream because of its prominent and dominant position in the information network.

[13] Personal communication with editorial staff, 2016.

[14] www.madisonmagazine.com/Madison-Magazine/About-Us/.

content on achievement disparities during the study, also did freelance video work for the Urban League, which Caire ran at the time of this study. Many Madison legacy sites hosted content produced not only by their journalists but also by activists, politicians, school administrators, teachers, and voting citizens. Throughout their sites, they linked to other content on the Web about achievement disparities. They also brokered knowledge by reporting the work of other institutions and community groups to actors who might not have that information otherwise. Online, participants also could access forums on thedailypage.com (the *Isthmus'* website).

Other media players who occasionally covered achievement disparities during my study period included the online-only news organization called Channel 3000,[15] three television networks, the student-run University of Wisconsin-Madison papers – *The Badger Herald* and *The Daily Cardinal* – and several radio stations, including various Wisconsin Public Radio programs. Another group of hubs also emerged in this information-exchange field: government and other institutional entity websites such as the Madison Metropolitan School District (MMSD) and the Wisconsin Department of Public Instruction – both of which hosted databases and content about Madison's racial disparities in K–12 education. In addition, the United Way of Dane County posted articles about achievement disparities on its site as well.

Individual Institutional Producers: In emergent local media ecologies, actors who worked for the institutional producers often became major influencers on their own terms. The major beat reporter for the *Wisconsin State Journal*, Matthew DeFour, posted regularly on his Facebook page, and conversations about achievement disparities in that interactive space prompted him to report anew. Many of the content producers we interviewed mentioned DeFour (operating at the macro-meso-micro level) *and* the *Wisconsin State Journal* (operating at the macro level in terms of its institutional scaffolding) as two major sources of information. This indicated they believed the two – reporter and news organization – to have separate credibility statuses in their minds. DeFour, an extremely traditional reporter, reflected a primarily organizational perspective, declining to give his own opinion in these spaces and always representing the *Wisconsin State Journal*. Similarly, *The Capital Times* reporter Pat Schneider, a veteran reporter at the progressive weekly, wrote a blog and tweeted

---

[15] Channel 3000 has a partnership with *Madison Magazine* as well.

about the Madison Prep debate and other achievement disparities in city. She also was often named independently as an influencer in the information-exchange field. Some of these individual institutional producers expanded the information flow into previously unreached spaces, helping to be a link between the meso- and micro levels of content in a way that institutional producers on their own could not achieve.

Alternative Sites: Alternative sites represent established niche-interest organizations that exist to "fill a hole" left by mainstream journalism. Alternative media have existed for generations as "new spaces for alternative voices that provide focus both for specific community interests as well as for the contrary and subversive ... to pursue a critical or alternative agenda, from the margins, as it were or from the underbelly of social life."[16] For Atton, alternative media "are crucially about offering the means for democratic communication to people who are normally excluded from media production."[17] Both of these seminal works on alternative media consider the position these organizations play in the media ecology, as opposed to any radical content they might offer. This player in our ecology exists at the margins where people normally excluded from or ignored by dominant institutional producers may gain voice. The problem is so many of these sites are isolated within the field. They are connected to very few, or even no other, actors in the network. In order to achieve viable positionality, these sites need to form connections to other actors. Some in my case site of Madison tried to do just this.

These sites in the Madison media ecology included entrepreneurial websites with organizational protocols but existed apart from the mainstream legacy sites. The citizen-run Dane 101, which folded in 2013, covered Madison Prep through irregular forum conversations and occasional updates by freelancers. Three young professionals in the city started Dane 101 as an alternative to the mainstream news organizations in order to "To report with honesty and integrity and without sensationalism" and "provide a prominent, public forum in which diverse people will have a voice."[18] In addition, the University of Wisconsin-Madison School of Journalism and Mass Communication hosted a citizen-focused Madison Commons[19] website that covered education news, with an emphasis on the achievement gap, in

[16] Roger Silverstone, *Why Study the Media?* (London; Thousand Oaks, Calif.: SAGE Publications Ltd, 1999), 103.
[17] Chris Atton, *Alternative Media* (London: Sage Publications, 2001), 4.
[18] www.dane101.com/about.
[19] www.madisoncommons.org/.

addition to city life, environment, and local food. Founded in 2006 by a White professor who was a former journalist, Madison Commons ran a newsroom with about a dozen students as well as partnerships with local media organizations. Also, several of the ethnic media outlets in the city published a few pieces on the charter school proposal or other aspects of the gap. In my data, the free, minority-owned, biweekly (and bilingual) *Capital City Hues*,[20] run by (White) Jonathan Gramling, ran the most stories or columns on the achievement disparities. His stories often showed up in various aggregations on the issue by mainstream media. Indeed, Madison was home to a handful of vibrant ethnic publications, also including *Madison Times, Umoja Magazine, La Comunidad News, Voz Latina*, and several others.[21] All of these actors or organizations follow intentional – and stated – organizational standards for coverage, which often (but not always) reflect mainstream journalism. Nonetheless, though all policymakers and reporters knew about (most of) these sites, very few of those interviewed reported that they used them regularly in their information production practices.[22]

Network Facilitators: The "network facilitators" enable and augment the information flow by reposting and curating what other actors are doing in the information flow. These would include sites with blog rolls and aggregations of content. Operating at the meso level, network facilitators often tend to be automated programs on websites or blogs and bring content to people who might not have seen it in other places in the information flow. Such a role is pivotal to information flows in which members seek broad diffusion and need information to be spread to build audiences and their own influence in order to improve their own position in the information-exchange field as an information purveyor.

In the Madison ecology, we might consider *WiscPolitics.com*, an online news service that aggregates not only mainstream news (institutional producers) but also that of blogs and other site content throughout the ecology. *WiscPolitics.com*. regularly posted content about Madison Prep from School Information Systems (SIS), AMPS, Ed Hughes School Blog, and other entities during my study period.[23] Bought in 2011 by *The Capital*

---

[20] www.capitalcityhues.com/about_us.html.

[21] Indeed, a rich conversation surrounding racial disparities had been happening in these alternative news sources for many decades before Madison Prep.

[22] One site that began after the study period for this section was Madison365, which would fall as an "alternative site." I will talk about this organization at length in the final chapter of the book.

[23] http://wispolitics.com/index.iml.

Times, the site enjoys thirty-six thousand unique visitors every month, but they are mostly into politics (as opposed to education). This opened up a new audience for the story of Madison Prep and the actors writing about it. Several of the actors I placed in other categories sometimes also acted as network facilitators, such as Madison Commons and SIS. Both regularly reprinted articles and blog posts from other sources without commentary. The Madison Metropolitan School District's website often collected all the news articles it could find on the issue of the day, including Madison Prep. This meant that these entities or people performed two or more roles in the ecology.

Niche Networkers: The least stable grouping of roles but the category most prolific and increasing in numbers is the "niche networkers." These specialists rule a particular topic, such as a food blog or an education blog (as in my case), and regularly produce and spread information. Many of these niche networkers were people whom Bourdieu might refer to as dominating actors – those people who have attained and spent a great deal of economic, cultural, political, or symbolic informational capital in the realm of K–12 achievement disparities. In my dataset, these niche networkers tended to be experts, such as political officials or others whose day job related to some aspect of the specialty, or activists in the arena of either civil rights, progressive politics, youth, or education. Activists and community leaders who post to Facebook publicly, such as Caire and Mertz, are niche networkers. In all, some 899 nonjournalists contributed content in this way in the study site.

According to my interviews and the network data, two of the most influential actors in this information flow were Caire (who proposed the charter school to the school district) and Rev. Dr. Alexander Gee of the Fountain of Life Covenant Church. Gee, an African American, stepped up in the wake of the failed Madison Prep proposal and began a series of racial talks he dubbed "Justified Anger" in the community. Both Caire and Gee posted frequently on their public Facebook pages throughout my study's time frame. Others who were often named as being influential in the community included the White progressive Mertz with his AMPS blog and Facebook posts, the Black CEO of the Boys & Girls Clubs of Dane County named Michael Johnson and his public Facebook posts, the White Ed Hughes, a long-time Board of Education member, and his Ed Hughes School Blog, and the White Jim Zellmer, a local entrepreneur who started the "curated" Schoolinfosystem.org (SIS) blog in 2004 with lots of guest posts and also snippets of mainstream news articles about education issues that reached fifteen thousand monthly.[24] The blog itself would be considered a Network Facilitator as well, as it often curated content from other places. Friedland et al. found that the discussion that occurred on SIS and other Madison education blogs around a controversial Madison Metropolitan School District referendum "radically altered" not only the tone and content of community conversations about the issues but also spurred the ultimate rejection of those referendums.[25]

Community Bridges: Some of these niche networkers also reached the level of what I am calling "community bridges." And indeed, some of the individual institutional producers could also be considered this. These are individuals or websites that connect otherwise disparate communities. They operate at the meso-micro level of the field and tend to be community leaders in some way such as activists, reporters, or even bloggers. The key here is that their influence extends beyond their niche circle, especially on social media (though much community bridging happens in private spaces as well). This is an important category because these people hold much potential to amplify voices that do not typically make it into the mainstream information flow. These bridges serve as grassroots-based links between groups or individuals to share information and facilitate connections. In this data set they tended to "do better" in the sense that they have access to more resources, gain more social capital, and achieve more success than people who are not multiconnected. They influenced the circulation of the information as well as the quality of the dialogue they spurred in their content production. As we saw earlier with our map of the four ego networks – the two journalists plus Kaleem Caire and TJ Mertz – these prolific content producers tie together groups that do not interact. Both Caire and Mertz could – although they did not in Madison during my study period – act as "community bridges" between policymakers and their niche communities (communities of color for Caire, middle-class White families and teachers for Mertz). All the reporters in this sample also have the potential to become community bridges. That said, not a lot of "bridging" really happened in the content that was produced on K–12 achievement gaps in Madison (as we saw in the network maps). Instead, reporters used people like Caire and Mertz as punctuation points rather than bridges, as singular sources representing their groups rather than as

[24] www.schoolinfosystem.org/.
[25] Lewis Friedland et al., "The Local Public Sphere as a Networked Space," in *Media and Public Spheres*, by R. Butsch (New York: Palgrave Macmillan, 2006), 198–209.

conduits to those groups. I will talk more about obstacles to public talk in Chapter 4.

Issue Amplifiers: Quandt[26] posited that as society's networked infrastructure has become more complex, the communicative components – that is, the information flow – have diverged, diversified, and fragmented, fueled by user-generated content – termed "participatory journalism." These users have been dubbed a number of different names over the years: Manuel Castells referred to these actors as "mass self-communicators,"[27] Axel Bruns labeled them "produsers."[28] Quandt called them "sensors." These individuals at the micro level are generally not producing significant amounts of original content beyond the occasional post, but they do redistribute information (albeit in less organized ways than the "network facilitators"). Their social networks overlap with each other but also often extend information into other geographies and throughout the local ecology. In addition to information from institutional producers such as news articles, they also share innumerable obscure, alternative-minded information from different kinds of sources from all levels of the system. In the digitally networked society, these online citizens are developing a sense of civic responsibility to find, verify, and redisseminate information and thus becoming a significant actor in the ecology, helping to shape the flow of content.

These engaged actors are one level above passive consumers. Typically their sharing comes with commentary, and their intentions are to gain social capital within their existing social and professional circles.[29] They become minor influencers within their own niche networks because others have learned these individuals regularly keep up on community news and are willing to share and distribute the knowledge they gain. In the Madison case study, I analyzed thousands of posts and comments under news articles, under blog posts, on Facebook, and on websites from people using both their real names and pseudonyms. According to our interviews, many of them regularly visited the same publication to lurk and (sometimes to) comment while others merely

---

[26] Quandt T., "Understanding a New Phenomenon: The Significance of Participatory Journalism," in *Participatory Journalism: Guarding Open Gates at Online Newspapers*, by Jane B. Singer et al. (Malden, Mass.: Wiley-Blackwell, 2011), 155–176.

[27] Castells, *The Rise of the Network Society.*

[28] Axel Bruns, *Gatewatching: Collaborative Online News Production* (New York: Peter Lang International Academic Publishers, 2005).

[29] This is according to extensive in-depth interviews I have had over the years with more than two hundred citizen commenters in this study and several other studies.

tweeted out the URL or posted it to their Facebook page. One of these frequent sharers of information said to me: "I think that's the most defining and best part of being an everyday citizen consuming daily events is that you can put it forward to any number of people in any way you want." With every "submit" action, content has the potential to go viral and its author, thus, has the opportunity to gain information capital, become more known, and achieve more prominence in the ecology and more power in the field.

In Table 2.2, I have formalized the typology I have just described. The "Roles" are the institutional producers, individual institutional producers, alternative sites, network facilitators, community bridges, niche networkers, and issue amplifiers that may be thought of as the signatures of the emergent ecology. Each "Role" has a "Function" that stabilizes or challenges the overall structure and encompasses the capacity to evolve the ecology. "Roles" exist on at least one – and sometimes all three – levels of the system – macro (such as the media system or institutions), meso (mid-range organizational level), or micro (individual). I also note who specifically might be performing as an "Actor" in these roles (understanding of course that some people in this ecology occupy several roles at different times, depending on the content they are producing). The "Platforms" offer the information channel most likely to be used by "Actors" to navigate the ecology and to try to improve his or her position in the field.

The documentation of signature roles within such a typology is useful as we seek broader understanding about how our communities are being reconstituted, communicatively, with new mediated platforms. The emergent media ecology comprises a networked information-exchange field that is constantly modified and recreated by the actors relying on their positions of power and capital. Some of these actors perform as bridges, connecting otherwise isolated groups and individuals in other parts of the field. These roles allow for relationships that comprise the whole, multi-dimensional, fluid media ecology, which expands and contracts as new actors take on new roles. The ways in which these actors function in these roles are determined by the field dynamics that govern the ecology, such as the exchange of capital and the dominance of the particular doxa (operating in these cities as progressive political ideology). When someone new wants to gain power, that blogger or alternative media organization must strategize carefully, struggling against boundaries that had been established long before their entry into the field. The next section explores the idea of boundaries associated with established information patterns that

TABLE 2.2 *Roles in an emergent ecology in local community*

Roles	Function	System Level	Actors	Platforms
Institutional Producers	Set hierarchy for information flow	Macro	Institutions such as the press or school district (as entities)	Newspapers, radio, television, website, social-media accounts
Individual Institutional Producers	Perpetuate hierarchy of flow	Macro-Meso-Micro	Individual reporters, politicians or others associated with institutions, offshoot websites	Reporter blogs, social-media accounts of employees
Alternative Sites	Groups or established entities challenge status quo	Meso	Nonprofessional journalism entities with general-interest content	Newspapers, radio, websites, blogs, forums, Facebook Group Pages
Network Facilitators	Maintain the network, aggregate content	Meso	Automated program	Website, blogs
Community Bridges	Individuals or sites that connect otherwise disparate communities	Meso-Micro	Community leaders (could be reporters, activists, bloggers)	Blogs, Facebook, Twitter, social media
Niche Networkers	Individuals not associated with institutions who produce copious content on an issue	Micro	Special-interest bloggers, activists, citizen journalists	Blogs, Facebook pages, websites, social media
Issue Amplifiers	Share, discuss	Micro	Engaged citizens	Facebook, Twitter, email

constrain influence and help explain why the media ecology looks the way it does at any given time.

STRUGGLES AND STRATEGIES IN BOUNDARY WORK

Kaleem Caire wanted to be heard on the issue of racial achievement disparities. It was summer 2010 and he had just arrived back in Madison as the new head of the Urban League of Greater Madison. Immediately he felt frustrated at the lack of action to improve the metrics on racial achievement disparities; for example, he found it took 30–45 minutes just to get a quorum at his Urban League board meetings to talk about the issue. Years later, he remembered thinking about that time period, "Man, I thought I told you all [Urban League] in the interview who you were getting. You know, I move. So this is not going to be a slow-motion game." And he vaulted into action. He sent the school district a nine-page request for data about the disparities. With the data in hand, he called Susan Troller, the education reporter[30] for *The Capital Times*. He called Channel 3000 and several other news organizations in town. He said he'd hold a press conference on the steps of West High School, his alma mater, in two hours. He promised a big announcement about a charter school for boys.[31] He posted an announcement on Facebook. He made some phone calls to people he knew around town. Twelve people showed up. Troller wrote a story. "And it was one, to get people's attention and to have my board really become leaders around this issue. Because guess what, if you don't sign up with me, this train is moving without you," said Caire.

The discussion began a circulation of information through the ecology as Caire set out to convince those in power of the wisdom of the charter school. He set up a Madison Prep website, Facebook page, YouTube channel, and Twitter account. He established relationships with other nonprofits in town dedicated to youth or race issues. And he laid the groundwork for the need by posting graphs of the differences between White children and Black and Brown children in terms of academic achievement, such as graduation rates. He strategized carefully: when he was asked to speak about the disparities, he sometimes sent his White colleague, lest he become known as an Angry Black Man and marginalize

---

[30] Susan Troller ended up leaving the paper right after this, which is why she does not show up as a major producer in our data.

[31] The announcement was later amended to include girls as well.

himself and his arguments. He set up a series of one-on-one coffees and meetings that involved Board of Education members, the superintendent, union officials, and reporters.

He did all of this because he knew he would be challenging some pretty rooted borders of power in the city. At the time, Wisconsin's Republican governor, Scott Walker, and conservative legislators were intent on defunding public education and crushing public unions, including the teacher's union. They had proposed a "budget repair bill," known as Act 10, that would end collective bargaining power for the teacher unions in the state, including Madison Teachers Inc. The city, so progressive at its roots, simmered and seethed as it continued to march well into that summer of 2011. Caire's proposal for the charter school would land in an information-exchange field that was not only already saturated with well-meaning ideas about the schools but also characterized by entrenched progressive ideals that were under attack. Caire would be engaging in what we call "boundary-work" in trying to attain a more dominant position of power. But the decks were stacked against him in this "stake of struggles."

Any individual's mobility within a field has always been limited by his or her historic position – that is, his or her position's boundaries. "The boundary of the field is a stake of struggles," wrote Bourdieu,[32] highlighting the intense competition in such a coup as the one Caire was attempting.

In each field ... there are those who dominate and those who are dominated according to the values internal to that field ... But heteronomy – the loss of autonomy through subjection to external forces – begins when someone who is not a mathematician intervenes to give an opinion about mathematics ... and is listened to.[33]

Could Caire successfully challenge the homophily that characterized this information-exchange field? Despite the plethora of new roles in our ecology previously laid out, information flows in fairly segregated streams, as the network maps reveal. Many new voices do not reach the inner circle of policymakers, for example. Much of this flow in the media ecology – and any change of position in the field – depended upon the accumulation and careful expenditure of capital – social and symbolic, political and economic. For example, Kaleem Caire had spent time in the city building friendships and making lots of connections; he had expertise and Washington experience

---

[32] Bourdieu, *The Field of Cultural Production*, 43.
[33] Ibid., 57.

around issues of education; and, he had a plethora of interactive publicity tools at his disposal to make his case. But he wasn't necessarily networked in the right way. Compare Caire to Mertz, who also was well positioned in the field with lots of connections and relationships. But Mertz had built the right kinds of capital with the right parts of this network – primarily, the progressive leaders and policymakers who held decision-making power at that time in the city. And we will see soon in our story what this difference in capital work meant for the fate of Madison Prep.

In all the cities in this study, activists, politicians, and bloggers worked to either become visible in the field or advance their positionality while those in power strategized to maintain their authority. People of color in particular were stymied by fairly widespread segregation – politically, economically, and socially – despite the fact that all were becoming increasingly more diverse; three of the five cities in fact had a majority of "minority" school populations by 2016 and the other two were quickly heading in that direction (see Table 1.1). In Evanston, one African American school board member, talked about the situation in an interview like this:

Evanston is physically a beautiful community. On the surface, the community appears to be most desirable. In addition, the diversity is a source I have heard many White Evanston community members boast about. However, the diversity is very superficial. For example, of the 3,322 students at Evanston Township High School, the 2015–16 enrollment demographics consisted of 43.2 percent White, 30.3 percent Black/African American, 1.5 percent Hispanic/Latino and 5.1 percent Asian. We call this "drive-by diversity" because driving by the school and observing this mix of students entering can be very encouraging . . . And then, reality sets in. Similar to the rest of the country, honest conversations about disparities based on race in Evanston are difficult and therefore frequently avoided. Many White community members live in a part of town that limits their contact with people of color on a regular basis. Until recently, the high school was described by many of the African American residents as "two schools"– as a way to differentiate the experience of White students from the Black students.

Rarely did White worlds collide with those of people of color, and this extended to the information-exchange fields. White bloggers appeared in each other's blogs and posts. White reporters ran in professional and social circles that looked like them. In this sense, I saw boundary-work happening on a number of levels with journalists in particular (but also some bloggers). They not only had professional borders to protect (from bloggers, from prolific tweeters, etc.) but also worked (unconsciously, inadvertently) to maintain the power structures of the place through their routines of sourcing. But first let's talk about what we mean by "boundary work."

A rich literature exists around the subject of boundary work in the social sciences, particularly sociology, and is starting to emerge for the field of journalism specifically.[34] Gieryn first coined the term "boundary-work" in 1983;[35] in his 1999 book, he documented the "science wars" between constructivists and naturalists in science domains by exploring how various agents in the field try to make claims of authority over "truth" and "reality." He concluded that "the meaning of such terms as 'rational,' 'empirical,' 'modern' – and even 'science' – are highly variable, negotiated and contingent rather than universal or transcendent" and calls such terminology "rhetorical tools deployed in the pursuit or defense of epistemic authority, or in efforts to deny legitimacy to rival claims."[36]

Journalists have always occupied just such a special position as they create a "professional logic" that helps set the industry apart from other content producers.[37] For scholars of the press, boundary work occupies at least three different domains – the realm of audiences (and participants), news gathering and production, and notions of professionalism.[38] Carlson offers a "matrix" of journalistic boundary work, breaking the phenomenon down into practices of expulsion, expansion, and protection of autonomy and suggesting that boundary work abounds within the profession and has for years.[39] For example, while journalists may be expanding the industry's own boundaries through their new-media practices such as blogging and tweeting, they work actively to protect their

---

[34] Carlson and Lewis, *Boundaries of Journalism*; Thomas F. Gieryn, "Boundary-Work and the Demarcation of Science from Non-Science: Strains and Interests in Professional Ideologies of Scientists," *American Sociological Review* 48(6)(1983): 781–795, doi:10.2307/2095325; Thomas F. Gieryn, *Cultural Boundaries of Science: Credibility On the Line* (Chicago: University of Chicago Press, 1999); Michele Lamont and Virag Molnar, "The Study of Boundaries in the Social Sciences," *Annual Review of Sociology* 28(2002): 167–195.

[35] Gieryn, "Boundary-Work and the Demarcation of Science from Non-Science"; Gieryn, *Cultural Boundaries of Science: Credibility On the Line.*

[36] Gieryn, *Cultural Boundaries of Science: Credibility On the Line*, 362.

[37] Seth C. Lewis, "The Tension between Professional Control and Open Participation: Journalism and Its Boundaries," *Information, Communication & Society* 15(6)(2012): 836–866.

[38] For a more nuanced understanding of this check out, Matt Carlson, "Introduction: The Many Boundaries of Journalism," in *Boundaries of Journalism* (New York: Routledge, 2015).

[39] This originally comes from Gieryn, "Boundary-Work and the Demarcation of Science from Non-Science."

autonomy by rejecting calls to be more partisan and criticizing public relations work. Through these ways of expelling interlopers, expanding their own norms, and protecting their independence, journalists work to maintain their authority to be the nation's storytellers.

Some research has begun documenting these protective activities. Singer showed how journalists respond to a challenge such as digital-era practice (social media, bloggers, etc.) by tracking their evolving ethical principles.[40] Singer calls transparency "a boundary-breaking norm." In addition to transparency, verification as an age-old norm for journalists[41] – and a key component of journalistic authority[42] – offers a lock for press borders, according to research on the BBC by Alfred Hermida. However, it is a lock that is not always latched these days, leading to an ever porous border indeed, ripe for interlopers such as bloggers with verification skills, routines, and ethics of their own to permeate. For example, Hermida noted how one key method of verification for reporters is their very presence at the scene. Yet, he noted how the ubiquity of cell phones and mobile devices means that the key border mechanism of verification via witnessing is now a shared practice. The profession is responding, noted Hermida, by "rearticulating" the ownership of norms as with the American Society of Newspaper Editors (ASNE), *Los Angeles Times*, National Public Radio (NPR), and other legacy news organizations' renewal of policies on fact-checking. Authenticity could also be thought of as a boundary strategy, certainly on the part of citizen journalists, but also for professional journalists as well. Stuart Allan argues that first-hand accounts offered in nonprofessional yet public realms engender a kind of audience trust journalists used to hold exclusively.[43] The "I'm there" anecdotes make people feel they are getting an unfiltered,

---

[40] Jane B. Singer, "Out of Bounds: Professional Norms as Boundary Markers," in *Boundaries of Journalism: Professionalism, Practices, and Participation*, by Matt Carlson and Seth C. Lewis (New York: Routledge, 2015).

[41] Alfred Hermida, "Nothing But The Truth: Redrafting the Journalistic Boundary of Verification," in *Boundaries of Journalism: Professionalism, Practices, and Participation*, by Matt Carlson and Seth C. Lewis (New York, N.Y. Routledge, 2015), 37–50. As Hermida points out, many press theorists have disaggregated verification as a journalistic practice. Kovach and Rosenstiel define verification as "the professional discipline of assembling and verifying facts."

[42] Carlson, *Journalistic Authority: A Relational Approach*. Journalistic authority is another much discussed topic in press scholarship. Besides Carlson's seminal and defining statement on the concept, see also Barbie Zelizer's 2004 essay called "Facts, truth and reality are God's terms" in *Communication & Critical/Cultural Studies* or Michael Schudson and C. W. Anderson's 2009 essay.

[43] Allan, *Citizen Witnessing: Revisioning Journalism in Times of Crisis*.

uncommodified version of the truth that is a direct challenge to journalism, even if it's an unintentional one. In turn, journalists must counter the strategy of authenticity with a number of rhetorical techniques, including suggesting that the authentic accounts are biased, unsophisticated, decontextualized, mundane, or too raw to be meaningful.[44] In her analysis of the *Guardian's* citizen journalism site, Wahl-Jorgensen showed how the traditional legacy organization segments citizen content into soft news that it moderates. These strategies are attempts to normalize citizens' content production, while mitigating any damage to professional boundaries by segregating it from the privileged, journalistic-sanctioned, hard news. One is emotional, anecdotal, and unverified; the other is well sourced, fact-checked, and objective.

More and more, the professional boundaries of the industry are symbolic constructions that are now very much in flux.[45] New actors have already stretched those borders. Digital technologies – and more importantly, actors' increasing savvy at employing them – help people in the network bypass media organizations. In order to do this successfully, nonprofessional journalist actors adopt the practices of reporters. Scholars Domingo and Le Cam assert that boundaries are only as permanent as the practices that enforce them and any event can shift the entire dynamics of a field. This is quite a bold statement. If it is true, then can we really say any field with any kind of discrete border exists at all? One cannot just examine mainstream journalism's take at any given event, but must understand that discourse within a larger, holistic flow.

Does it matter what Madison's Kaleem Caire does if he performs his work from a marginalized position? What about in my other cities? In Ann Arbor, a Black school board member told us she constantly challenged the status quo when it came to race in that liberal city dominated by the University of Michigan, pushing the boundaries as it were. It seemed to her that little progress was made. Years later, Ann Arbor had moved the needle significantly on K–12 achievement gaps, and by 2016, three of the seven Board of

---

[44] Karin Wahl-Jorgensen, "Resisting Epistemologies of User-Generated Content? Cooptation, Segregation and the Boundaries of Journalism," in *Boundaries of Journalism: Professionalism, Practices, and Participation*, by Matt Carlson and Seth C. Lewis (New York: Routledge 2015), 169–185; Kperogi F. A., "Cooperation with the Corporation? CNN & the Hegemonic Cooptation of Citizen Journalism through iRepo rt.com," *New Media & Society* 13(2)(2011): 314–329.

[45] David Domingo and Florence Le Cam, "Journalism Beyond the Boundaries: The Collective Construction of News Narratives," in *Boundaries of Journalism: Professionalism, Practices, and Participation*, by Matt Carlson and Seth C. Lewis (New York: Routledge, 2015), 137–151.

Education were females of color. All of the case studies represented progressive or very liberal suburban-urban microcosms attached to universities with documented intentions of trying to resolve large achievement disparities. This was said in a Cambridge, Mass., interview but some version of it was said in all the cities:

> The city of Cambridge is a liberal haven and so I think that there is this willingness and the spirit of equality that is really calling us out . . . because this is the ground zero of liberalism. And I think that because that is the case, a lot of times people become blinded by their blind spots, for lack of a better word, and that really blocks the community and the city from seeing how they're standing in the way of really being able to do some radical things that relate to tackling the achievement gap in the city.

This book explores the various field actions in these cities in terms of what ideologies are at work, how actors' positions keep in place certain legitimacies, and more importantly, how some dynamics might change and a new discourse might emerge – one perhaps a bit less racist and more inclusive and empowering for those taking part (as well as for those who decline to speak in public spaces). If we alter the field operations, then one outcome must be a reconstituted media ecology as well.

In my information-exchange field, we have two institutionally bounded subfields: professional journalists and education officials. For these actors, their day job is exchanging information about the K–12 achievement disparities for public consumption. At the boundaries of these subfields, however, exist a slew of actors with agendas – progressive bloggers, youth activist Facebook posters, engaged parents – and who are interested in gaining authority in the overall information-exchange field. Some are motivated by political ambitions, a special-interest cause, or to advocate for their children. Their legitimacy increased or decreased according to their actions, including how they moved about in the media ecology.

In my case studies, bloggers, positioned on the edge of the information-exchange field, built symbolic information – and political – capital if they were able to successfully move within the boundaries. They did this in part by employing the dimensions of expertise to develop this capital. Let's see how this plays out when we think about an "expert" like TJ Mertz, who began this chapter. Who gets called an expert depends as much on the person making the declaration as it does the declaration itself and, in particular, their motivations in these realms. Capital can take the material form of "expertise" represented in degrees and other credentials,

---

Box 2.1: An interlude: Public talk in Cambridge, Mass., about race

Home to world-class universities Harvard and the Massachusetts Institute of Technology, Cambridge, Mass., has a reputation as a progressive, highly educated community. Despite being adjacent to Boston and filled with residents who work in that large seaside metropolis, many Cambridge residents believe that their town has its own distinct identity with a school district, six-member school board, and a population of more than 107,000 in just 7 square miles. Cambridge's biggest racial group is White (62%) – though that number is declining – followed by Asian (15%), Black (11%), and Hispanic (8%). The racial diversity of Cambridge is something that residents take pride in, but the city is fairly segregated, socially and culturally, according to interviews. It's one of the most expensive real estate markets in the country: In 2014, the median price for a single-family home increased from $858,000 in 2013 to $1.2 million in 2014 with monthly rent for a one-bedroom at a whopping $2,583. This increasing cost has priced out many or sent families and individuals to public housing. For example, in Kendall Square, MIT and the offices for big-name tech companies such as Google, Facebook, and Amazon exist alongside housing projects and significant poverty.

Twenty public schools and fifteen private or charter schools educate six thousand children, about 40 percent of whom are White. It is one of the wealthiest districts in the country with more than $27,000 spent on each student. Their access to financial resources, in many ways, makes them an anomaly. At the same time, however, the achievement gap and discussions of racial equity have been persistent, and the gap itself has been difficult to surmount. The schools report a declining enrollment but a dramatic increase in the percent of students who need free and reduced lunches – more than 40 percent of students qualified for free or reduced lunch in 2015. The achievement gap has been persistent in Cambridge with lots of explicit frustration within the community that it hasn't been closed. Cambridge has a long history of working on the achievement gap, from desegregation of schools and busing to the more recent "Innovation Agenda" launched in 2010.

Talk about all of this occurs in segregated ways as well, with a small core of affluent, "uber-active" parents talking in a Yahoo!

Box 2.1: (cont.)

online forum and who comment on schools blogs such as the popular Public School Notes run by a woman with a doctorate in
education from Harvard. These would all be "niche-networkers"
and "issue amplifiers" in the typology. On the other side of the
spectrum, people who were working with lower income families
reported developing phone trees and getting phone numbers so they
could text each other. Meanwhile, the major hub for school news –
the district website and its affiliated newsletters, social media, and
emails – were widely reported to be full of jargon, with community
leaders of color reporting that they are asked routinely to translate
for parents. Other institutional players included three news outlets:
1. *The Boston Globe*, was focused on the larger school system in
Boston; 2. The *Cambridge Chronicle*, the oldest weekly newspaper
in the United States still operating and now owned by the large
GateHouse Media, was the only mainstream paper that focuses on
just Cambridge, but did not cover many school-specific issues with
depth during our study period and reaches less than 18 percent of
Cambridge households; 3. The online-only *Cambridge Day* represents the only consistent school-board coverage. The city had some
local radio as well as high school and college media, such as the
Harvard Crimson, all of which published stories on the achievement
gap. No Cambridge-dedicated ethnic media existed that we found.

One of the biggest obstacles to fixing the achievement disparities
mentioned was the ideology of the city. The city's liberal and progressive bent often leaves policymakers with "blind spots," said
interviewees. Communicative distrust reigned; for example, school
officials, community leaders, and others noted that parents were
intimidated to speak at the imposing City Hall where school board
meetings took place. Many believed that criticizing the schools for
the persistent disparities was politically incorrect and would result
in repercussions in the classrooms or at work places. Schools
attracted much disdain for the lack of progress in resolving the
gaps. Like all of the cities in this book, Cambridge viewed itself as
unique when it came to school issues, and more than one person
suggested that an overarching sense existed that if they can't figure
out the achievement gap in progressive Cambridge, then the gap
couldn't be solved anywhere.

connections to power, job title, and other attributes attained through one's ability to work the field to her advantage. Keranen noted how boundaries of authoritative realms such as science can be mapped differently depending on who is speaking and what they are saying; these borders are inevitably influenced not just by the norms of the technical, personal, or public spheres that the actor is speaking in, but also the background and networks of the speaker.[46] Mertz is an expert in our K–12 achievement disparity realm because of his professional position as a professor and his educational background in education history. But it was the exercising of that expertise via his blog – his prolific presence in the information-exchange network – that propelled him to prominence in the field. He used his weekly public statements and his weekly presence throughout the field to network a campaign to become a Board of Education member. He achieved that status two years into the study and moved from information-exchange actor to policymaker with significant new power. He blew through all boundaries and ultimately become a more prominent player in the field because of his ability to manipulate the information flow, network with power elites on their turf, and organically work through the media ecology. Progressive bloggers in three of the other cities also used their blogs to enhance their political capital; all of them were elected to local office before the end of the study period.

Not all actors were able to accrue this symbolic information capital, let alone transform it into political capital; much depended upon the actor's acceptance of the dominant doxa of the field such as abiding by a progressive ideology. For example, another one of our actors in the Madison, Wisc., case study was a biracial mother of three who became interested in achievement issues when her kids experienced racial disparities. She started a blog and attended meetings about the disparities but after the Madison Prep vote, she faded from the ecology as she removed her kids from Madison schools and shuttered her blog (temporarily). But what would happen to Kaleem Caire? In our datasets, he easily achieved the top ranking for most influential in the information-exchange field, the most prolific player in the ecology overall. His quotes in news articles and blog posts, Facebook status updates, YouTube videos, tweets, and website content played a significant role in directing the information

---

[46] She explored how stakeholders talk about an accusation of funding fraud in some scientific research about breast cancer. Lisa Keranen, "Mapping Misconduct: Demarcating Legitimate Science from 'Fraud' in the B-06 Lumpectomy Controversy," *Argumentation & Advocacy* 42(2)(2005): 94–113.

flow over the course of this year in Madison. He was highly connected and knew how to work his networks. How successful would he be in his boundary challenges? Would he too disappear into obscurity? As the reader will see, the answers always depend on field positionality and the ability to network within the dominant doxa.

These examples reinforce the importance of recognizing the many different varieties of boundaries for our actors, especially as we consider the full range of media in play. Four important boundaries emerged in my study: First, physical boundaries, such as the meeting room where the school board members deliberate, represent a powerful border for actors – a place where only a select few may act on information via policy and where others go to raise their own prominence and attain legitimacy in the field. Second, virtual boundaries proliferated in the ecologies of my study sites. Facebook profiles are a bounded space, webbed with social networks but whose influence only extends to one's friends and followers. A news website may demarcate between work by a professional journalist and writings from "regular" people, sometimes with a "comments" tab physically distinguishing the two kinds of content. Third, journalists engage with rhetorical boundaries often, using specific professional lexicon and conventions such as "confirmed" or quotation marks. Last, mediated boundaries also exist. Information channels, such as a television broadcast or an emailed memo, came into play in my datasets as people shared links to other media on Facebook pages, for example, or when a reporter wrote about an emailed memo passed along through social networks. Many of the recommendations in the concluding chapter will address how these boundaries need to be explicitly understood and overcome to improve dialogue.

My case studies showed Caire, Mertz, and many actors – new and established – traversing many of these boundaries, or at least trying to. Within the very site of "institutional producers" were spaces where interlopers undermined journalistic content and thus became boundary objects that engendered challenge.[47] In the margins of the media ecology were socially networked places that helped people typically marginalized from mainstream information flows amplify their voices. In the next chapter, I track information as it circulated in local community and then explore why it flowed in the way that it did.

---

[47] I wrote a bit about this in a book chapter called "Redrawing Borders from Within: Commenting on News Stories as Boundary Work," published in Matt Carlson and Seth Lewis' *Boundaries of Journalism.*

CONCLUSION

As Kaleem Caire was sitting in his private meetings with school officials, union representatives, youth activists, and others and posting publicly on the need for the charter school, the White progressive blogger TJ Mertz was also ubiquitous in the information flow. Mertz was showing up at every public school board hearing and meeting on the issue of Madison Prep. He was posting publicly on his blog, Facebook, under news articles and on other people's blogs and Facebook updates. Both (as "niche networkers") were highly networked in their niche circles, but also served as "community bridges" in connecting information to people who might not otherwise have it. One community leader pushed the charter school and the other did everything he could to derail it. At this writing in 2017, neither were professional journalists but each had the technologies available to seek better positions for their cause, themselves, or their organizations. New actors have arrived in the form of commenters and bloggers, digitally connected activists and parents, and organizations with a desire to bypass journalists. In their ambition to alter the information dynamics within this field, these newly networked content producers discover their ability to change information-flow patterns and diffuse knowledge in different ways. As a result, the field shifts and resettles with every new actor or bit of information that enters it.

What do we make of these new actors and the way they relate to those already in these fields? As I was analyzing this data, I was seeking a way to understand this networked field in conjunction with the media ecology I knew existed in Madison and my other cities, especially as that ecology was evolving because of digital technologies and the way that people were using them. The internet and, more specifically, interactivity provide regular (that is, nonnetworked) individuals with the ability to communicate in a mass way (that is, becoming instantly networked). So I found myself asking the question: Is the change in the network composition an indication of the change in the field, particularly when it comes to sources of information? Bourdieu certainly argued that a field also has the capacity for agency and change:

A structured social space, a field of forces, a force field. It contains people who dominate and people who are dominated. Constant, permanent relationships of inequality operate inside this space, which at the same time becomes a space in which various actors struggle for the transformation or preservation of the field. All the individuals in this universe bring to the competitive all the (relative) power at their disposal. It is this power that defines their position in the field, and as a result their strategies.[48]

And changing the ways in which actors are networked is one way to change a field. For example, social movements are no longer defined by formal, offline methods of meetings, protests, and pamphlets organized by an established entity but by a patchwork of informal, technologically enabled connections largely through weak ties. Now, people self-organize through the logic of connective action, which is characterized by little or no coordination, large-scale personal access to multilayered social technologies, shared personal expressions, rejection of organizational forces, and other factors.[49] This also has drastic implications for the overarching media ecology that serves as a scaffolding for these networked fields.

When Benjamin Page[50] was writing his book *Who Deliberates?* in 1996, the media ecology comprised newspapers and broadcast news, cable television and radio, "populist" and alternative media such as underground newspapers, one-person zines, pundits and talking heads, as well as ethnic media. Although some news organizations were building websites and recognizing how email and other new technology could facilitate the profession, most conducted business as usual. Page urged a more holistic appreciation of what might be happening: "We should look at what *all* the media have to say ... We need to pay attention to the totality of political information that is made available, because much of it may make its way, directly or indirectly, to the public."[51] He suggested that public deliberation in the modern era is a mediated exercise whose actors include professional communicators, public officials, and experts, but can extend to "populist" communicators such as the zine editors. "When mainstream media are out of touch with the citizenry,"[52] he wrote, these alternative outlets offer a more representative form of deliberation. In 2017, we can add blogs, tweets, posts, and other information channels to his list of participants in the media ecology. C. W. Anderson in an unpublished manuscript also called for becoming more rhizomatic in our approach to media, considering not just the actors at the center of the information network – e.g., journalists, citizens – but also the news

---

[48] Pierre Bourdieu, *On Television* (New York: New Press, 1999), 43.
[49] Lance Bennett W. and Alexandra Segerberg, "The Logic of Connective Action," *Information, Communication & Society* 15(5)(2012): 739–768.
[50] Benjamin Page, *Who Deliberates?: Mass Media in Modern Democracy* (Chicago: University of Chicago Press, 1996).
[51] Ibid., 7.
[52] Ibid., 120.

network and information flow themselves.[53] Such comprehensive description is aided by a mediated, ecological approach to analyzing news
coverage.

By studying how digital technologies help renetwork a media ecology,
and thus reconstitute its field of information exchange, we can begin to
understand how public conversation about racially charged topics in
education can be improved via digital technologies. In this chapter I laid
out a typology made up of the signatures characterizing the media ecology
emerging in the local community of Madison, Wisc. (corroborated in the
four additional case studies). Institutional producers and their associated
individuals create a fluid foundation for the ecology and help establish the
power dynamics of the field of information exchange for K–12 education's
racial achievement gaps. Institutions in the local community such as the
press and the school system manipulate and adapt their information
vehicles to maintain order and extend their power in the field. Each
community also had a handful of alternative sites seeking status in the
field and contributing to the ecology with special-interest – often nonprofessional– websites. These places of content all purport to provide an
alternative to the media system – "to fill a hole" in coverage left void by
mainstream news sites; in describing their mission in this way, they
situated their role as being in competition with core domain sites, the
dominant actors in the field. Network facilitators helped keep all this
information flowing through aggregation features.

Meanwhile, niche networkers like Mertz or Caire and the blogging
activists in all my study sites used digital media to either challenge or
maintain the status quo (depending on their motivation), hoping their
digital media production would have some impact on shifting the field
dynamics at any given time. In the process, however, their content both
recirculated existing information in the ecology and added abundant new
data, comments, perspectives, and other actants that open up the networks to new nodes for flow. Finally, issue amplifiers embody citizens
contributing in some way in these realms by sharing, commenting, and
exchanging information through their own social networks. In the process, these issues amplifiers increase the presence of certain content producers throughout the ecology and buoy their production position (and
authority) in the field. Their participation – fleeting, ephemeral – can shift

---

[53] Anderson C.W., "Media Ecosystems: Some Notes Toward a Genealogy of the Term and
    an Application of It to Journalism Research," in *Professional Journalism, New Producers
    and Active Audiences in the Digital Public Sphere*, 2013.

both the direction and the volume of the information's current. To extend an ecological metaphor, envision a small trickle of water constantly coming down a mountain and depositing into a stream. This forces the water to accommodate the new drops in aggregate, and ultimately that stream becomes a new river, forever altered. The same is what occurs with aggregate trickles of information from network sensors as they alter the local media ecology.

In the next chapter, I will take a closer look at this river of information to understand just how much faster and farther our reconstituted ecology circulates. A key goal in the next chapter is to examine where power manifests throughout the flow and what roles our sites, nodes, and sensors play in supporting or undercutting dominant structures, messages, and acting positions. Are marginalized voices present in the ecology, and if so, how and where? How are status-quo challengers like Kaleem Caire using both traditional and digital media platforms to contest field boundaries, and how are actors part of the dominant ideology like TJ Mertz working to fend them off via these same platforms? Subsequent chapters will drill down even further into the obstacles, strategies, and opportunities in conducting boundary work at a time of communicative upheaval.

3

Power, Trust, and Authority in a Local Information Flow

In mid-2009, Matthew DeFour was about to get married, had no children, and harbored grand ambitions to be a state political reporter for Madison's largest news organization, *The Wisconsin State Journal*. He had the credentials, with a BS and an MS in journalism from top-ranked Northwestern University plus two years under his belt at a small paper. Previously he had jumped at the chance to cover Dane County, all the time with his eye on a bigger political beat. When an editor approached him, DeFour, a 28-year-old White man, was ready for a big move. But instead of his coveted state political reporting gig, the editor offered the K–12 education beat. Disappointed, DeFour pondered the opportunity but didn't see the pathway to politics in the new beat. He declined. A few months later on November 4, 2009, President Obama visited a local middle school – one located right next door to the newsroom, in fact – to kick off his national education program.

"That could've been you," the editor said later, after DeFour had watched the education reporter cover national politics in the K–12 beat he had turned down.

Something akin to regret tugged at DeFour.

When the K–12 beat came open again a year later in summer 2010, DeFour accepted. He inherited a giant beat folder of story ideas and sources that had been handed down from reporter to reporter. He set out to expand its state breadth, cultivating lobbyists, state education officials, and other politicians. By August 2011 when I first met DeFour, he had already made a name for himself in journalism circles for hard-hitting stories that were more political in nature than the traditional programming and cute features that characterize much school coverage. At that time, just after Gov. Walker had been elected and was cutting back on public education, DeFour was fully immersed in one of the largest school issues he'd encountered on his beat to that point – one that had both state and local ramifications. Can you guess what it was? Kaleem Caire's Madison Prep charter school proposal.

In our data, DeFour was the most prolific reporter writing about the charter school. During his two-plus-year stint as a K–12 reporter, he wrote 384 stories, including 202 front-page stories that take more time and are more heavily sourced and edited. DeFour was responsible for two to four stories a week, with at least one a larger centerpiece feature for the front page. Stories at the *Wisconsin State Journal* tended to require three or more sources and included named people. These sources included Board of Education members, the teachers' union ("for when it's an issue that affects teachers," DeFour told me), and a variety of activists and advocates. He received a weekly email blast from Jim Zellmer's Schoolinfosystem.org, the type of website that I dub a "niche networker" and also a "network facilitator." He noted that he deemed blogger TJ Mertz credible because Mertz either showed up or watched every school board meeting. In contrast, DeFour tapped those who pursued a narrower agenda as sources only for those topics: "Obviously Kaleem Caire is advocating on that specific issue but I don't think of him as somebody I would necessarily go to just get sort of general reactions." He went to Parent Teacher Organizations (PTOs) when he needed a parent perspective because "there's not really a good way to get at parents otherwise" even as he was aware that Madison's PTOs tend to be dominated by White, middle-class "booster" people. His menu of media includes various blogs such as Mertz' AMPS as well as other local news organizations, aggregators, and institutional web-sites such as the Madison school district. He received a few trade publications, such as *Education Week*, from which he got the idea to do a long feature story about how Madison schools with a higher percentage of kids in poverty had less-experienced teachers compared to schools with less poverty.[1] He did not receive feedback on the piece: "It's hard to tell how much impact the story had," he said in our interview. And he added that he rarely read ethnic media.

---

[1] Matthew DeFour, "State Journal Analysis: In Madison, Poorer Schools Get Less-Experienced Teachers," *Wisconsin State Journal*, September 16, 2012, http://host.madison.com/news/local/education/local_schools/state-journal-analysis-in-madison-poorer-schools-get-less-experienced/article_10472fa2-ff62-11e1-bcad-001a4bcf887a.html.

In these ways, DeFour was also one of the most mainstream, traditional reporters we interviewed, describing his job as primarily an information disseminator who used "fact-based" evidence to tell stories: "My value is in the ability to get information about the topic I'm covering. Maybe that's changing but I don't think it's necessarily changing in a good way." He reported being wary and disdainful of "bad information," which he called "self-serving and through a lens that tries to put the person providing the information in the best possible light." Meanwhile "good information is factual; it's honest." For DeFour, the biggest constraint in covering K–12 education in Madison was the "sense among people you are covering that they are doing this very good work, so any critical reporting is viewed as being antithetical to their mission and not helping society. In K–12 it was like, 'why are you hurting our kids and trying to expose things'?" It was a tough beat because of all of these moving parts: he needed to be conversant in statistics and databases, understand how to talk to all of Madison communities, cover meetings that lasted for hours with often very little publishable information, schmooze with a wide array of stakeholders, and be fluent in the esoteric policy and confusing acronyms that pepper conversations about the schools – especially in a college town with world-renowned education schools.

At the time of the Madison Prep discussion, four very different bloggers around the city were reporting and writing as a way to either supplement what DeFour was publishing or openly undermine his content. One, a well-off White school board member, used his blog to explain the thinking behind his votes and to clarify the school district's policy. This was Ed Hughes, a highly visible progressive in town who had been on the Board of Education for many years. The second was a White middle-class college instructor in education policy and father of two with ties to the incumbent (Dane) Progressive Party of the city. He was driven to philosophize about local education policy, much as he did in his day job, with the subambition of making a name for himself so he could run for city office. We have met him already – TJ Mertz, whom I described in the previous chapter. The third, an upper-middle-class Black civil rights activist with four kids, used his Facebook page like a blog to fundraise and garner support for a charter school that would educate Black kids as well as to raise awareness about achievement disparities in town. This was Kaleem Caire. Finally, the fourth was a middle-income biracial attorney and single mother writing in a blog she called "Obsession with Education" that she hoped would counter popular opinion about the city's schools. Her name was Chan Stroman and she was active on several nonprofit boards in town and networked among community leaders as well. "I will be blunt," Stroman told me in our interview when asked about the local media in relation to racial achievement gaps in the schools. "What they are doing is recycling the school district press release. The local media need to stop being boosters for a system that is not working for a lot of kids."

Taken in aggregate, these four nonprofessional writers challenged DeFour's journalistic authority, (re-)directed the information flow, and used social digital platforms to expand the media ecology. They linked to reports, analyzed data, provoked conversations, and offered comment sections where people contributed their own perspectives. Often they would link to local news sites, but when they did, they often challenged or otherwise "repaired" those accounts. By the time this study finished, two of the four bloggers would no longer be participating in the information-exchange field on K–12 achievement disparities in Madison. The other two remained in the public spotlight, producing content and collecting information capital. Can the reader guess which two disappeared from the public eye? The two White individuals continued in this information ecology, attaining authority as their production continued. The two people of color withdrew from the field, though both remained active for the cause in more private settings. And as for DeFour? He was ultimately promoted to that political beat he so coveted in Spring 2013.

This chapter examines the information flow of the Madison, Wisc., ecology, asking "What does the information flow look like and who gets to take part in it? How is content being shared, by whom, and why, especially considering the intersection between traditional media and social-media platforms? How do power and authority shape this content and direct how it flows through a community? Where are boundaries erected and challenged in this sharing economy, and what do these shuffles mean for traditional notions of authority, if anything?" In examining the five information streams around racial disparities in our cities, we note how much dialogue is happening in spaces such as Facebook and other online forums – but among fairly isolated groups. These silos contain White progressive politicians and active citizens on the one hand and those challenging the status quo in our liberal cities on the other. The higher volume of content produced by any individual boosted that person's influence score (quantitatively) and also his or her authority among their communities (qualitatively determined). Their offline positions in the field also determined the ways in which their content entered and circulated through the ecology. An individual's status or position meant their content was shared, reposted, and linked to throughout the network.

However, content that adhered to the dominant ideology, reified the existing macro structures, or buoyed the status quo was picked up and shared more frequently. This was particularly true in mainstream journalism but also happened throughout ethnic media or in niche public spheres dominated by African Americans, for example. Using the major case study of Madison, Wisc., let's see what these flows look like in a local community and how its direction, volume, and speed matter for power, authority, and boundary work. First, I will explore why information flows in the way it does, governed as it is by institutionally situated journalists, even as new technologies emerge and boundaries are tested. Then this chapter details how those flows are being diverted at times, according to my data. These reconstitutions lead to changes in how authority manifests in because of the changing ecology; specifically I argue that the dimensions of authority as have traditionally been understood have evolved. The conditions by which authority seemed to manifest in this dataset included not only those with institutional positioning, longevity, and exclusivity over information, *but also* those produced in high volume, with immediacy, on multiple platforms throughout the media ecology. This mix produced a significant amount of information capital that could also garner political capital. As long as someone was properly networked and working to gain capital in these ways, one could achieve a certain level of information authority in this digital world. Finally, I conclude with an examination of two incidents from the Madison case study that reveal the boundary work that characterizes digitized information flows.

NEW TECHNOLOGIES, JOURNALISTIC AUTHORITY, AND BOUNDARY WORK

In 2010, Matt DeFour wasn't big on social media, but he knew it was going to be an essential part of his job as a reporter going forward. At the time, he had a cell phone for personal use, no laptop, and had only just started Twitter and Facebook accounts. He was contemplating a blog about Madison schools, trying to decide between the titles "Extra Credit" and "Report Card" and asked coworkers for their preference. To him, these platforms represented mere tools to continue to do his job in his traditional way. He refused to draw information or quotes from public tweets, posts, or blogs unless he talked to the author first and verified the information. He thought carefully about what he wrote in these social spaces, always aware that he remained steadfast in his commitment to be an ambassador to the organization's brand, saying "I'm not a big fan of the personality-driven journalism." When he wanted stories, crowdsourcing was not something he considered.

The manner in which information has circulated in our culture structures our particular ways of being and thinking, interacting, and creating meaning.[2] Every time a new communicative technology emerges, we spend a lot of time heralding its potential and lamenting what it will change. Inevitably, these specific predictions fail, for existing hierarchies and institutions entrench systems of practice. Yet, technologies also undoubtedly alter how we exchange information – just not always in the ways we think they will. Social theorist Anthony Giddens suggested that humans developed linear rationality after the printed word encouraged people to structure their thoughts in logical orders of sentences and paragraphs. According to cultural studies theorist James Carey, the telegraph disentangled communications from geography as well as physical carriers such as horse or train. He described the telegraph as "an agency for the alteration of ideas" that "brought into existence new forms of language as well as new conceptual systems, and brought about new structures of social relations, particularly by fostering a national commercial middle class."[3] Medium theorist Neil Postman noted how mediated channels of technology helped formulate the way humans think, attributing our notions of equality, democracy, and even happiness to the rationalized print medium, in part "because it undermined the oral tradition and placed great emphasis on individuality."[4] But he argued that whereas print fostered a sense of community, electronic media, such as television, created isolated humans who exist alone.[5] And he worried that our dependence on these channels would nurture not the love and kindness in our human nature but the capacity to hurt each other. Nonetheless,

---

[2] Anthony Giddens, *Central Problems in Social Theory: Action, Structure, and Contradiction in Social Analysis* (Berkeley: University of California Press, 1979); James Carey, "A Cultural Approach to Communication," *Communication* 2(1975): 1–22; Neil Postman, "The Humanism of Media Ecology," *Proceedings of the Media Ecology Association* 1(2000): 10–16; Lewis Mumford, *Technics and Civilization* (Chicago; London: University of Chicago Press, 2010).

[3] James W. Carey, *Communication as Culture, Revised Edition: Essays on Media and Society* (New York: Routledge, 1992), 203.

[4] Postman, "The Humanism of Media Ecology," 13.

[5] This is a thesis put forward by a number of influential scholars, including this book by Robert Putnam in 2001 as well as this book by Sherry Turkle in 2012, to name just a couple: Robert D. Putnam, *Bowling Alone: The Collapse and Revival of American Community* (New York: Touchstone Books by Simon & Schuster, 2001); Sherry Turkle, *Alone Together: Why We Expect More from Technology and Less from Each Other* (New York: Basic Books, 2012).

each new communication technology has provided new vehicles for information in a way that has altered communication flows, how people received information, and how they turned information into knowledge. In turn, these evolutions created spaces for new ways of relating to each other, new kinds of networks (whether social, political, economic, or cultural), and, as a result, opportunities for power manipulations.

But whether we are talking about the printing press, the telegraph, or broadcast and cable television, these new technologies have long been political artifacts,[6] reflective of power structures already in place. Humans' particular use of these communication devices helped establish capitalism, set the division of labor, regulated time, and ordered a class system, all while each new invention disrupted existing social and other relations, such as private versus public or individual versus community.[7]

Furthermore, new technologies have been used to perpetuate discriminatory practices. During Colonial times, rich White newspapermen dominated the printing press, and then, later in the 1800s, only those who could afford to send telegrams roamed the world of privilege, literacy, and relevance. Carolyn Marvin demonstrated how those who could attain technological literacy exchanged it as a kind of social currency used to become "expert" and thus achieve prominence in elite circles. Those without access or the wherewithal to gain said literacy remained marginalized. Meanwhile, those in control continued to set policies that perpetuated the dominant power dynamics, including a systemic institutional racism that traveled across new technologies and throughout American history and its policies.[8]

Even as the telegraph, telephone, computer, and other media fundamentally changed how information flowed through the United States, journalism reified these power structures. For with each new tool, journalists and the news-media owners still maintained control over the selection of sources, the nature of the narrative, and the diversity of the employees in the newsroom. Shanara Rose Reid-Brinkley, studying how news

---

[6] Langdon Winner, "Do Artifacts Have Politics," *Daedalus* 109(1)(1980): 121–136.

[7] Mumford, *Technics and Civilization*; Langdon Winner, *The Whale and the Reactor: A Search for Limits in an Age of High Technology* (Chicago: University of Chicago Press, 1988); Carolyn Marvin, *When Old Technologies Were New: Thinking about Electric Communication in the Late Nineteenth Century* (New York: Oxford University Press, 1990); Joshua Meyrowitz, *No Sense of Place: The Impact of Electronic Media on Social Behavior* (New York: Oxford University Press, 1986).

[8] John A. Powell, *Racing to Justice: Transforming Our Conceptions of Self and Other to Build an Inclusive Society* (Bloomington: Indiana University Press, 2012).

accounts depicted "successful" kids from the ghetto, showed how these seemingly positive portrayals in fact reinforced stereotypes about poor people of color. These constant frames dictated how people thought about people of color by reiterating "scripts" that become the default narrative and are "incessantly reproduced."[9] Many others have documented these frames regarding people of color, showing how binaries of good versus evil and superficial depictions of victim or athlete or perpetrator have prevailed in American news coverage through the years.[10] Such constant portrayals nakedly display and perpetuate the subjugation/domination between the races.[11]

Reporters have been so essential in establishing dominant power structures in American society, that some researchers have implied journalist workers are mere cogs in political regimes.[12] Reporters' "indexing" of power, relying on story sources and backdoor networking among politicians and others in political, economic, social, or cultural power, reinforces a hierarchal structure.[13] Their authority comes from this institutionally constructed protocol that audiences have accepted.[14] Norms such as "objectivity" keep these power systems in place because they assure

[9] Shanara Rose Reid-Brinkley, "Ghetto Kids Gone Good: Race, Representation, and Authority in the Scripting of Inner-City Youths in the Urban Debate League," *Argumentation & Advocacy* 49(2)(2012): 84.

[10] Jack Lule, *Daily News, Eternal Stories: The Mythological Role of Journalism* (New York: The Guilford Press, 2001); Catherine R. Squires and Sarah J. Jackson, "Reducing Race: News Themes in the 2008 Primaries," *The International Journal of Press/Politics* 15(4)(2010): 375–400, doi:10.1177/1940161210372962; Hemant Shah and Michael Thornton, *Newspaper Coverage of Interethnic Conflict: Competing Visions of America* (Thousand Oaks, Calif.: Sage, 2004).

[11] Murali Balaji, "Racializing Pity: The Haiti Earthquake and the Plight of 'Others'," *Critical Studies in Media Communication* 28(1): 50–67, doi:10.1080/15295036.2010.545703.

[12] Herbert J. Altschull, *Agents of Power: The Media and Public Policy* (White Plains, N.Y.: Pearson, 1994).

[13] Tim Cook, *Governing With the News: The News Media as a Political Institution* (Chicago: University of Chicago Press, 2005); Bartholomew H. Sparrow, *Uncertain Guardians: The News Media as a Political Institution* (Baltimore: The Johns Hopkins University Press, 1999).

[14] David Mindich, *Just the Facts: How "Objectivity" Came to Define American Journalism* (New York: NYU Press, 2000); Stephen D Reese, "The News Paradigm and the Ideology of Objectivity: A Socialist at the Wall Street Journal," *Critical Studies in Mass Communication* 7(1990): 390–409; Michael Schudson and C. W. Anderson, "Objectivity, Professionalism, and Truth Seeking in Journalism," *Handbook of Journalism Studies*, 2008, 88–101; Gaye Tuchman, "Objectivity as Strategic Ritual: An Examination of Newsmen's Notions of Objectivity," *American Journal of Sociology* 77(4)(1972): 660–679.

audiences that experts and officials and data will relay the single truth.[15] However, most of these measurements tend to be based on a world where credentialed experts and elected officials have historically been White.[16] Objectivity and other evidence-based measures of rationalized truth are rooted in the policy of White-dominated institutions. "Objective" techniques came to be associated with civilization; those without literacy or education were dubbed to be lesser and uncivilized and not included in the "universal."

Notions of how to arrive at the "truth" have generally remained unchanged in newsrooms today, particularly among those mainstream journalists in my dataset. Policies in news organizations such as DeFour's *Wisconsin State Journal* discourage anonymous sources (to make sure the information holds accountability and to reveal potential agendas), emphasize balance and fairness (that is, getting "both" sides), prohibit "conflicts of interest" (reporters cannot fraternize with sources or even the communities they cover), and demand "evidence," (privileging government databases, reports from "experts," and first-person accountings). These practices comprise the very heart of reporters' job, their raison-d'etre. These "neutral" reports and entrenched policies, however, reflect a generations-old dogma of American policy that had privileged White men – and discriminated against others – without many reporters being conscious of this. These constructs ultimately exclude those who are uneducated, non-credentialed, and unfamiliar and intimidated by meeting protocols as well as those who are scared to speak out, have irregular work schedules, and lack transportation or childcare.

Journalists are trained in these norms in journalism schools and on the job. Even when management has mandated change, the habits are entrenched.[17] Indeed, these tenets are so closely aligned with democracy

---

[15] Powell, *Racing to Justice.*

[16] By the time of my study, which began in 2011, many of the cities we investigated had made great strides in diversifying their school boards and administrations. In fact the Board of Education in Madison around 2011 when DeFour took on the K–12 beat, comprised of five women, one White man and one African American man, who was also President of the BOE at that time.

[17] I conducted a yearlong ethnography of a newsroom that ended its print product to concentrate on the online venue, watching its reporters struggle with the transition with new standards. See: Sue Robinson, "Journalism as Process: The Labor Implications of Participatory Content in News Organization," *Journalism & Communication Monographs* 13(3)(2011): 138–210; Sue Robinson, "Convergence Crises: News Work and News Space in the Digitally Transforming Newsroom," *Journal of Communication* 61(6)(2011): 1122–1141, doi:10.1111/j.1460-2466.2011.01603.x.

that many consider their job more of a calling.[18] Asking reporters to be less reliant on officials or more inclusive of people not necessarily in traditional power structures is often fruitless. It is akin to trying to alter a field's enduring, routinized path dependency, which has been notoriously difficult to modify or its entrenched professional doxa. And with each new technology – cameras, the telegraph, the telephone, television, computers – reporters adopted the new media into their existing routines and structure of protocol; technologies did not radically change their professional ideology.

In my study, reporters such as Matthew DeFour covering the achievement disparities in K–12 education were beat reporters who cited the superintendent and school board members as their go-to sources and attended formal public meetings as their main pool for information. Many of these sources in all the cities studied were White men, but not all. In Madison, Wisc., their stories focused on logistics and procedures, documenting the votes at the meeting or explaining how a charter school proposal worked. Only a few of the reporters profiled a family who might consider the Madison Prep charter school, visited any of the neighborhoods from which the school might draw, or quoted any people of color other than the activists and community leaders calling for the school. Occasionally, they quoted parents who showed up at meetings. One reporter suggested delving into the racial aspects of the proposal would be too "sticky" – that is, interrupt his objective reporting practices and create tensions that he didn't feel he had the time or expertise to resolve. Another said she worried about offending someone and losing sources or credibility in the community she was trying to cover. Still another argued that after sourcing the superintendent and all the "usual suspects," the article didn't need any more information; it was balanced, informative, and met the deadline. One other noted that he had a hard time getting people of color to agree to go on the record and give their names, and tight deadlines prevented him from spending much time convincing them. At school board meetings he knew the activists would not only give good sound bites but also their names.[19] The end result of these protocols was that those who attained visibility in these mainstream news accountings of achievement disparities in Madison were familiar names of politicians,

---

[18] Journalists I have interviewed over the years like the word "calling" when talking about their job; I myself adopted this rhetoric as a reporter during my first career. It helped rationalize the low pay, for sure.

[19] I will discuss these obstacles more in the next chapter.

school officials and administrators, and major activists – mostly White or White "sanctioned" or single, vocal, visible individuals supposed to "represent" entire communities of people.

Furthermore, there is the reality that most reporters are White and increasingly come from higher income families. This affects the attitude and enthusiasm with which reporters – particularly reporters not directly on the "race" beat – are willing to engage on racial issues. Few reporters today come from working-class backgrounds, ignoring unions and working class issues.[20] In my study sites, all the education-beat reporters were White people. Most had grown up in or near the place where they were reporting, and only a few had had any African American friends growing up. These demographic differences are exacerbated by what Rodney Benson calls "the habitus gap."[21] These gaps represent significant differences in the practices and attitudes of professional communicators. In other words, the ways in which reporters go about their jobs – and lives – differ radically from poor people's and/or people of color's realities. These realities represent field dynamics; these differences reflect different field positions. The habitus gap is a structural relationship, and affects what is happening in the field of journalism.[22] Structural chasms lead to reportorial and narrative disconnects that result in superficial coverage, distrust in interviews, ignorance of cultures, or outright exclusions in copy.

I saw this tension as well as boundary work playing out in a May 2013 Facebook post by a Black community leader named Michael Johnson, President and CEO of the Boys & Girls Club of Dane County in Madison. With several "Person of the Year" awards and the successful operating of multiple large-scale organizations around the country, Johnson enjoyed mover-and-shaker status in the city and was someone whom media, politicians, and community leaders turned to when racial chaos simmered in Madison. One such time came in 2013 when a report titled "Race to Equity" was published, determining Dane County to be the worst in the country for racial disparities. It came as no surprise that a national network, NBC, contacted Johnson. They wanted to interview Johnson and also to connect themselves with people of color for a story on the report.

---

[20] William Serrin, "Labor and the Mainstream Press: The Vanishing Labor Beat," in *The New Labor Press: Journalism for a Changing Union Movement*, by S. Pizzigati and F. J. Solowey (Ithaca, N.Y.: Cornell University Press, 1992), 15–16.

[21] Rodney Benson, *Shaping Immigration News: A French-American Comparison* (New York: Cambridge University Press, 2013), 126.

[22] Benson, *Shaping Immigration News*.

Johnson requested a pre-interview with producers and a written note as to the intent for the story before he would help. The news organization declined and Johnson pushed back, posting the situation on Facebook. His post elicited a long discussion between people of color and reporters about the "right" way to handle such a story. Johnson wrote: "I am not trying to steer their story. I receive requests on a regular basis and they will usually tell me in writing what the story is about. I can't be part of a blind story." A reporter answered:

I would never be able to tell you in writing up front what our story was about, and I assure you this is why they declined. If they do, then they've put themselves in a position of having to stick with a predefined narrative which isn't good for you, Madison, or them. I can tell you what we want to discuss, what we're hoping to cover, and our general angles and goals – and be honest about them. But if I tell you in writing what I'm coming to do specifically, then I do a week's worth of newsgathering and my story shifts or changes, then I'm stuck with what I promised you or run the risk you'll use it against me. See where they're coming from?

A woman from Johnson's community responded:

I do not see Michael's attempts at story clarification as steering a story or promoting group think, but rather being proactive in gathering information about the direction of the piece. Many times public stories shared in our mainstream media, are promoted in our community in order to increase consumption, and profits, for those outlets, but do not promote the best interests of the community. If having your story be shared means it must be defined and told, without oversight or accountability, by another entity, then I would also be apprehensive.

In these exchanges, how journalists perceived the ground rules of public information production conflicted with how activists and those in the Black community understood the goal of the content. For reporters, the process of creating an objective, true-to-the-facts story trumps the community's concerns; for Johnson and his supporters, unknown journalists must first earn some trust that the story will help the community.

The inability of journalists and community members to meet in the middle on these habitus gaps created distrust and apprehension. It also meant Johnson was ultimately excluded from the story because he didn't play by the rules of the journalistic field. This represented a classic example of what was described in the previous chapter as boundary work: Johnson pushed back on the norms that journalists rely on to maintain their authority in the information-exchange field. Examining the broader information-exchange field (outlined in the previous chapter) allowed us to see the struggle over roles. The NBC reporter and all of those commenting in this post worked to maintain their authority to tell the story "correctly." For the press, this meant according to protocol (thus avoiding having "to stick with a predefined narrative which isn't good for you, Madison, or them"). The press, therefore, is the one who gets to determine what *is* good for the community by evoking their standards of objectivity. However, this exchange took place in public, involved diverse voices, engaged both journalists and nonjournalists about professional news-room policies, and contested authority. The Internet allows regular citizens to become a part of the mass conversation in a way that telegraph, telephone, or television did not. This unique two-way connectivity will change the field. But how?

INFORMATION FLOW EVOLUTIONS

By mid-2011, everyone was talking about K–12 education in Madison as the debate about Caire's proposal to build a school only for Black boys and girls highlighted intense disparities that had been present (and discussed) for generations but not really commonly known among the majority of White Madison. The *Wisconsin State Journal* reporter Matthew DeFour found himself inundated with information coming from online and offline plat-forms and administrators, lobbyists, activists, teachers, parents, and other citizens – all with an agenda around the issue. The information came not only into his email inbox, on the phone, and through the mail or fax, but also on the numerous blogs, websites, newsletters, listservs, trade publications, Facebook posts, tweets, and other spaces of content production that he was required to follow as part of his job. As the century moved toward adolescence, this kind of information ubiquity had been heralded as holding the potential for making something like journalism less concentrated on news just from power elites.

The hope was that as we move to digitally networked worlds, people from all socioeconomic positions will improve their situations by being able to access previously unavailable power sources. Interactivity allows every person to be a "mass self-communicator" who can diffuse and redistribute power across networks. Castells argued that people organized power into vertical, hierarchal structures to be more efficient and information had to be centralized for society to successfully operate.[23] But now, he argues, we have entered a society whose structure has been

[23] Manuel Castells, *Communication Power* (Oxford: Oxford University Press, 2013). A similar argument is made in Yochai Benkler, *The Wealth of Networks: How Social Production Transforms Markets and Freedom* (Yale University Press, 2006).

reorganized into networks with a host of mediated power players and other, new intermediaries. Networks are home to a "space of flows" within which people in their micro networks identify with one dominant position – mother, business woman, journalist, activist – and act accordingly, creating a "power of flows." Optimistically he goes on to write that the "the space of flows takes precedence over the flows of power."[24] In the past, journalists have been a major information authority in civil society dominating macro networks, concentrating information. But in today's reconstituted media ecology, the nature of that authority will evolve. Now community leaders, activists, involved citizens, and others can bypass journalists' frames, craft their own narratives of empowerment and of equality, and make bids for their own information authority over specialty interests. Or at least, that's been the idea.

So far scholars are finding some reasons to uphold this optimistic viewpoint about power diffusions. Studies show blogging and other kinds of online production generate feelings of community, incite more offline civic engagement, and increase connectivity among and between niche groups.[25] Bloggers use fewer officials and more "regular" citizens in their copy. Interactivity encourages multiway dialogue and "reciprocity"[26] among contributing authors online, which adds "emotion"[27] and other dimensions to the copy that is typically absent from professionally constructed news accounts. Tweeting can strengthen ties to local community and create "peripheral awareness and ambient community."[28] Within journalism, Hermida discusses how today's information system is dominated by 140-

---

[24] Castells, *Communication Power*, 467.

[25] Sue Robinson and Cathy DeShano, "Citizen Journalists and Their Third Places," *Journalism Studies* 12 (5)(2011): 642–657, doi:10.1080/1461670X.2011.557559; Sue Robinson and Cathy DeShano, "'Anyone Can Know': Citizen Journalism and the Interpretive Community of the Mainstream Press," *Journalism*, August 15, 2011, doi:10.1177/1464884911415973; Weiai Wayne Xu and Miao Feng, "Talking to the Broadcasters on Twitter: Networked Gatekeeping in Twitter Conversations with Journalists," *Journal of Broadcasting & Electronic Media* 58 (3)(2014): 420–437, doi:10.1080/08838151.2014.935853; Homero Gil de Zúñiga, Nakwon Jung, and Sebastián Valenzuela, "Social Media Use for News and Individuals' Social Capital, Civic Engagement and Political Participation," *Journal of Computer-Mediated Communication* 17(3)(2012): 319–36, doi:10.1111/j.1083–6101.2012.01574.x.

[26] Seth C. Lewis, Avery E. Holton, and Mark Coddington, "Reciprocal Journalism," *Journalism Practice* 8(2)(2014): 229–241, doi:10.1080/17512786.2013.859840.

[27] Zizi Papacharissi, *Affective Publics: Sentiment, Technology, and Politics* (New York: Oxford University Press, 2014).

[28] Erickson I., "Geography and Community: New Forms of Interaction among People and Places," *American Behavioral Scientist* 53(8)(2010): 1194, doi:10.1177/ 000276 4209356250.

character constant messages that have created a form of "ambient journalism" where people are always aware of the news on some level.[29] C. W. Anderson traced the path of a breaking-news crime story in Philadelphia and found information disseminated through the mainstream media as well as several key blogs, which "positioned within highly particular communities of interest acted as bridges to larger, more diffused digital communities."[30] Damien Smith Pfister documented the flow of bloggers into the media landscape and demonstrated how their content offered new arguments and changed doxa.[31] The online space is a space of changing authority and diffused information flows.

This study set out to document some ways in which the use of digital technologies might be reconstituting media ecologies in local, mid-sized communities where information exchange had been characterized by hierarchal processes (that is, top-down, institutionally driven coverage of K–12 news). First, the network analyses we conducted demonstrate how different voices were brought into the community dialogue on the issue of Madison Prep by different authors. Then, this data will reveal how people's networking changed the information flow in this community, at this time, on this issue. Finally, I discuss how information authority evolves because of these new dynamics associated with social platforms.

Different Authors, Different Sources

In all, ten people in Madison's information flow accounted for 56.51 percent of all the content produced in news articles, blogs, and Facebook, and these ten cited directly or mentioned more than six hundred people. In this information flow, our intrepid reporter, Matthew DeFour, was only the eighth most prolific author of public content. Of the 54 journalists who authored content in the coverage we coded, only two (one was DeFour) engaged on the achievement gap or Madison Prep in other media channels, such as Twitter or Facebook (although several, such as Pat Schneider of *The Capital Times*, had blogs at this time). For the

[29] Alfred Hermida, "Twittering the News: The Emergence of Ambient Journalism," *Journalism Practice* 4(3)(2010): 301.

[30] Anderson C. W., "Journalistic Networks and the Diffusion of Local News: The Brief, Happy News Life of the 'Francisville Four'," *Political Communication* 27(3)(2010): 290, doi:10.1080/10584609.2010.496710.

[31] Damien Smith Pfister, *Networked Media, Networked Rhetoric: Attention and Deliberation in the Early Blogosphere* (University Park, Penn.: Penn State University Press, 2014).

most part, these journalists published on the home pages of the news organizations. Traditional journalists (who act as "individual institutional producers") operate in a profession with entrenched, uniform protocols. DeFour and several other reporters who worked for Madison's major news organizations covering K–12 education and/or race adhered to standards of objectivity, balance, and credible sources to report. Much research documents how information flows into news, including from primary sources such as experts, government officials, nonprofit actors, activists, and other sources. Work routines, professional expectations, audience feedback, and reporter ideology, among other elements, complicate the content that is produced and even the direction of the news flow.[32]

Ahead of DeFour and all the other journalists (by many pieces of content) were: bloggers TJ Mertz and Jim Zellmer, Kaleem Caire, and a White progressive named Jackie Woodruff as well as the entity Madison Preparatory Academy (basically Caire or his employees at the Urban League), and columnist and White radio host Alan Ruff. These authors were producing content throughout the ecology, on a wide variety of social platforms as well as under news articles on the sites of news organizations. One, Jackie Woodruff only appeared online, mostly Facebook, but she was prolific. As an "Issue Amplifier," Woodruff commented in ongoing conversations and throughout the ecology, linking to news articles, citing fellow progressives, and reporting on meetings and hearings she attended. The presence of these authors changed who and what kinds of sources were brought into the information flow on K–12 racial disparities during this study time period.

Figures 3.1, 3.2, and 3.3 provide a visual representation of how the pattern of sourcing changes according to platform and content producer – journalist in news articles compared to bloggers and Facebook posters. These figures were drawn using the data from the Madison case study. As the different size arrows show, the bloggers and Facebook posters tap fewer sources for their content. According to the interviews we did, many of these actors preferred to use these channels to criticize media or comment on news events. However, in the process, Facebook in particular introduced more nonofficials such as students and parents into the discussion, with commenters mentioning their kids under posts about 17 percent of the time.

---

[32] Pamela J. Shoemaker and Stephen D. Reese, *Mediating the Message: Theories of Influences on Mass Media Content* (White Plains, N.Y.: Longman, 1996).

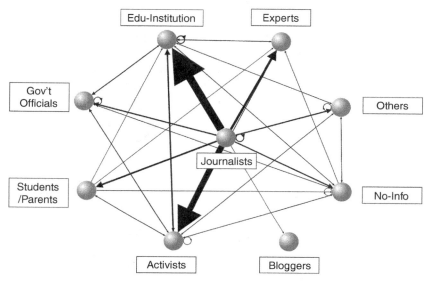

FIGURE 3.1 Newspaper articles. In this map, we can see that Madison's professional journalists heavily relied on education and institutional sources for their information about Madison Prep and K-12 racial disparities, followed by activists, experts, and government officials for news stories. This data reflects what other scholars have found in terms of sourcing patterns for journalists.

Networked Conversations

In interview after interview, activists, officials, journalists, active parents, and others reported how they used the Internet to share, attack, criticize, deliberate, ask questions, and otherwise engage on achievement disparities. Their Facebook pages teemed with public posts with links to blogs, reports, news articles, and other sites with the latest information about the topic. Just after the Madison Prep vote in January 2012, Kaleem Caire took to his Facebook page to help get his Urban League colleague Nichelle Nichols elected to the Madison Board of Education. Without this kind of mass medium, this announcement would have taken the form of flyers and door-to-door conversations. Now, we "like" the pages of politicians and community leaders and activists can work the information network, easily mass-distributing their perspective. Bloggers purposefully scour the information flow for worthy things to post. One left a comment for a national PBS reporter who had posted a video about Madison's achievement disparities: "Hari: Where is the report on this (I found it)? I would like to read

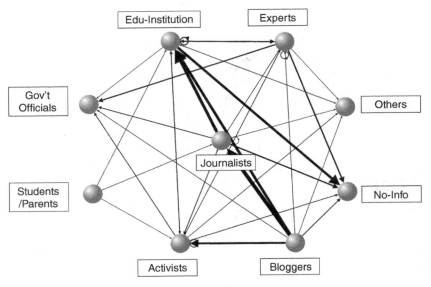

FIGURE 3.2 Blog posts.

it and potentially write on the topic over at Angry Bear Blog." The typically behind-the-scenes process of information gathering is laid bare in this public request for primary-source material. The blogger also uses the first name of the reporter, "Hari," as if they are colleagues. In addition to comment sections, Facebook and Twitter became the medium for information exchange in a way that disrupted the normal flow of content. In one example, our reporter Matthew DeFour posted a link to a news article he wrote about school board candidate Nichol's speech. After a lengthy conversation ensued in the comments that called into question the candidate, DeFour asked Nichols to respond to the thread. She posted her response to her own Facebook page (also public), which DeFour shared on his page.

Nonetheless, despite these expansions of the ecology and intriguing changes to the normally predictable information flow, the sharing trends reinforce the existing hierarchy in the city of Madison. A close examination of how these authors and their sources posted what, when, and where show that the most prolific producers were also the most influential in the information-exchange field and purposefully used their information production to maintain their position. The mainstream journalists, bloggers, and activists in Madison all cite each other in their articles, blogs, and posts. Those who were not as centrally networked, were not as well

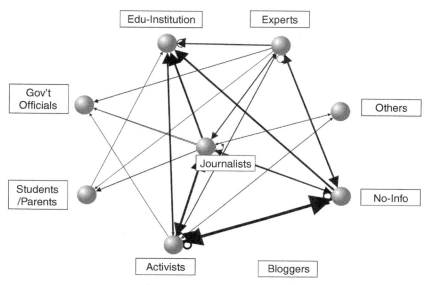

FIGURE 3.3 Facebook posts. In Figures 3.2 and 3.3, we can see visually how the information sources change between media channels. Bloggers (Figure 3.2) cite or mention journalists most, followed by experts. "No-info" means we didn't have enough information to designate the person's affiliation. These tended to be commenters with pseudonyms or names of people we could not identify from the surrounding content. In the Facebook posts we see a significant number of these "no-info" connections between activists, journalists, and education officials. The posts allowed for much more cross-discussion among people of different roles. For example, comparing Figure 3.1 (news) to Figure 3.3 (Facebook), these nonjournalistic authors brought into the information flow a more diverse set of people, drawing from different kinds of expertise, anecdote, opinion, and stories. These maps are also directional, meaning that you can see who is responsible for the information. Whereas journalists are responsible for all of the content in articles (Figure 3.1), we have a wide range of people in different roles authoring content in blog posts and on Facebook.

positioned to amplify their voices. To see this dynamic, we can look at the public Facebook page of Alan Ruff.

Alan Ruff was a White American historian at the University of Wisconsin-Madison, wrote a popular blog, produced a popular radio show, and was generally highly connected to the most active progressive politicians and community leaders in the city of Madison. He came out against Madison Prep early in the debate and launched a campaign to demonstrate that Caire and others behind the charter school proposal were the puppets of wealthy conservatives. Ruff was one of several progressive bloggers in town who connected to one another via sharing and linking, constantly reinforcing the authority of particular voices and establishing boundaries for others. In a series of posts and comments showing a history of Republican funding connections to Madison Prep, Ruff showed how an instrumental actor online can perpetuate the progressive information network in the city. For example: "For those interested in the ongoing battle over Madison Prep, this piece from the irrepressible TJ Mertz, posted last October affords some important perspectives," he wrote on his blog in December 2011. This post was months after Mertz's original post, but Ruff uses the ability of the web to scale time – that is, to keep alive past information contributions in a way print media or broadcast have difficulty doing. By calling Mertz "irrepressible," Ruff set up his fellow progressive blogger (and friend) as a dogmatic and persistent underdog, implying that others are trying to "repress" him. Many of Ruff's posts during the time period of Madison Prep echoed this sentiment, waged war on the charter school's supporters, and perpetuated the theme that the supporters are trying to get away with something through hidden agendas or outright lies. Here he boosted another progressive blogger, Rebecca Kemble who often wrote for *The Progressive* magazine and had come out against the charter school as well:

Rebecca Kemble has been following the "Madison Prep" story from its inception and has been on top of it all along. As a parent, community activist and damn good thinker, she has consistently pierced holes in the claims, assertions. emotional pitches and "selling points" put forward by the project's marketers. If you have any interest whatsoever in the issue of public schools and the ongoing attempts to undermine and privatize them, then you should read this piece and pass it along. Especially if you're in Madison.

Ruff described Kemble as someone who "pierces holes" in the "claims" of the proposals "marketers" (note the decision not to use the term "supporter"). In his endorsement of both Mertz and Kemble, Ruff continued to establish the position of this particular information network in the overall field. I will talk more about these kinds of legitimation strategies in Chapter 5, but for now it suffices to say that Ruff, Kemble, and Mertz made up a huge, influential part of this information flow in part because of their prolific posting and in part because of their consistent maintenance of their positioning in the field as dominant actors, declaring and then reinforcing each other's authority on this topic.

These strategies of information production by these highly engaged actors worked to maintain very clear boundaries for the field in terms of who can have power and who cannot, who can achieve symbolic informational capital and who cannot. And most of those we interviewed who were producing during this time period stated they were very intentional about what they wrote and where they posted it. For example, in his K–12 news stories, DeFour frequently linked to his own past articles. This *Wisconsin State Journal* protocol perpetuates the core institutional producer's position as a major field player. The result of this practice was that DeFour continued to maintain his authority as an important, exclusive, and authoritative information source on the topic. Furthermore, he generally cited only those with elite status in his stories; although sometimes he quoted from his Facebook page, these tended to be experts, proving his ability to access major power players in the field and earning him informational capital with both audiences and potential sources, not to mention the editors from whom he wanted a promotion to the political beat. And it worked. Just about all of the sources interviewed for this study listed DeFour (specifically, not just his news organization) as someone they relied on for information. But people participating in my study *also* mentioned a host of other nonprofessional content producers.

The main goal of the "niche-networked" actors in Madison tended to be "getting a message out" and essentially improving their own, their organization's, or their cause's position in the information-exchange field. They were adept at using blogs and other social media to achieve these means, tapping into information networks and trying to build capital. Community leaders and activists in all the case studies knew reporters well enough to call them on the phone, attended a large number of public meetings where they usually spoke, and said they often met privately with the city's officials and other power elite. Most also shared information in email listservs, posted on their Facebook pages, and commented on their topic throughout the media ecology. Reporters quoted them in stories, bloggers linked to each other, and nonactivist citizens cherry-picked from their content to make points in various forums.

These online postings reflected offline relationships as well. In surveys and interviews, my sample of contributors to online dialogue in Madison reported socializing offline with those they mentioned in their blogs. Online and off, most were known among their social circles as influencers and information hubs. This participation at various levels of the ecology – the institutional and organizational as well as the social and individual – ensured that these citizens helped shape the conversation a city was having about these issues of disparities on one level.[33]

In Madison, many community leaders reported about their encounters with the journalists and marketed any pieces they were featured in. Many also asked Facebook communities for ideas when asked for commentary by journalists. Boys & Girls Club CEO Michael Johnson, for example, asked his "friends" and followers whom he should suggest the reporters talk to in town and Rev. Dr. Alexander Gee, founder of Madison's Justified Anger group, solicited interview questions through his Facebook page. Thus, a group of information producers played a significant role in providing the fodder for the public talk about civic issues, while engaging others at the boundaries of the information-exchange field through online platforms.

Finally, we have another loose grouping of citizens on the edges of the media ecology who commented only on Facebook in public groups and on activists' public pages. They rarely comment under blogs or on news sites where their perspectives might enter the mainstream of information flow. In the previous chapter I called these people "issue amplifiers." They are sensitive to the information flow and help to shape their part of the network. These people generally "know" the activist or community leader in some capacity socially or professionally but don't generally comment in other public spaces. These people tended to be part of a niche community, compared to those commenting in the more exposed places of news article forums. Yet they responded to the activists, for example, when asked for input and in doing so, helped shape the ecology and its information flow as well. One woman contributed to Johnson's request for sources, propelling the conversation and expanding the network while simultaneously commenting on it: "Good! Hopefully when Dane County's horrific statistics – free and reduced lunch, incarceration, arrest, families living in poverty, graduation rates, and more become a national conversation THEN appreciable action will be taken. Lynne Green also needs to be tapped as does the DA's office including the Juvenile division." The female poster inserts a new actor for the reporters to engage, offering a new node in the network, and more information into the stream.

---

[33] And it should be mentioned, offline, private familiarities were not kept out of their online, public writings. Slights from years before would surface in bitter posts. Frustrations born from inaction in the past despite what some saw as copious efforts to lessen achievement gaps exacerbated the intensity of defensiveness. Rumors circulated widely in emails and phone calls before making it online.

This was the environment in which DeFour was trying to cover Caire's proposal. As the newsrooms around him were contracting significantly, DeFour was keenly aware of the fiscal pressures to be not only productive on his beat, but also relevant and essential. In professional terms, that meant maintaining *the* authority in the community to lead this conversation around the charter school. In digital-era information flows, we see time and again how interlopers in the information-exchange field can alter the information flow, expanding the media ecology. But ultimately what this comes down to is a battle over information authority.[34]

INFORMATION AUTHORITY DIMENSIONS CHANGING

Certain dimensions of authority evolve in new environments, shifting for each channel in the moment of content production. Four aspects of authority become altered in digital environments, according to my evidence: 1. volume of content generates information authority; 2. exclusivity no longer is a requirement for authority when everyone has access not only to mass publication but also to power elites through social media; 3. immediacy can be just as important as someone's longevity in the ecology; and 4. offline histories and dynamics still influence authority.

First, volume of content collected in aggregate challenge professional boundaries of production online, but are reestablishing authority and power dynamics between journalists and contributing citizens. Consider how one accounting of citizen "microbroadcasting" and "microblogging" (e.g., "sending timely, location-tagged bits of information to the members of a community" that is geographically bound[35]) might do so:

> In the way that citizen journalists use their voice and distributed geographic location to provide depth and breadth to newscasting, the citizen microbroadcasters use their mobility and understanding of their community's needs to provide broad-ranging and timely information to that community. No one can be in all places at any one time, so the organization of Twitter users in the field acts like an octopus whose tentacles feed information to the head.[36]

The idea that "no one can be in all places at any one time" implies that the power of citizen microblogging is about aggregation of information to

---

[34] Matt Carlson shows how Scotusblog, a new node in the media ecology around Supreme Court news, is challenging the mainstream press' authority to be a watchdog.

[35] Erickson, "Geography and Community: New Forms of Interaction among People and Places," 1200.

[36] Ibid., 1202.

capture everything that is happening. It used to be that it was journalism that held that power to define and be in all places at any time to form the pictures in our heads. They were there so we didn't have to be, and they decided "where" was important enough to cover. Now, the power in social media in terms of authoritative content production comes from a multitude of hyperengaged actors in different parts of the field generating information at the same time. This implies that volume trumps singular expertise. The collective approaches authority. The more sharing by citizens on Facebook and Twitter, through blogs and other interactive spaces, the more credible that information seems through the repetitive corroboration.

Second, if mass collaboration creates content that audiences can accept as authoritative in addition to, or even in place of, news articles, then this also challenges the established dimension of authority of exclusivity. One source of journalistic exclusionary power emerges from the press' autonomy. Matthew Powers explained how this power worked hitherto. Separated from the business operations, journalists worked within an organization that "was mostly hierarchical (e.g., reporter, editor, managing editor, executive editor). This form of organization is a social system; its primary feature is centralization. In a centralized network, all activity travels from the center to the periphery; so news happens when 'journalists' report on it."[37] When the Internet distributed power sources – or at least created the potential for this to happen – journalistic autonomy, which is an essential necessary ingredient for authority, became moot. Once everyone has the capability to be an information authority, does autonomy hold meaning anymore? This change means the information flow in any media ecology today could turn on the whim of a random posting, that someone untethered to an institution could have the power to shape a conversation in that flow.

Third, we must also consider whether the notion of longevity is still required in an authoritative relationship if nonprofessional citizens can pop into an ongoing story only to disappear. Traditionally, authority requires longevity because it must be built up over time and then reified repeatedly. Even algorithms online that measure a blogger's "authority" ranking take into account the length of time present in the web space. But then there are the cases where relative unknowns achieve prominence online because of some information production that gets circulated in

---

[37] Matthew Powers, "Forms of Power on/Through the Web," *Journalism Studies* 10(2) (2009): 274.

the network. Or when the commenters are so articulate (or poignant, smart, timely, or connected), their content is shared again and again on Facebook. The line between authority and popularity depends on who is the author, the relationship between the person and the community, why people are sharing it, as well as the channels through which it went viral.

Finally, offline circumstance, networks, and relationships inform online ones, and these interactions can stymie voice in production. Just because power seems to be flowing in new ways does not mean it is no longer settling into familiar niches. Public policy, cultural norms, corporate co-optation, societal expectations, economic inequalities, and real digital divides impede utopian realizations. Moreover, these new communicative streams might be reproducing a chaotic world. Anderson and Erickson both found that outside traditional media, information facts of the story were manipulated and that microblogging content fell into the realm of rumor, advice, gossip, and informal conversation. Others have shown how many bloggers tend to link back to mainstream news sources and other institutional databases or how media companies merely subsume "alternative" perspectives online into their website simply as free content.[38]

AN EXAMPLE IN THE INFORMATION FLOW

Now I detail how this played out in specific Madison examples. On September 7, 2011, the Urban League of Greater Madison held a listening session for parents of children of color to discuss Madison Prep, the charter school they had proposed. *The Capital Times* advanced the meeting in a September 6 story that focused on whether a quorum of school board officials would be present – thus, constituting a meeting that must abide by open meeting laws.[39] In the story, Caire is quoted as saying, "We'll have to kick one of them out ... I'm serious." As promised, during the meeting, Caire and others asked reporters and bloggers to leave.

The next day a flurry of news articles and citizen posts reported on the incident. Mertz, Kemble, and former city councilor Brenda Konkel were some of the most visible progressive community leaders in town, and

---

[38] Beckett C. and R. Mansell, "Crossing Boundaries: New Media and Networked Journalism," *Communication, Culture & Critique* 1(2008): 92–104.

[39] Samara Kalk Derby, "Urban League Meeting Closed, Unless It's Not," *Wisconsin State Journal, Madison.com*, September 6, 2011, http://host.madison.com/news/local/educa tion/urban-league-meeting-closed-unless-it-s-not/article_fb0ab360-d876-11e0-8359-00 1cc4c002e0.html.

online they frequently cited and commented on each other's prolific writings. This incident was no different. The most angry and in-depth appeared on *The Progressive* magazine's blog by freelancer Kemble under the headline "Secret meeting on controversial charter school in Madison."[40] Kemble, who had biracial kids, attended the meeting and was not recognized as media and so allowed to stay. Her blog did not allow for comments, but other bloggers, including Mertz and Konkel, wrote about the slight in columns and Facebook posts throughout the ecology. Konkel, incensed, posted three times about it and collected some 34 comments; both Mertz and Kemble took part in these online socially mediated discussions. One Board of Education member (and Madison Prep supporter) entered the fray on Konkel's page, defending the closed meeting:

I have been in rooms as a parent when these conversations happen. It is painful, personal, and often humiliating to the speaker who is describing the way they or their child were treated by a school employee or official. It is more important to me that they be able to speak their truth without the added pressure of media in the room. Some people may feel comfortable speaking in public about their experience, others would be silenced under a media presence. I can sympathize. I can talk with friends and in groups about my experience as the grandparent of a child who was the victim of child abuse. I am not ready to say that with cameras and tape recorders running, much less with bloggers who may or may not respect what I have to say.

As the week wore on, the discussion in these spaces continued. With the exception of the comment above on Konkel's page, all the online dialogue focused on being kicked out instead of on the charter school or why parents might need a closed meeting to discuss sensitive issues.

Meanwhile, the local media also emphasized the closed aspect of the meeting, rather than the event itself, in their coverage. In a *Wisconsin State Journal* column,[41] Chris Rickert used the incident to suggest Caire missed an opportunity to force mainstream Madison to talk about race in stark ways. DeFour, interviewing people breaking from the meeting, wrote about the meeting as a forum for the proposal and as a way to document the process: "Andre Nelson, a black business owner who attended the

---

[40] Rebecca Kemble, "Secret Meeting on Controversial Charter School in Madison," September 8, 2011, www.progressive.org/charter_school_madison_wi.html.

[41] Chris Rickert, "Chris Rickert: Maybe It's Time to Stop Tiptoeing around Race," *Wisconsin State Journal, Madison.com*, September 8, 2011, http://host.madison.com/ne ws/local/chris_rickert/chris-rickert-maybe-it-s-time-to-stop-tiptoeing-around/arti cle_d5bf3770-d99d-11e0-a10f-001cc4c002e0.html.

meeting, said he hopes the Urban League will schedule more meetings to highlight the issue."[42] DeFour also quoted Kemble, who wrote frequently for media around town, particularly *The Progressive* magazine, as she left the meeting. DeFour had trouble getting other people to talk to him as named individuals – a requirement all the local media in town, including the *Wisconsin State Journal*, followed. He knew Kemble would not only give him her name but provide him with a different perspective. Similarly we find Mertz quoted in a Channel 3000 piece, telling his story of being kicked out. Caire also is quoted:

"There was a concern about the media being there. We like to provide a space for families where they feel comfortable. We know a lot of people don't like speaking in front of cameras," Caire said. "So we really put ourselves out there to make a judgment call on something, and we'd never done that before. We won't do it again."

Mertz and Caire were the only two quoted in the piece, and in the end, Caire changed his position and backed down with a "we won't do it again."

During this time, as the progressive writers and the reporters were caught up in the closed-meeting debacle, Caire and Madison Prep supporters were also scrambling to call attention to what they saw as a more important meeting – a last-minute school board meeting to discuss the Madison Prep proposal's viability going forward. Caire himself was filling up his Facebook pages (including the Facebook page of the Urban League, his own page, and that of Madison Preparatory Academy) and his Twitter with the news that the Board of Education had "hastily scheduled" a vote on whether or not his proposal could advance to the next level for September 8: "We urgently need your support Thursday, September 8 at 5:30 PM at the MMSD Admin Building for a special public meeting about our charter school. Please attend! We need you there – but if you cannot make it, please send an email NOW to board@madison.k12.wi.us to share your support of Madison Prep." This generated about a dozen likes, half a dozen shares, and several comments voicing support. His concerns that sufficient notice was not given were also reported in the mainstream news accounts of the logistical process of the charter school proposal. One Channel 3000 article headlined "Urban League Voices

[42] Matthew DeFour, "Meeting Focuses on Achievement Gap," *Wisconsin State Journal*, *Madison.com*, September 8, 2011, http://host.madison.com/news/local/education/local_schools/meeting-focuses-on-achievement-gap/article_d994ec77-f032-564a-8467-b7b29 dd3531a.html.

Concern about Meeting on Charter School" cited an email that Caire had sent to supporters of the charter school.[43] *The Capital Times'* education reporter Susan Troller[44] also mentioned Caire's concern in a blog post on September 8, 2011, titled "Will Madison School Board pull the plug on Madison Prep's planning grant?"[45] In this piece, Troller cited not only the memo that Caire had sent to supporters but also an email he had sent to Board of Education members in which he wrote: "For an issue of such great importance and implications as Madison Prep, I want you to know that the Urban League of Greater Madison does not agree or support your moving forward with the closed meeting without our view being presented, and holding a 'public meeting' on Madison Prep on such short notice." Her sources also include other school board members. DeFour also mentioned Caire's disdain in a very process-oriented piece citing not only the same email but the very same excerpt. He wrote: "The meeting scheduled for Thursday conflicts with a plan he and Nerad discussed last week over how to move forward with the revised proposal, Caire wrote in the email. That plan included holding a public hearing on the proposal after DPI[46] decided on whether or not to approve the planning grant." No comments appeared on any of these news stories.[47]

In this flow of information, we can see how mainstream journalism and social-media platforms informed each other as important parts of the media ecology. Both sides used content platforms as a way to question the ulterior motives of the actors. In this examination, we can see obstacles to public talk such as issues of trust (which I will explore further in the next chapter) as well as the ways in which distrust is perpetuated and disseminated through this information stream. Who posts what, when, and how shaped field dynamics and, thus, changed the composition of the information flow of the media ecology. Furthermore, we can see how

---

[43] Channel 3000 Web Staff, "Urban League Voices Concern About Meeting on Charter School," *Madison South News*, September 7, 2011, http://madisonsouth.channel3000 .com/news/education/57744-urban-league-voices-concern-about-meeting-charter-school.

[44] Troller left *The Capital Times* shortly after this to change careers. Pat Schneider took over the coverage for *The Capital Times*.

[45] Susan Troller, "Chalkboard: Will Madison School Board Pull the Plug on Madison Prep's Planning Grant?" *The Capital Times*, September 8, 2012, http://host.madison.com/ct/n ews/local/education/blog/chalkboard-will-madison-school-board-pull-the-plug-on-madi son/article_f4a1284e-9012-574e-a911-aedb9d7ed708.html.

[46] DPI stands for Department of Public Instruction, the Wisconsin education department that approved the Urban League grant to research the charter school.

[47] All the local media regularly remove the ability to comment if they become too vitriolic or if editors feel the topic will generate racist and other hate speech. The editors I interviewed did not remember whether this was the case in these specific stories.

reportorial authority is made more complex because of social media – comments, blogs, and Facebook posts. Though comments were not allowed on Rebecca Kemble's *The Progressive* piece decrying the meeting, it was shared three times on Facebook, attained 66 likes and linked in 18 tweets. Instead of remaining an episodic item, the issue rose again and again through the study period. For example, former city councilor-turned-blogger Brenda Konkel referred to the September 2011 meeting again in January 2012 as a way to disparage the very idea of more charter schools being considered in Madison:

Madison Prep wants another vote in February. Smells like an election's stunt to me. I really wish instead of cramming their ideas down our throats, we could back up and Urban League would lead an open, transparent and inclusive discussion (that bloggers aren't banned from) about what we need to do about the achievement gaps.

This post reignited the outrage at the closed meeting with those that had been kicked out recounting their stories all over again. At the end of the post Konkel implied that her voice and others were not heard during the debate, calling for a summit where "all views" can be amplified. Meanwhile, Caire and the charter school supporters worked their networks and were able to be published in mainstream circles as well to call attention to their position.

At this time in Madison in the waning weeks of 2011, a communal conversation was not happening in Madison's media ecology. Instead, silos of talk emerged in which those most active in our field publicly vocalized what used to be backroom diatribes. In the digital age with interactive social platforms such as Facebook and blogs, insiders of the field could seize the opportunity to publicize niche-oriented details of events from ideological perspectives. Furthermore, dialogues were hierarchal and segregated depending on spaces and who was present. Madison, Wisc., was not unique. A Cambridge, Mass., activist of color and local politician described the Cambridge information ecology in this way:

You have these community forums. They're on the Yahoo! group list serves, the Google list serves, and in those communities you have the uber-active parents. And those parents just so happen to be middle-income, upper-income, White families. And that's where they congregate. Of course, there's some diversity there. It's not all 100 percent. But it just, it begs to show how, the way these conversations are happening are very much segregated because the kids that fundamentally need the most support, their parents need the most support. [They] don't have the time, energy to be a part of those conversations cause they're working two or three jobs to make ends meet and things of that nature. So it's just a very stratified conversation.

These silos, where parents, educators, activists, and policymakers aren't hearing each other, lead to distrust (to be tackled in the next chapter) and a constant grappling for information authority.

Dialogues, we see from tracking the information flow, take place among not only journalists citing the most powerful in our fields (e.g., Board of Education members, superintendents, credentialed experts) but also prominent activists using these platforms to improve their position in the field. These online social spaces also became a resource for new actors who hoped to make themselves or their pet issue more prominent. They could post on the walls of those with more visibility (and capital) than they might have. For example, during the back-and-forth that Mertz had on his AMPS blog about the closed Madison Prep meeting, one commenter wrote:

TJ, if I had known that was you speaking to Kaleem last evening I would have introduced myself to you. I was standing off to the side, with another individual who was also pulled out of the room and asked to leave because we were perceived as media . . . we were there as citizens and active community members . . . I too like open PUBLIC meetings . . .

This commenter made a move for more exposure in the information-exchange field, hoping to be a player in the know. Whether intentionally or not, Mertz did not reply to her publicly (as he was apt to do), signaling that interacting with this woman publicly was not an essential action for his own position in the field. Commenters who disagreed with the posts wrote as well and the bloggers and posters strove to repair any criticisms. But more importantly, these posts – especially those that adhered to the dominant ideology – entered the information flow and were liked and shared throughout it; their sheer volume helped ensure the authority of their position as well as its efficacy.

Even users with a small number of followers published posts that ended up being viewed by hundreds. Mertz reported that he had "a handful of followers" on his blog at this time (with an average of 200 hits daily and hot posts reaching 500 views), 1,432 friends on Facebook, and 200 followers on Twitter. During this study period, before he became a Board of Education member, Mertz posted every week, sometimes daily, often about achievement disparities. His posts contained on average 12 links to academic reports, government databases, and news articles. Many of his links were fairly esoteric pieces that probably would have remained unknown in the pre-online media ecology. The journalists, policymakers, and others I talked to knew Mertz, occasionally read his blog, but generally did not reshare his material (with the exception of the other progressive writers such as Ruff, Kemble, and Konkel). Those who declined to relink to Mertz cited concerns about his stated "agenda" as progressive against school privatization. For example, one reporter I interviewed distrusted activists' blogs and "would never" directly quote from them or even link to them, lest he be seen as supporting the perspective. That said, the wary journalists had no problem quoting him, as we saw in the Channel 3000 story.

If we conceptualize all these posts, links, and comments as boundary objects as defined in Chapter 2, we can understand how the ways in which our actors are manipulating the information flow work to challenge and maintain field dynamics. For journalists, it was control over the presentation of information and sources (like Mertz) in their stories. Mertz, the Madison blogger and activist committed to working on social-justice issues, particularly around education, also harbored ambitions for elected public office. He ran a failed campaign for city council in early 2011 before running for the Board of Education two years later. Commentary by Mertz, always signed and usually with links, popped up in virtually every platform we coded: news articles, other people's blogs, and other people's Facebook pages in addition to his own platforms and other well-attended Facebook group pages such as the Stop the Charter School Bill.[48] Mertz spent huge chunks of his day scouring the web, reading academic articles, and using Google Alerts to find blog posts and news articles on his favorite social-justice topics.[49] He also spent a lot of time on listservs, emailing with those most influential in the field (including journalists), meeting people for coffee, and attending meetings. And he rarely hesitated to share or reply. He said to me in our interview how "coalition building," "community organizing," and "getting out the message" were his main incentives for all his communicative activity: "I think that when you have dominant framings, that often there's a need to question the framing and offer alternative understandings ... In terms of organizing and advocacy, face-to-face stuff is still the best. But in this day and age, you have to do the other. Keep hammering your talking points. Keep expanding on or offering new evidence and new angles of vision but maintain the same themes."

[48] Mertz began this public group of about 400 members in 2011 during a state legislative initiative to create a Charter School Authorizing Board to help more charter schools operate in Wisconsin. But the group remained active around education issues (and was still regularly updated as of 2016).

[49] It helps that this is also part of his day job as an education professor.

Mertz' stated intention was to question those in power, those who have already framed the debate.

These posts became boundary objects for him, policing two different borders. First, he perpetuated and reified the progressive political ideology of Madison throughout the ecology, using his comments to counter boundary challenges to progressive tenets. Second, he used his posts to propel himself into a new sphere of power within the progressive ecosystem of education politics and policy. His posts (serving as boundary objects) contained links that represented authoritative pitches for credibility in both the information-exchange ecology and the education political field. Mertz himself had this to say about the amount of evidence he links to in his writings: "It gives you some kind of authority, that this is not just what TJ says, he has evidence behind it. I genuinely want people to know more and think more. I want them to consider the evidence. I don't want them to not take my word for it. I want conversations around it to start." Almost without exception, those I interviewed who wrote copious amounts in public spaces about the achievement disparities expressed the same motivation: some version of "getting information out" so that "conversations" could start. The prolific nature of the postings, their immediate presence, their display of insider knowledge, and their connections to offline networks of power helped amplify these dominant viewpoints in a way that gained traction among policymakers, according to interviews. And, I might add, they bypassed traditional institutions to accomplish this as well.

CONCLUSION

Media ecologies have always comprised different types of platforms with content that flows in fits and starts. Some pieces emerge for a brief moment only to wither on a WordPress site with few readers. Other pieces become part of a conversation linked to on Facebook or in a well-read blog, which propels the information into the universe to be dissected, heralded, and criticized. As people take up these pieces of information, the content becomes discursive symbols that formulate identities and spread values in a way that establish exclusion and inclusion patterns. Although journalists can establish a launching pad for these constructions, bloggers, Facebook posters, and commenters throughout this ecology negotiate (e.g., contest, mock, prove, and otherwise manipulate) any ultimate meanings. If the right conditions are in place – high volume, pervasive immediacy, offline status, efficient networks – someone without institutional standing as a journalist or communication officer can achieve a preeminent level of information authority.

When citizens wanted to counter or augment journalism on some issue, social media offered a space to produce content. For example, in Ann Arbor, Mich., race in journalistic coverage emerged in 2010 when a group of African American students were taken to see an African American rocket scientist to get them excited about college. Several White parents were upset their kids were not included and, thus, took to Facebook and other platforms to drive the he-said/she-said stories that appeared.[50] In Chapel Hill, N.C., one of the best discussions about race as it was being taught (or not) in the schools occurred during a class field trip when a girl posted a photo of herself carrying a Confederate-era flag with the caption "South will Rise." The picture went viral on Instagram when another student left the racist comment "Already bought my first slave."[51] In an interview, the school district's superintendent said:

The next school board meeting had 100 people all focused on the two girls in the picture. Comments from angry speakers like "no wonder we have an achievement gap" and "we demand harsh punishment for the two girls." No one ever asked about the context of the trip. Assumptions were made that the girls posted the comments. The fact that the two girls were assigned to the Confederate side and were instructed by the teacher to carry the flags until the end of the battle was lost in the emotion of how viewers interpreted the picture. It was the picture that became the focus and the girls were the targets of a huge outcry on social media because they were holding the flags and smiling. They arrived at the top of hill and their picture was snapped. The school was chastised for not educating the students about the meaning the Confederate flag has for African Americans. Although in reality it was part of the curriculum. Nothing could quell the furor over the picture. The repercussions went on for months and it all started with a posting on social media.

In these events, the reporters and the school officials framed these controversies as singular incidents and misunderstandings and used the discussion happening on digital platforms as the main focus, rather than taking the opportunity to engage publicly on why the viral communication may have happened at all. The institutions were called out

[50] David Jesse, "Field Trip for Black Students Sparks Controversy at Ann Arbor Elementary School," *The Ann Arbor News*, May 3, 2010, www.annarbor.com/news/black-student-only-field-trip-sparks-controversy-at-ann-arbor-elementary-school/.

[51] Reema Kharis, "For Many, Teenage Instagram Photo of Confederate Flags Speaks to Larger Problems," *WUNC 91.5*, May 8, 2015, http://wunc.org/post/many-teenage-instagram-photo-confederate-flags-speaks-larger-problems#stream/0.

Box 3.1: An interlude: Public talk in Chapel Hill, N.C., about race

The 17-year-old high school student in Chapel Hill, N.C., posted a picture of herself and another girl carrying a Civil-War era North Carolina regiment flag with the caption "South will rise" to her Instagram account in May 2015. They were on a class field trip, learning about Civil War history. Quickly, another individual posted a comment that said "Already bought my first slave." Though the girl deleted the photo, a screenshot went viral. In all, more than a dozen mainstream outlets – from the local *News & Observer* to the national website Salon – in the first two days reported on the incident. Discussion raged in social-media spaces such as Instagram, Twitter, and Facebook. Much attention turned to one of the loudest voices in the conversation – the girl's father who was quoted extensively in media defending his daughter. All of this resulted in several offline forums discussing issues of race in the schools, but still our interviewees called for more productive dialogue.

Chapel Hill is a liberal town in the southern state of the very conservative North Carolina. It is a city where no one can remember ever electing a Republican to the school board. The town had a population of 59,233 as of 2013 with a 21.6 percent poverty rate. Many know Chapel Hill because of the Tar Heels, the name of the University of North Carolina – Chapel Hill athletic teams, which are based in the city. This research university is well known internationally and thus the city attracts and retains highly educated people. Chapel Hill remains predominantly White (73%), but increasing in diversity among Hispanics and Asians with Blacks decreasing (now at 10%). As in Cambridge, Mass. and our other cities, Chapel Hill is pricing out many lower-income families with rising housing costs.

The school system has a reputation as one of the best in the state, but it became clear that this was true only for White, middle-class children in the early 1990s when a superintendent at the time disaggregated the data on achievement for minority students at the request of an African American school board member. A number of initiatives to close the gap followed, but today its K–12 achievement disparities remain persistent and pervasive across all grades. For

Box 3.1: (cont.)

example, at the end of third grade, 90.1 percent of White students are proficient in their end-of-grade assessments, while 36.4 percent of Black students, 43.9 percent of Hispanic students, 75 percent of multiracial students, and 80.2 percent of Asian students are proficient. There are 19 public schools as well as a dozen private and charter schools with about half the student population being White kids and a growing demographic of students of color, particularly Asians and Hispanics. The school board's seven elected members hear regular complaints from frustrated parents about the noxious disparities. In a theme we heard repeated across our cities, one interviewee noted a "fear of retaliation" from people still involved in the district either as students, parents, or teachers. One person reported in an interview that a Chapel Hill school stopped a student newspaper from writing about what was going on with achievement disparities, as one example. Whether or not this vengeful environment existed, the perception chilled dialogue.

Nonetheless, the schools work hard to communicate with parents, such as hiring social workers. But, the changing demographics have inhibited their ability to engage, with growing Hispanic populations often absent from the discussion. Black members of the community are much more vocal, aided by the very active NAACP and other community groups in the city. While some White parents are social justice-oriented, many were described as "consumers" of the school system, who moved to the city because of the good schools, work at the university, and have little incentive to change things up.

Chapel Hill, like our other cities so close to major media markets, itself has little in the way of regular journalistic coverage. Though unacknowledged by most interviewed, the UNC-run *Daily Tar Heel* – the only daily paper in Chapel Hill – provided consistent coverage of the achievement gap. The local radio is another source of news, but does little in the way of critical reporting. While only one city blog called Chapel Hill Watch covered schools (its author was elected to the Town Council), social-media spaces were rife with content about the schools. The school only uses social media to push information. Coverage in general is episodic surrounding an

Box 3.1: (cont.)

event. In comment sections on news sites, the dialogue often centers on how parents are responsible for underperforming children, implying that African American parents are lazy, addicted, not around, or setting bad examples. That said, some of our participants noted that race work in the South was easier because people couldn't "hide" from the history of the region, which pervades discussions in Chapel Hill more than our cities in the North and Midwest. Others in our case studies, however, noted that people get uncomfortable when talking about race. Like in Madison, some of our districts entertained proposals for charter schools or other programs to focus on students of color and/or low-income kids. But in all of our cities, such suggestions were considered to be calls for "segregation" and politically unviable in these liberal places.

not in journalism but in social media. And a new stream of information flow appeared.

Indeed, it is online where we find a much greater diversity of voices on the topic of race in these cities, during this time period. In Madison, linked through Caire, Mertz, and others, parents, teachers, and retired citizens spoke out alongside ministers, national civil rights leaders, reporters, and bloggers on these issues. But they spoke in niche spaces such as Caire's Facebook page or the Stop the Charter School Bill Facebook page. As "community bridges," "niche networkers," and "issue amplifiers," social-media users connected with other people, often "tagging" sources to bring them digitally into the conversation, in these spaces. In all the cities, long commenting threads cited external reports and linked to other information, bringing information into the ecology that would not have otherwise been there. While they introduced new players into the ecology, these producers rarely left the spaces themselves. The result is that while we have 798 authors of all colors and ideologies in the Madison ecology, those whose content is influential is limited to about 10 who are all major players offline. These 10 people, to varying degrees, are bridges or brokers who can amplify voices or silence them, who can illuminate alternative perspectives and add new actors into discussion, and who are most trusted to funnel content into the information flow.

With every blog, and every post, Mertz, Caire, Hughes, and other activists, community leaders, politicians, and nonjournalists challenged the mainstream, reportorial version of events. They forced openings to the information flow to admit hundreds of new voices not otherwise heard in the public information streams. They asserted themselves into the field as monitors of the press – sometimes praising news stories, often criticizing. They even commented on procedure and protocol long established as part of "objective" journalistic routines. They rallied their communities in support of this role as well. The evidence also demonstrated that those who speak the loudest and most often attain influence in the field unmatched by any journalists. In order to advance the field, it seems from this data, a content producer needs to be constantly visible in the ecology, always maintaining the field position.

Our *Wisconsin State Journal* reporter Matt DeFour tried to ignore the "noise" except when it seemed to encroach into "news value," and he had to respond. He and other mainstream reporters posted their stories and avoided the commenting spaces unless they felt the need to repair mis-impressions to protect the boundaries of their information authority. In the social-media realm, reporters were on the defensive. For example, DeFour tried to maintain control over a conversation on his Facebook page; and other journalists visited the Facebook page of Boys & Girls Club of Dane County CEO Michael Johnson to "explain" why NBC wouldn't meet his demands. Many of our institutional actors, such as journalists and school officials (our "institutional producers" and "individual institutional producers"), however simply avoided the interactivity available online because of the intense criticism in social-media spaces. This was true across the cities studied for this book. For example, a Cambridge, Mass., school administrator told us a story of inviting a critical blogger into his office to discuss the achievement disparities. He spent an hour and a half thinking he was having a civil discussion about policy. A couple days later the blogger compared him to a serial killer with disingenuous charm. The incident reaffirmed the administrator's avoidance of blogs and comments online, preferring face-to-face dialogue about these issues. His absence likely led to a less nuanced conversation in these realms.

Information authority depends upon being listened to, and though regular people have the *capacity* to produce, they have only limited control over whether audiences pay attention. As an example, let's return to our four bloggers whom we mentioned at the start of our chapter – the White school board member, the Black activist, the White activist, and the biracial attorney and parent. I noted how of the four, only two remained producers in the ecology by the end of the study period in 2014. They were Ed Hughes, a White school board member of more than a decade, and the White TJ Mertz who was elected to the board after the Madison Prep vote. Meanwhile, Caire left the Urban League after Madison Prep failed. And the biracial attorney withdrew her children from Madison public schools and stopped blogging regularly.[52] All of these – some of our most prolific and influential content producers – represented roles of authority in offline worlds as directors of centers, union representatives, school officials, and longtime political activists. Each of these content producers "understood" the unwritten "rules" of providing information that was credible and accurate, linking and verifying. Each also "marketed" their writings through their networks. Chan Stroman's "Obsession with Education," for example, showed up occasionally in Jim Zellmer's Schoolinfosystem.org, was reboosted by her Twitter account, and was filled with facts gleaned from academic journals and other formal evidence caches. But in the end, she said she got busy with other things and realized "nothing was going to change." She added in our interview, "I knew it would be a lot of talk and there is a temptation to regard talk as substance. I'm not interested in conversations that are merely about people kind of confirming their affiliation with a particular group and parroting the official party lines. That is not interesting to me and that tends to be the nature of a lot of policy discourse in Madison. And not just Madison, but especially Madison." Stroman was not cited in any of the mainstream news articles on K–12 racial disparities in our dataset. In the mainstream flow, Black and Brown people were represented by established community leaders like Caire or those credentialed by institutions like Gloria Ladson-Billings, a frequently cited African American education professor at the University of Wisconsin-Madison. Those who became a solid part of the ecology tended in these datasets to be those with structural advantages offline who had mastered the field dynamics. Similarly, after analyzing millions of websites and their linking structures, Hindman found that hierarchy ruled in political blogging: "The hierarchy is structural, woven into the hyperlinks that make up the web; it is economic, in the

---

[52] Although years later, by 2015, "Obsession with Education" was being populated again, if somewhat sporadically, http://eduphilia.blogspot.com/.

dominance of companies like Google, Yahoo!, and Microsoft; and it is social, in the small group of White, highly educated, male professionals who are vastly overrepresented in online opinion."[53] My evidence shows that new influencers are affecting how information travels through a media ecology. In essence, community leaders, activists, and others who hold (or aspire to hold) public offices offline and who are creating space for information production online are becoming part of a new expanded newsroom that is not bound to one organization.[54] But the evidence also clearly indicates that one's position in the field (offline) mitigates this influence.

In December 2011, the week before the big school board vote on the charter school proposal by Kaleem Caire, he and the Urban League of Greater Madison introduced a flurry of content to the information flow. Our most prolific reporter, Matthew DeFour, knew it was going to be a huge (and exhausting) week for him. He knew the vote would be well attended; it was the first time in twenty years that school officials had moved the hearing out of administrative offices downtown to the far West location of Memorial High School. And he knew the evening was going to be fraught with tension. Everyone was talking about it and the various social media and blogs he monitored were blowing up with last-minute pleas and arguments both for and against. People were already setting it up as an "us" versus "them" battle with some in communities of color suggesting the vote would serve as an indication whether the Board of Education was really committed to closing Madison's K–12 racial achievement disparities.

This dichotomy put DeFour in an awkward position as the major reporter covering the upcoming evening. On the one hand, he could highlight this evident chasm in the community, even knowing the binary being set up would inevitably lead to more polarization and was, frankly, artificially constructed. The alternative was to try to write more systemic stories he didn't have time for and wasn't sure he had the expertise for. DeFour began his week talking to as many Board of Education members as would answer his calls. He wrote half a dozen articles and blog posts and wrote one Facebook post about the looming

---

[53] Matthew Hindman, *The Myth of Digital Democracy* (Princeton: Princeton University Press, 2008), 18–19.

[54] In one early paper of mine, I dubbed this the "cyber-newsroom." Sue Robinson, "The Cyber-Newsroom: A Case Study of the Journalistic Paradigm in a News Narrative's Journey from a Newspaper to Cyberspace," *Mass Communication and Society* 12(4) (September 30, 2009): 403–422, doi:10.1080/15205430802513234.

event. He and his editor strategized how to cover what would be a long, complicated, and fraught meeting. Thus, as the big night of December 19, 2011 approached, he had a feeling for which way the vote would go. But as he had seen over the years, anything could happen in such an event and often did.

PART II

4

Obstacles to Public Discourse About Race

For weeks ahead of the vote, Kaleem Caire and the supporters of Madison Prep blanketed social media with pleas to "come on out!" and "let your voice be heard!" The Board of Education will listen. They just had to. The schools were failing their kids, and finally people seemed to be taking note. Long dialogues on Facebook preceded the night – December 19, 2011 – with parents asking how they could get their children into the school and back-and-forths about the chances of the charter school proposal passing. Everyone knew that three BOE members had declared themselves against it and two for it. But the remaining two votes were unknown and people figured it could go either way. They strode into the auditorium, some full of cautious optimism and others feeling as if they were on a fool's errand. But they all came anyway. And they spoke up! One by one, they offered up personal experiences of racism, of disparity, of inadequacies of the schools and laid out an argument in support of Madison Prep. But after several hours, they found themselves just sitting, listening in stunned silence as one by one the school board members read from prepared statements pulled out of pockets and bags. The members spoke of legalities associated with charter schools and teacher unions, of disproportional expenses for a small segment of the population during times of public-school funding strife (including what some saw as unreasonable administrative fees of $900,000 to the Urban League over five years), and of worries that the school would be leaving out many of the children who most needed the one-on-one attention. They also disliked that the plan would give unprecedented oversight to the Urban League instead of the school district in its management. Little of the people's long hours of testimony seemed to be considered or even acknowledged in these prepared statements. Little of the people's words seemed to have been heard. At least that's the way attendees felt.

And long after the Board of Education members had gone home – the verdict of the 5–2 no to Madison Prep hanging heavy in the air – the supporters of Madison Prep sat still with their disappointment, not quite successful in squelching the resentment choking them. Caire rose to address the morose, defeated crowd. He reminded people to keep up the good fight, that they would just take the school to the people, do some fundraising, do it themselves. He urged people to run for school board to change up the power dynamics. He talked of filing a racial discrimination suit. "We are going to challenge this school district like they've never been challenged before, I swear to God," Caire told the emotional crowd.

Slowly, people started to leave the room in trickles, comforting each other as they went. Some talking to themselves, saying "I can't believe what I just saw." And they trudged out of the hall, back to their families. As they left, and in the weeks and months that followed, distrust sidled in, replacing the optimism. Caire left too and soon after, left the Urban League, nurturing the seeds of an idea to privately fund Madison Prep.[1] Five years later, in focus groups and interviews, people who had been at that meeting spoke of that moment as a turning point for them, the moment where any hope they had that the school district would somehow respond to the intense racial disparities flittered away. They spoke of that moment as the moment they "gave up."

The theme of "giving up" echoed throughout our cities in Wisconsin, Michigan, Illinois, North Carolina, and Massachusetts. Some citizens refrained from participating in public forums about the opportunity gaps – a problem plaguing each city. These cities hosted huge racial academic and economic disparities: 40 percent or more of the entire school population received free-and-reduced lunch and had large gaps in their high-school graduation rates, while a majority of the White population consisted of multigeneration college graduates. These chasms led to segregation in communicative patterns in all of our cities as well. The superintendent of the Cambridge, Mass., public schools described the information-exchange problem as one of income and education gaps:

Basically, what you had here was: . . . you have a very educated and very savvy half of a population. The middle class wanted to preserve the status quo because it was

---

[1] This endeavor culminated in Caire founding a private preschool called One City Early Learning Centers for communities of color in 2016, after seeking private funding for Madison Prep failed.

working for their kids . . . And then you have the voiceless who were not at any of those hearings, who were too busy working three jobs.

Those absences of voices carried into the media. When many of the local reporters in these cities approached Black or Brown parents to find out more about their children's experiences in the schools, they heard an earful of stories. But when it came time to catch the sources' names for the published story, the answer was often no. "Honestly it got to the point that I stopped trying," said one Wisconsin freelancer who wrote frequently about Madison Prep. On this point, many of the journalists interviewed for this study agreed: finding parents to talk to about issues involving racial achievement disparities in a publishable way was nearly impossible. Few wanted to go on the record and have their names associated with negative information. One network television reporter in Wisconsin remembered making a beeline for Black and Brown community leaders and public meetings rather than seeking sources in neighborhoods:

You went to these people because you knew you could trust that they would go on camera in a timely, reliable way. If I go into neighborhoods, I cannot reliably and quickly find someone truly engaged in the issue who would also be willing to speak publicly on TV. The timing of the public hearings was often an obstacle, too. We have a 10 p.m. deadline and a constraint on the length of the story, so you could only share so much. That is always our frustration.

One parent whom reporters frequently asked for comment understood this difficulty perfectly. "People are afraid of repercussions," explained Ms. Jones. "I mean, I applied for jobs I didn't get because of my outspoken comments on certain topics that didn't make people comfortable." She added that people of color feel judged when they speak out, with every word scrutinized and constant confrontations by random White people. At work the morning after she spoke at a Madison Prep public hearing, a coworker came up to her to challenge her on her views about charter schools:

She got really upset with me. Even though this coworker had no child in the school district, she wanted to tell me that my view was totally wrong. And I had to stand up for myself and let her know, "we can talk after work . . . but I am not going to discuss this with you at work because this is not the proper place."[2]

---

[2] All but two of the Black or multiracial parents I interviewed spoke in a focus group, with the promise of anonymity. They are listed here with pseudonyms. They were given $25 gift cards for their participation.

Cynicism, wariness, fatigue, and frustration flowed from the focus groups we held with other parents who had Black or Brown students in the schools as well. They told story after story with anecdotes about offenses and incidents that they perceived as being racially motivated. Most of their stories had to do with their children's schools – they spoke of PTO functions that White parents dominated, disproportionate punishment for their students of color, and principals and teachers who implied that parents didn't care, worked too much, or did drugs. They also mentioned the difficulty of having a physical presence at meetings concerning their children's education. They often learned about school hearings on proposals like Madison Prep at the last minute, only to find out the meeting was across town. And even if they made it to the meeting, these meetings typically resulted in ... well ... nothing. "So why would we bother anymore? At some point, you just give up," said Mr. Joshua, a Black man.

Over and over, we heard how the progressive politics in these cities inhibited good deliberation about solutions. A school board member in Ann Arbor, Mich., described similar dynamics in the home of the University of Michigan's flagship campus:

Oh, we love to talk. We're great in Ann Arbor. We're very smart people. We're very engaged ... It's nothing for us to get 200 parents in an auditorium at one of our board meetings around certain issues. I mean, that's just nothing ... And schools ... see education is what we do in Ann Arbor. That is our income. It's our base. It's our livelihood. It's our brand. But we struggle, I mean, you know, we're quite a liberal town but we're also very conservative. So when you start talking about race and disparity, you see very ugly signs and evidence of how not liberal and not equitable we can be at times when it comes to those that are disadvantaged, particularly socioeconomically.

The advantaged people in these cities, comfortable with reports, statistics, and academic jargon, effectively dominated conversation while the institutional and organizational structures that perpetuated the disparities remained unchanged. Said a national YWCA Black activist (who grew up in Madison, Wisc., but lived in Washington, D.C., and was knowledgeable about all of these cities): "The progressive liberals have never figured it out. But they are quicker to congratulate and pat themselves on the back." In Cambridge, Mass., one Black city official noted how the progressive mindset reflected the social segregation at work and exacerbated the disconnect:

People with good will try to do things, but it doesn't change the structure. And I think for a lot of White people, not all, there's just obliviousness. Even people who can do anti-racism trainings and articulate theories about class and structure, they can tell you lots of facts about what's wrong, but they still live in a world ... of privilege ... Because you want to talk about race and you want to talk about how, how the kids of color and their achievements in school is not the same, but you don't want to talk about ...what percentage of kids of color spend the summer in their apartment in the public housing? And what percentage of the White kids spend their summers on the coast of France or in Vermont or in Maine or visiting relatives around the country?

Often, attempts to change the institutional structures were met with resistance, or proposals watered down to the point of ineffectiveness. In the wake of the Madison Prep charter school rejection, the Madison Board of Education and superintendent at the time – a man named Dan Nerad – promised to address the achievement gaps. Nerad spent the spring working on a plan, holding more hearings, looking at research, and crafting a $105.6 million plan over five years. The BOE whittled down the proposal, finally passing a vastly scaled back $4.5 million for the year with no plan for the future. In the wake of the Madison Prep rejection, this perpetuated the feeling of inaction. In October 2013, The Wisconsin Council on Children and Families published the *Race to Equity: A Baseline Report on the State of Racial Disparities in Dane County*, which aggregated evidence to show Dane County was the worst in the country when it came to racial disparities from education metrics to unemployment and incarceration. A social movement named "Justified Anger" began that raised a bunch of money and sparked a lot of community forums but soon left the front pages. Then in March 2015, a White police officer shot and killed an unarmed biracial 19-year-old man named Tony Robinson. The city erupted in protests, reinvigorated after the district attorney declined to prosecute the officer in May 2015.[3]

More violence, more journalism, more meetings, little improvement, said some in the city.

And Madison wasn't alone in this frustrating cycle – all of our communities found themselves trapped in the obstacles to public talk to some degree. In Evanston, Ill., one Black city official recounted how her constant dismay at the inaction made her so cynical it took some personal work on her part to appreciate when real change was afoot and for her then to have an open mind to the ideas being proposed. In Chapel Hill, N.C., a Black high school specialist described how difficult it was to

---

[3] Catherine Shoichet and Jethro Mullen, "Tony Robinson Case: No Charges for Officer – CNN.com," *CNN*, May 12, 2015, www.cnn.com/2015/05/12/us/tony-robinson-madison-killing-investigation/index.html.

Box 4.1. An interlude: Public talk in Ann Arbor, Mich., about race

With a population of about 118,000, Ann Arbor, Mich., is near Lake Erie, just outside of Detroit in the nation's Midwest. For half a century, the city has been known as a hotbed of left-wing politics and was a hub for the civil rights movement during the 1960s and 1970s. In 2010, it was predominantly White (73%) with Asians the next largest group (14.4%), African Americans (7.7%), and Latinos (4.1%). And as home to the University of Michigan's main campus, it's well educated with 70.6 % holding a bachelor's degree. The Ann Arbor Board of Education oversees the public-school system, and is made up of seven members who serve two-year terms; nearly half at the time of this study were people of color. The district was described as a "whistle-and-bell destination district," which offers a variety of programs for students and families in the know, but leaves out many who are unaware of these resources. This was very similar to all of our districts. The graduation metric gap in Ann Arbor was not as large as our other districts (while 89 percent of White students graduated in four years, 77 percent of Black students and 71 percent of Hispanic students did), but testing showed a larger divide with White children scoring in the 87th percentile in 2013–14, Black children in the 58th, and Hispanic children in the 61st percentile for third grade MEAP testing.

For three decades, Ann Arbor has been trying to close the achievement gap between its White, Black, and Brown students through various strategies, including the hiring of an achievement gap administrator in 1997, consultation with Glenn Singleton's Pacific Educational Group, and a Rising Scholars Program with the University of Michigan. Still the disparities continued and the failed outcomes frustrated administrators and people of color alike. One Black public official blamed the lack of real resources toward change, as in the dearth of support for the achievement-gap specialist:

So they gave her the title of Academic Achievement Gap Czar and they gave her a respectable salary. And yet they gave her none of the resources. She had no leverage as far as, you know, being able to invoke change, [be]cause she had to work with the superintendent, work with the principals. She had no support staff. So needless to say, she wasn't very successful. So that was deemed a critical failure.

Additionally, a reluctance within the community to talk about systemic issues, such as racism, contributed to the problem as well

Box 4.1. (cont.)

as high administrative turnover and a lack of institutional memory among many influential roles such as journalists and top school officials, according to interviewees. Finally, a lack of political will also hindered progress in the progressive enclave, according to some of our community leaders.

Major media stories related to the achievement gap have tended to focus on controversial issues. In particular, Singleton's consulting fee attracted much media attention, as well as comments (often in excess of one hundred on individual stories). Another incident involved an elementary school club called the Lunch Bunch, started in 2010 for Black students. The school's principal coordinated a field trip for Black students to meet with an African American rocket scientist. Complaints ensued that White students were turned away. The outcry highlighted the lack of support for certain initiatives to close the achievement gap as White parents worried that new programs for African American or Hispanic students would take away from the opportunities for their own children.

Many interview subjects noted the decline of education coverage. Local news is covered through MLive.com (Michigan Live), which publishes the *Ann Arbor News* online. Other publications included a newsletter by the *Ann Arbor Public Schools*, a blog called Ann Arbor School Musings, a new online newspaper named the Ann Arbor Chronicle, and a monthly magazine, *The Ann*. In the comment sections of these publications, racist vitriol ran rampant. Several interview subjects noted that when the conversation turns toward race and disparity, "you see very ugly signs and evidence of how not liberal and not equitable we can be at times when it comes to those that are disadvantaged, particularly socioeconomically." Commentators frequently portrayed the gap as a deficit and faulted African American communities – Black parents lacked the skills necessary to help their children, or Black children lacked the temperament required to be successful in school. One Black Ann Arbor school board member told her son to carry the card of a lawyer when in school in case he was unduly targeted, according to *The Ann*. All that said, Ann Arbor – like all these school districts – worked diligently on these disparities with myriad programs that had varied successes.

bring up the issue of racism in the schools and the community at large because of people's discomfort as well as lack of training on how to facilitate those dialogues; furthermore, discussions tended to spur from specific incidents and last only a few weeks without lasting change. In Ann Arbor, Mich., several participants noted the dearth of follow-through – particularly resources – from seemingly productive community conversations. This chapter explores the obstacles to public talk that prevent the successful dialogue and productive deliberation. And in the next two chapters I look at how to overcome them.

Three Obstacles to Public Talk

The data from the five case studies points to three categories that feed off each other:

1. Missed *connections* in dialogue such as logistical impediments or isolated networks that keep talk from even happening;
2. *Structures* of public talk such as worn tropes, racist assumptions, entrenched routines, and polarizing ideological statements that occur during what is supposed to be safe dialogue;
3. *Outcome failures* where no action results and a historical repertoire builds that prejudices future communicative action.

After describing the obstacles in our Madison story, I revisit the concept of trust/distrust that I spent some time laying out in the introduction of the book. The absence of trusting communicative relationships in the five cities included in this study has served as a major stumbling block for deliberative change in our information fields. With everyone so caught up in defending their various borders – of their profession, of their cultural space, of their very identity constructs – they lose opportunities to effect change.

(MISSED) CONNECTIONS

First, we explore the *missed connections* that plagued these cities. They occurred at every level of opportunity for dialogue – among public officials and reporters, disengaged citizens and activists, White people, and people of color. Yet, this major obstacle is the easiest of the three to resolve. It requires a commitment on behalf of those in power to make an effort and a commitment on behalf of others to communicate clear expectations and check personal cynicism. An understanding of these missed connections is essential to enacting change, from the institutional producers in our communicative networks to engaged citizens such as "community bridges," "niche networkers," or "issue amplifiers."

Institutional Actors: Journalists and School Officials ("Sometimes the Gods just drop one")

In 2013, about two years after the Madison Prep proposal failed, Erica Nelson was ready to release a 90-page report called *Race to Equity* in conjunction with the nonprofit Wisconsin Council on Families and Children. The report showed how Dane County in Wisconsin ranked as the worst in the nation on racial disparities. It did not release any new data per se, but rather aggregated statistics from dozens of different sources to present a narrative about life for Black people in Wisconsin. Nelson helped the YWCA build the annual Racial Justice Summit around the report and sent out press releases to local press, embargoed with the news of the release.[4] All the news outlets publicized the report, but not quite the in-depth pieces Nelson and her colleagues desired. One editor sighed with frustration when I mentioned the *Race to Equity*'s limited coverage around its release:

Here is why it was this small: [It was] [t]wo or three months before when I asked to get whatever data they had and promising a big cover story if we have time to work on it ... I knew about it months before and they just stonewalled and so they obviously thought they needed to do some kind of media event rather than frankly having a good piece. Had we ... been able to do the storytelling and do all the interviews and we would have done more.

Across town, two other reporters also worked on the report's release. Both said they received news of the report at the last minute because the reporters who would normally cover the news were absent. "I really didn't have time to do a lot of preparation, and, I think I told myself what I'm doing right now is meeting coverage, you know?" said one. None of the reporters went to the YWCA conference where the report was announced amidst hundreds of activists, people of color, and others who may have given unique stories to buoy the numbers. "I did not go to the conference," said the other. "I could either go to the conference or spend my time doing the story." The only reporter to quote someone other than the report's

---

[4] "Embargo" means that the reporters could read the report and prepare a story, but not publish it or tell anyone about it until after an agreed upon date and time.

author explained that she "used my community contacts" to find someone from a prominent Black neighborhood to supplement the report.

This example demonstrates a common "missed connection" between reporters and communities of color resulting from deadline pressures, cynicism about motivations, and insular networks. Many barriers inhibited information flow between schools and their communities about achievement disparities, including inaccessibility to officials for parents, decreasing amounts of education news, and unavailability of some parents to school officials or reporters.[5] Obstacles range from the logistical – missed meetings, deadline pressures – to more abstract missed connections, such as feeling disconnected from people of other races.

As I noted in the beginning of this chapter, journalists had difficulties convincing Black or Brown parents to give their name for publication. Their Rolodexes held the names of few people of color who were not the heads of nonprofits or national experts on race issues. Most sources came from existing networks, such as names gleaned from past stories or connections made through regular sources. In my entire sample, only two reporters ventured into neighborhoods or community centers with the sole purpose of networking and building relationships, though almost all expressed a deep desire to do more of that kind of grassroots reporting. One reporter noted:

> It's really difficult to find parents to speak on the record and [there are] many of those middle-income Black parents who will speak in kind of a general sense of that, when asked to come up, when asked to tell a story, and I really try to mine those contacts for someone to tell a story and was you know, pretty desperately doing so for this. You know how sometimes there is a God? Sometimes, the gods just drop one. I think that woman called me because she heard my name so much. I picked up the phone and there she was.

Here, serendipity represents this reporter's strategy: her African American source already knew her name and called her. When asked why they cited the people they did, reporters used words such as "accessible" or "straight-shooter" and "it's just a big issue for him," showing how logistical concerns

[5] Gerstl-Pepin C. I., "Media (mis)representations of Education in the 2000 Presidential Election," *Educational Policy* 16(1)(2002): 37–55; Michelle LaRocque, Ira Kleiman, and Sharon M. Darling, "Parental Involvement: The Missing Link in School Achievement," *Preventing School Failure* 55(3)(2011): 115–22, doi: 10.1080/10459880903472876; MacMillan K., "Narratives of Social Disruption: Education News in the British Tabloid Press," *Studies in the Politics of Education* 23(1)(2002): 27–38; Stack M., "Constructing 'Common Sense' Policies for Schools: The Role of the Journalists," *International Journal of Leadership in Education* 10(3)(2007): 247–264; Amanda Williams, "A Call for Change: Narrowing the Achievement Gap between White and Minority Students," *Clearing House* 84(2)(2011): 65–71, doi:10.1080/00098655.2010.511308.

mix with assumptions about motivation and expectations about interest in talking publicly. This meant that sources who were inaccessible or whose motivations were suspect or unknown received little exposure in mainstream publications.

Thus, journalists' networks recreate a local community's dominant hierarchies. They use official sources that tend to be White or regular contacts that tend to be outspoken at meetings or confident in approaching reporters. Few sources were contacts outside of the dominant information-exchange networks already in place. Research demonstrates that reporters and those in power share a symbiotic, dependent relationship that provides journalists with the access they need for their authority and helps those in power stay in power.[6] Deadline pressures and declining resources in the newsroom mean that reporters have little time to develop the necessary relationships in communities of color, and become frustrated after repeated rejections from people who don't know them or who have had poor experiences with media. Said the most prolific reporter on the education beat at the time of the Madison Prep debate, "That was kinda one of my weaknesses as covering the beat as I was a lot more up in the, you know, power structure and the academia."

Furthermore, the White reporters in our cities were keenly aware of their white skin as they covered stories about racial disparities – so much so, they felt their difference prevented them from truly being able to get at the core of the story. Said a television reporter from Wisconsin: "I am not Black, so I do not have a sense for what it is truly like to be a minority in the metro school district. Viewing the issue at hand with that lens, you do come at it without the perspective you might need for the story." An editor from a publication in Madison echoed this sentiment: "At its most basic level can White reporters really report well on race? Is it coming from a standpoint or an experience where you don't really understand and therefore you are not getting the story, and is there a real story that is being missed?" Another reporter from Cambridge, Mass., talked about the need to be well versed in background of the disparities, and cautioned: "You don't say 'White' without checking if you are including Asians and White Hispanics. You don't say Black if you mean African American as opposed to, say, Haitian or Dominican. You have to be very specific about what it

---

[6] In Nikki Usher's account of the *New York Times* digital transition, Usher noted how little real commitment to interactivity and participation was happening among individual reporters: Nikki Usher, *Making News at The New York Times* (Ann Arbor: University of Michigan Press, 2014).

is you are measuring so that you get it right." Really delving into the racial part of the disparities would entail deeper stories about racism and institutional bias – stories that would take longer and also might provoke reactions from sources journalists depended on for access, such as the teacher's union head or the superintendent. "I think I stuck with procedural and meeting coverage to maintain impartiality on a sensitive issue," said one mainstream reporter about the coverage of Madison Prep. The result was those stories – the ones that examined racial and institutional biases, historic struggles with educational disparities, and challenges to institutional authority – rarely got written during our study period.

But logistics of communication connections also served as an obstacle for other institutional actors throughout our information-exchange field. Information bottlenecked in multiple places. Two staffers at the Madison Metropolitan School District administration office talked to me about the difficulty connecting with Black or Brown parents.

Ms. HUMPHREY:[7]   We find from the district standpoint that we have a lot of parents that do not have access to the internet, and as such they probably would not subscribe to a paper and so it is hard for us to get the information out to parents. We have cell phones, but it is hard to share information in a two-minute phone call to parents. We have a biweekly parent newsletter ... but every year when we download the list, there are so many parents where there is no email connected to so many families. So how do you get the information out?

Ms. LOVEJOY: I have heard that some people might have email but they never check it, so then they tell us "well I am not going to check it anyway why should I even give it to you."

Ms. HUMPHREY: So that is a big barrier.

Ms. LOVEJOY: We send information to the schools but we don't see those being picked up.

Ms. HUMPHREY: [Sending information home with kids] might work at the elementary level. Kids are still bringing stuff home to mom and dad. But at the middle- or high-school level it is a lost cause. It never hits the home. So that's a problem.

7 These are pseudonyms.

Administrators in all of our other cities expressed similar problems with getting information out to families as well as working within schools to facilitate frank conversations about race. School administrators in Evanston, Ill., have worked with race-dialogue consultant Glenn Singleton of the Pacific Educational Group, but "it gets beyond some people's comfort level," said one school official. And they contend with the nearly impossible reconciliation of the progressive identity of teachers, for example, with the reality that the schools are failing an entire population of children. Said one White school official in Evanston, Ill.:

It's hard to work as hard as you do as a teacher day in and day out, with a deep dedication to all children and a real fundamental belief in what you are doing. Then look at your data and see that ... one segment of the population is doing really well and another isn't. And if that's split along racial lines, that's a painful thing for a professional to face.

With both mainstream journalists and school officials facing challenges in connecting with all parents and even internally with all school personnel and students, these opportunities for broad community dialogue get lost in discomfort, inertia, deadline pressures, and logistical problems.

"Regular" Citizens: "I want the steak too!"

For their part, parents said they do not get the word that school hearings and meetings were happening, and when they did, it tended to be last minute and not convenient. "The meetings they do have, they make them far away," one parent said. "A majority of White people have cars but we don't." Another added, "We never know about these meetings ... Next time you have a meeting, you invite me and I'm going to invite some people and we can sit down and you can see where we are coming from." Here we see a cultural difference in how some in the two groups approached communication. For some of the Black and Brown people I talked to, information needed to be exchanged on a personal, individual level rather than via mainstream, traditional, impersonal networks that dominated this information-exchange field. School officials, journalists, and others needed to enter Black and Brown communities and embrace those networks if they wanted to engage them.

Although most activists kept abreast of local news, few of the parents we talked to watched or read local mainstream journalism. One African American parent said, "They will give 15 minutes to whatever horrible thing is happening and then five minutes about the sports thing and that's it.

So I stopped watching." And, "Whatever they print, it is negative. If it's hardcore, every 30 minutes it's on the news. You are not going to see the single mom who just graduated on the news." Or "they never talk about education. They talk about crime. They talk about sports." And, finally, "There is no Black news. The one Black woman who was on the news, they took off." They do not feel connected to the news because they do not see issues relevant to them or people who look like them.

These obstacles combine with the feeling that their input is not really desired. Parents agreed that reporters don't seem to care about what is happening in the Black community, and that school districts didn't seem interested either. One Black reverend in Madison, Everett Mitchell, invited some reporters to the first-ever gay marriage between two Black women at his church (or in Madison), and no one showed. "But when there was some conflict between me and other Black clergy . . ., that leaked out, and I got phone calls from the press. I said, 'I am not talking to you about this'." One woman concluded that they held meetings far away from their neighborhoods and didn't publicize them because "They don't want us to go." Mr. Ford, an African American with several children in the Madison school district, explained what was going through his head when someone asked him to come to a meeting about Madison Prep or the achievement gap:

You want me to talk about racial disparity? Put me in a room with other people who are having the same problems. Don't say, I want you to come. Say, I NEED you to be there. Tell me you need me to make the difference . . . But if you had a meeting on the east side of town and you want me to come, well I don't have no car. It takes me two hours to get from this part of town over to the east side of town. I am not going to make it. And that means my voice is not heard. My vote is not taken . . . We are getting nothing because we don't get a chance to put our two cents in, our opinion in, a true conversation. Don't ask me if I want to come. Make me come. Proof is in the pudding. Don't bring me to the kiddie table for the mashed potato. *I want the steak too!*

These parents desired substantive conversation, news, and information in these meetings and on their television. They wanted to feel as if their perspective mattered to the process of deliberation – and ultimately to the decision. The lack of meaningful opportunities for input contributed to the widespread sense that a conspiracy was at work to keep them marginalized and from being a true actor in the information-exchange field: "There is no Black information. It's like placing a secret vote, 'I'm gonna tell who I want there'." These parents reported in our focus groups that they want to be a part of the decision-making, not merely tapped for token input. They not only feel unrepresented but deliberately shut out in general and completely powerless.

Finally, an innate distrust of media and of school officials pervaded. Several activists reported to us that White journalists and school officials shouldn't even try to build trust in neighborhoods until they make good on promises to hire more people of color into positions of power within their organizations. "These White people have no idea what my experience is," said one Black parent. Said another, "How can you understand us? You don't know the struggle. A White reporter is not going to understand what I am going through."

These communicative dynamics that resulted in missed connections were exacerbated by the ways in which the education political networks worked in Madison and in all the other case cities. A core group of activists and some key administrators and politicians command most of the dialogue. As we saw in the previous chapter, only 10 people produced the majority of the content during the study time period. For example, the school officials and journalists complained that the same vocal activists and parents show up, drowning out other voices. Said a school communication specialist, "Every time we do reach out to the community and ask for input, we always get the same people coming." One White school board member in Madison echoed this dismay, saying the district's hearings on the superintendent's achievement gap plan, "weren't all that illuminating. I don't think it was the fault of the format or anything ... You just tend to see the same few people there and it's hard to get a sense of the community because people have to show up and be willing to say what they are thinking and that can be a hard thing to work out together." People, he added, were "stuck in their networks" and this prevented more effective and inclusive public deliberation. The names of the most dominant actors in the field of information exchange around achievement disparities appeared over and over in our interviews and surveys to map key influencers on the topic. These active players worked both publicly – in blogs, Facebook pages, on websites, and in news media – and also privately – in meetings, phone calls, texts, and emails – to network. But they networked mostly with each other. On social-media spaces, these core groups held exchanges with each other, sometimes even meeting in alternative virtual spaces such as a reporter's Facebook feed on a story.

These core networks thrived because they also contained all of those with the power to make decisions or to offer proposals. Consider the following comment from a Black woman involved in getting Madison Prep passed about trying to generate support among the city's power players:

We met with John Matthews [the union representative]. We met with the superintendent. And those were endless conversations going back and forth. We had breakfast with John Matthews at Perkins [restaurant]. I told Kaleem at the end because he was so excited because John was giving on this and "Oh yeah you can do this," . . . Kaleem was just giddy. John left, and I told Kaleem, "Don't be all excited about this. He hadn't written down a thing. He's going to go outside and put his finger to the wind and see which way it's going." That accord didn't last 24 hours. We shouldn't have had to be doing the negotiation. If it was something done correctly, then the school folks would have been carrying the water on that, and they would have been talking to him. We shouldn't be talking to him.

In all of our case-study cities, we found the information-networks mirrored the political power circles, with key people – a union representative in Madison, a couple school board members in Evanston – occupying roles of influence. Without their support, proposals faced an uphill battle.

Those supporting Madison Prep also worked these same networks. But because their network position was not as strong as that of MTI and Matthews, they ultimately could not muster the influence necessary to move their position or effect change. These core networked actors engaged in boundary crossing, but when crisis hit, the groups circled the wagons, as Caire lamented in an interview after the vote:

I met with each person individually. Yeah. And they all said they would support it. All of them. And then (Gov.) Scott Walker happened. I don't think there was anything we could do to stem the tide on that because the unions had their horns up. They weren't going to let anything pass. And they mobilized their base. Had this not happened, I don't think the reaction would have been as strong against it . . .

Mobilizing the base in this situation meant a slew of content production in places such as blogs that were picked up by local news organizations. The White progressive blogger Alan Ruff produced a damning, widely circulated piece that connected Caire to the conservative Koch brothers and other Republican-oriented entities actively working for the privatization of public education – a death blow in hyperprogressive Madison where the teacher union had ruled for decades as the symbol of the independent worker and the home of the Progressive Party.[8] The piece characterized the debate as a matter of honor, values, and identity, and reinforced the existing hierarchy – who is valid (progressives in power) and who is not (the conservative Koch brothers, Gov. Walker, Caire). It became another article that circulated in the power networks of Madison, influencing Board of Education members who would make the final call on Madison Prep.

For those not in these influential networks, they missed out on communicative connections. One was the White parent of a biracial child, who expressed extreme frustration at this insularity she saw in Madison:

When I attend things ... where people are trying to make changes and there are more White people than Black people ... I don't feel like African Americans have a platform in Madison. I don't know how their jobs go, but it would be really nice if journalists who are doing certain stories get both sides. So if you are interviewing a school district or a government entity ... [it is important] that you also get some public comments ... because the public has a right to know ... what actual people are talking about ..... I want [to read about] regular people like myself or others.

This woman, a stay-at-home mother, tried to make connections by commenting on Facebook, sharing news on social media, and commenting on news stories about the disparities she saw between White students and Black and Brown students in Madison. But she came up against a wall of defensiveness and disbelief. And her existing networks tended to be insular to her low-income social class. She didn't know any reporters or even how to go about calling them, and doubted they would be interested in what she had to say anyway.

Black activists in Madison as well as in the other cities worked to change the innate power structure by inserting their actors into a more powerful part of the field. Kaleem Caire and the Urban League endorsed candidates from Black and Brown communities such as Ananda Mirilli, a Latina with a prominent position at the YWCA, an organization that worked for racial justice in Madison. But Mirilli's school board campaign sputtered when two White well-known progressives ran. One of them, a woman named Sarah Manski, won a majority of the votes. She was the wife of a high-ranking member of the Dane County Progressive party and had the teachers' union's backing. But the day after the primary, she

---

[8] Allen Ruff, "Ruff Talk: History, Not 'Conspiracy': Kaleem Caire's Connections," *Ruff Talk*, January 27, 2012, http://allenruff.blogspot.com/2012/01/history-not-conspiracy-kaleem-caires.html.

announced she would be moving to California where her husband would be attending graduate school. The news slammed into the information flow, becoming another communicative flashpoint for blogs, articles, and Facebook conversations. Manski's announcement did not sit well with those who believed her campaign to be part of a conspiracy to keep even liberal Black and Brown from networked places of power. This of course was denied, but the lingering suspicions further created disconnect among network actors and discord in the community as a whole.[9] Said one Black activist about the election debacle:

It stunk to high heaven. It was the blatant manifestation of White privilege that somebody would treat a school board race as a back-up race . . . Look, these people will go to any lengths to maintain their status quo. They will trample over people of color who don't deserve it . . . This isn't about educating the kids. You want to be right. You want to be the saviors. You want to be the people. You want to be the people to turn things around.

But another major obstacle engendered missed connections: Few people wanted to *really* talk about race in public. This was true for all of our cities, though attempts at lasting public dialogues were made in all. Black people told me they felt a sense that White people would never understand their position. "We have to discuss things that have to do with race in our community because we are the ones going through it. We are the only ones who can understand it," said Mr. Coates, one Black parent in a focus group. Parent after parent in these groups told stories about their isolation and their unique experiences with racism in a city that prided itself on its progressive ideals. Said Ms. Lovely:

As a child at four years old, I was the only Black kid in the school. They chased me home. Called me names. As a kindergarten kid. They set our car on fire. This is what I grew up with. When you see your parents try to make more opportunities but you still see the other side and they can't be in my shoes. They cannot understand . . .

---

[9] Several articles publicized this feeling, including the city's Black paper, *Madison Times* (whose story is no longer available). The alternative weekly *Isthmus* ran a column by *The Progressive* magazine editor Ruth Conniff that said in part, "Both sides are wrong about their worst conspiracy fears. Mirilli is a sincere and independent advocate for kids, not a tool of the right. And, contrary to a lot of commenters on Facebook and Madison.com, Marj Passman, TJ Mertz, John Nichols and teachers union director John Matthews did not hatch a plan to keep Black and Brown people down during secret meetings in the organic produce aisle at the Willy Street Co-op." See Ruth Conniff, "Community Members Are at Each Other's Throats after the Madison School Board Catastrophe," *TheDailyPage*, 2013, www.thedailypage.com/isthmus/article.php?article=39317.

Even the long-time civil rights activists in these samples noted how carefully they had to approach the topic, lest they be labeled "angry." When drumming up support for Madison Prep, Caire and his staff strategized who should appear where, considering color of skin among other factors.

Meanwhile, White people, from school administrators to reporters covering race to White parents, acknowledged their inability to really understand and desire to appreciate others' perspectives. Yet, they were unsure how to listen productively, when the accusations seemed so far from their reality. As I mentioned above, White reporters worried that no matter how carefully they sourced or worded their pieces, they would miss the "real" story, impede progress on race relations, or inadvertently offend someone. School officials felt the same way. Two White school administrative staffers noted how awkward the hearings for the achievement disparities could be:

MS. HUMPHREY: There was one that I remember being at and taking comments and registering people to speak ... I think that was when they voted. I think it went until like two in the morning. And just the people standing in line there was such, I don't know, just so much tension just standing there. And you felt uneasy. If people did say something and another person would not let them finish. I don't think people felt free to speak for some reason ... you could tell that people were having conversations with one another but instead of speaking with someone who might have a different view, they just wouldn't have any conversation at all. I think at the board public hearing, people felt open and that they could speak. But it was not a debate. You go up there and say what you wanted for three minutes and people were quiet and respectful but I don't know if there really was a way to debate the topic.

MS. LOVEJOY: People are very sensitive when it comes to anything involving race. They are very careful about what they say about race. They don't ever want to offend anybody. That is not specific to Madison or this issue but it is more a general thing. I don't know if that is something we can solve with the achievement gap plan or anything.

Their hesitation colored the way they handled communications that might have a racial component. The school employees noted how this sensitivity informed their approach to social media and the Madison Metropolitan School District website:

Ms. HUMPHREY: I have to say that I am sort of wary of putting something on our Facebook page without going to an administrator and saying "what do you think?" Maybe [the reason] why we don't have many comments on our Facebook page is because we don't get into those topics. One that came up recently was an op-ed piece about extending the school year.[10] And both of us were thinking "oh maybe we should ask how we feel about this." But no one would give us the yes or no, so we decided against it.

Ms. LOVEJOY: We try to not make too much controversy but we also try to get the news out. We just have to be careful about how we do that.

ME: Why is that?

Ms. HUMPHREY: I don't know. Good question. Maybe because we just don't ... If there is something that is so straightforward, I don't think about not putting it on Facebook but if there is something where you go in the back of your mind, "Would this upset the teachers?' Would there be a segment of the population that it might offend?" That sort of thing. I feel uneasy and uncomfortable posting something like that."

Ultimately, these were venues for information input, not interactive discussion.

These feelings contributed to the small size and insularity of these core networks. People talked about race in their silos of *private* talk – around the dinner table, in an email listserv of like-minded people – but also in pseudo-*public spaces* such as on their friends' Facebook pages. Hearings were carefully structured to avoid debates that might break down into name-calling and accusations of racism. Reporters stuck to meetings and process stories to avoid deep discussions about race that didn't fit into

---

[10] Extending the school year is one effective strategy to alleviate achievement disparities because it helps low-income students who don't have the same summer camp, travel and other educational opportunities from falling more behind.

short-form articles. Time after time, connections failed to happen, and networks remained static. As someone who watched Madison Prep fail in part because of these dynamics, Kaleem Caire had this to say:

Leaders of Madison. They've been impatient. The mayor. The county exec. They've been impatient about the pace of the problem, and they're like "where is this going? All they're doing is having conversations?" And I'm like, "You guys, you've gotta have relationships in order to get anything done." The same thing goes for people in neighborhoods, and even more there because now you're in their turf, in their world. And even if they don't feel a connection to their world, now that they might be able to feel a connection to you, their relationship is warm when you hear their voice and feel you're involved.

He encountered resistance to changing protocol that had been in place – and worked well for the White majority – for years. And the result is, the relationships don't happen and those with existing links to people in power dominate the microphone, leaving out "others" – those without emails, without cars, without connections.

STRUCTURES OF PUBLIC TALK

Rev. Dr. Alex Gee and several other Black activists arrived at a meeting of city officials in 2013 after the release of the *Race to Equity* report, ready to talk about achievement disparities. It did not go well. The problems started after one official questioned the root problem and one activist bluntly stated that it was all about racism. "You could see them just check out at that point," Gee said. The accusation of "racism" became rampant as Black and Brown people felt more and more frustrated by the status quo that endured. Such accusations shut down conversation. And, White people's guilt and defensiveness – rather than a willingness to change – reigned.

Even when connections have been made and communication flowed, *structures of public talk* instilled obstacles into the dialogue, stalling its productivity. The structures I witnessed came down to two in particular: domineering political ideologies and threatened individual and group identities. As previously mentioned, these mid-sized cities – all suburban-urban microcosms – skew liberal, even progressive, with well-funded public-school systems. In Madison for example, school referendums rarely failed – only twice in the last thirty years. In Chapel Hill, N.C., no one could remember a Republican elected to the school board. Cambridge, Mass., boasted one of the highest per-student spending amounts in the country. In every single district, task forces and reports, collaborations with nonprofit entities such as Boys & Girls Clubs, and interventions such as Spanish immersion programs, four-year-old kindergarten, or detracking[11] grades proliferated through the years. And still, the disparities remained, and even grew in some places.[12] Major structural changes such as extending the school year or establishing charter schools to educate only students of color with taxpayers' money would radically alter the status quo – especially when it came to teacher contracts and funding for programs such as gifted and talented children.

All the cities in our study express pride at their histories of civil rights: several of them were ahead of the nation in making progress in the areas of desegregating schools, busing, and conducting protests during the 1960s and 1970s. Let's take a closer look at the macro case study of Madison, Wisc. Long a bastion of union support, Wisconsin, and in particular Madison, fiercely protected its workers. Indeed, some of the nation's very first trade unions emerged from Wisconsin.[13] Its first-in-the-nation Progressive Party, which came into power in the early 1900s, strengthened the state's already strong stance on worker rights and passed the first workers' compensation law in 1911. The state remains one of the most unionized states in the nation. Its Progressive Party roots stand as well, especially in Madison, where the name Evjue – after William T. Evjue, who founded the progressive *The Capital Times* in 1917 to publicize the Progressive movement – adorns buildings and a foundation that grants money to community projects. The current editor of *The Capital Times*, still half-owned by the Evjue Foundation, evokes this identity and its mission to "comfort the afflicted and afflict the comfortable" in nearly every speech he does in town. The philosophy guides every move the paper makes.

But in 2011, Gov. Scott Walker passed Act 10 Wisconsin Budget Repair Bill, which dealt a serious blow to unions by limiting their ability to collectively bargain contracts and increasing pension and other benefit contributions. Walker's Republican Tea Party stances, combined with a conservative majority in the State Legislature, threatened the state's iden-tity as a union-friendly, progressive haven. Nationally, a movement to privatize education and defund public schools gained momentum. In the

---

[11] Detracking is when classes are no longer determined by level or ability (e.g., no honors versus remedial classes).

[12] Abigail Becker, "Wisconsin's black-white achievement gap worst in nation despite dec-ades of efforts," WisconsinWatch.org, December 16, 2015, http://wisconsinwatch.org/2015/12/wisconsins-black-white-achievement-gap-worst-in-nation/.

[13] See the website of the Wisconsin Labor History: www.wisconsinlaborhistory.org/resources/milestones.

following months, teachers, school officials, and progressives felt helpless, angry, and on the defensive. The Madison Prep charter-school proposal couldn't have come at a worse time, ideologically.

This ideological defensiveness and the ensuing frustration on the part of people of color merged with identity – both group identity (as teachers, as a community, as White folks, as Black folks) and individual identity. Collectively, White progressives had been in power so long, the identity of a Madisonian reflected their ideology: pro-worker, pro–public schools, pro–government safety nets, pro–social justice (and postrace), etc. Individually, people who identified as progressive felt threatened in this environment, and specifically, that their position in the fields they performed in were in danger. As the only Black school board member in Madison during this study's time period said, "People are more concerned with individual status and individual positions, and they don't want to jeopardize or sacrifice any of that, you know?"

The last thing Madisonians (or any person in any of our cities) thought of themselves as was racist. But for more than a century, Wisconsin reflected a dominant democratic set of principles that equated the American sense of self with a White sense of self. Early public policies privileged the propertied, literate, and those with the power to vote, excluding women and anyone not White. Researchers have shown how a tacit White supremacy has long ruled education policy, for example.[14] Additionally, race has played a key role in communication flows, for it implicates "powerful ideological and institutional factors for deciding how identities are categorized and power, material privileges, and resources distributed."[15] White-dominated institutions, market dynamics, historic cultural traditions, and racialized social systems also dramatically affect communication patterns in local communities.[16] This has created racial tension that combines with inaccurate cultural assumptions and (often unwitting) marginalization that excludes minority groups from important public conversations, particularly in regards to the schools. Madison – and my other cities – has been no exception, where the White majority determine decisions, social norms, and culture. "There is not a strong sense of African Americanism here in

[14] Gillborn D., "Education Policy as an Act of White Supremacy: Whiteness, Critical Race Theory and Education Reform," *Journal of Education Policy* 20(4)(2005): 485–505.

[15] Giroux H. A., "Spectacles of Race and Pedagogies of Denial: Anti-Black Racist Pedagogy under the Reign of Neoliberalism," *Communication Education* 52(2003): 200.

[16] Eduardo Bonilla-Silva, *Racism without Racists: Color-Blind Racism and the Persistence of Racial Inequality in America* (Lanham, Md.: Rowman & Littlefield, 2006); Kinder D. and L. Sanders, *Divided by Color* (Chicago: University of Chicago Press, 1996).

Madison. Period," said one of my Black parents in the focus groups. The Black and Brown people in my study consistently mentioned their feeling of isolation and exclusion in the city. Said one White official with the Madison YWCA, which works on racial justice issues:

I think parents of color, despite all this hue and cry about how much everyone wants them to be involved, have been dis-involved through a whole long history and a number of methods in which everyone says they are wanted at the table, but the tables are not designed to be in places or times that work for them.

Instead, worn tropes about "poverty"[17] and "parental laziness" pepper forums and any hint that problems might reside in the schools – such as criticism of teachers – is lambasted throughout the ecology. The comments under news articles reveal constant conjectures about parents' work ethics, value systems, and family "culture." Stereotypes pervade both public and private dialogue. One African American parent described how a teacher bought her child gym shoes, assuming she didn't have the money. "Stop making assumptions," she said. Another told of a principal who accused her of being on drugs. Several Black activists talked about an omnipresent narrative they constantly confronted:

Oh it's ridiculous, it's crazy. They tell kids like "you ain't graduating" ... Like teachers will tell students that and, you know, if you tell people in the White community that they say that kind of stuff, they're like "oh, nobody will say that." I've sat in these meetings with principals and administrators and teachers and parents, and I was getting all these crazy, disrespectful people and [here I am] trying to be an advocate, and I'm just sitting there looking at the people in power like "you do realize I'm an attorney?" And they still will just say it, because they're so preoccupied with this narrative that they have to maintain.

When I told White reporters and politicians about these conversations and incidents, they furrowed their brows and wondered aloud whether there is any truth or justification to the accusations. Here was one exchange with a White reporter covering Madison Prep at the time:

This is sort of where I get into the whole sociological underlying factors, like when you take their comment that Blacks are lazy it is sort of skipping over relevance to what they might be saying ... clearly what they're saying is wrong and racist, or it's like, is there any truth to it? It's easy to jump to it being racist and dismissing it ... It's

---

[17] The causes of the disparities are regularly debated. It is true that of Madison's 3,247 Black children, more than 75 percent live in poverty and that income is correlated with school achievement. However, the disparities hold true even for middle-class Black students. In addition, the reason for that poverty is at least partly a result of poor education for Black and Brown children.

difficult to go to the minority community and really try to figure out, well, what is happening here? Is there a struggling fifth grader a product of a single parent home who I don't know … I'm not saying there's laziness there, I'm saying, there's sociological reasons.

And MTI's Matthews discussed the racial achievement gap through a sociological lens: "This is a poverty issue in my opinion. Almost solely a poverty issue."

These persistent declarations create stalemate in the dialogue and stagnate progress toward a solution. Such proclamations absolve the schools and laser the "problem" onto the home life of Black people rather than spotlighting possible structural dynamics in the White-dominated institutions. At its heart, this is a problem with identity and ideology. Bouncing the problem back to the Black community implies the fault lies within Black individuals, rather than within the institutions in this progressive city built on White power structures. Even those who recognize that race and racism contribute to the stalemate for the achievement disparities, defer to their own ideological constructs when it comes time to make policy.

The very term "progressive" in these cities had morphed away from the original Progressive Party reform mandate to change public institutions and programs. Instead, the label "progressive" – or even "radical" – comprised a commitment to the institutional status quo for these places. When I asked Ananda Mirilli – the Latina and former YWCA Director of the Restorative Justice Program who ran unsuccessfully for the Board of Education in Madison – whether she considered herself a "progressive," she demurred at first and then tried to explain: To declare oneself "progressive" in Madison embodies a very specific understanding, she and others told us – namely a White person who *intends* to force disruption but ultimately declines to challenge principles these cities identified as core. As someone who wants to effect significant change in these progressive-built institutions, Mirilli wasn't sure she could call herself a "progressive" in the Madison evolution of the term. She told me in an email, "In essence, Madison progressiveness is centered in Whiteness, consequently marginalizing and further perpetuating the invisibility of POCs." Since 2008, Mirilli has lived by her commitment to social/racial justice and education and served in many supportive roles to reduce opportunity gaps between White people and Brown/Black people. For example, in 2015, Mirilli accepted a position with the Madison schools as the Family, Youth & Community Engagement Coordinator to improve the experience of *all* of the district's students and their communities. And, in 2017, Mirilli accepted a position with the Department of Public Instruction, as Educational Equity Consultant, working with districts and educators to address disproportionality across the state. She has publicly stated her commitment to addressing achievement disparities by "finding solutions" that will "transform" the existing protocols and policy and hold the current system "accountable" in the search for equity.[18] In the formal definition of "progressive,"[19] then, Mirilli is indeed a progressive but it was striking she couldn't immediately answer my question in the affirmative without caveat.

Madison Prep supporters saw stark divides in how those in power received suggestions from White progressives, compared to people outside these dominant networks. We saw in the Madison Prep debate a calling out. Now I want to go through a lengthy exchange in which we can see this intractable difference in locution play out. This exchange occurred on the public Facebook page of Black radio personality Derrell Connor, a strong supporter of the charter school. The dialogue was between Connor and the White progressive blogger, TJ Mertz, who had not yet declared a run for school board but was heavily involved in the public information exchange about Madison Prep. Both men held prominent positions in the information-exchange field, and appeared frequently in my sample. Both were also named as key influencers on the topic. This exchange exemplifies the kind of public dialogue I witnessed. It began when Mertz posted on Connor's wall following a news article that quoted Connor in support of the charter school.

DERRELL CONNOR: TJ, I've never said that Madison Prep was THE ANSWER. I've stated from the very beginning that I felt that this was a starting point in addressing a problem that has existed in this community for a long time ... But here's another discussion that Madison needs to have. There are folks in this community that feel that the White liberal establishment in Madison believe that they and they

---

[18] See for example her website at https://anandamirilli.com or any number of news articles during her race such as Schneider, Pat. "Ananda Mirilli: I was falsely depicted as pro-voucher," *The Capital Times*, February 28, 2013. Accessed July 4, 2017 from: http://host.madison.com/ct/news/local/writers/pat_schneider/ananda-mirilli-i-was-falsely-depicted-as-pro-voucher/article_3db8bf4a-8140-11e2-972f-001a4bcf887a.html.

[19] Remembering from Chapter 1 that: Progressivism focuses on "improving the lives of others" and presumes that "human beings were decent by nature, but that people's and society's problems lay in the structure of institutions."

alone know and should decide how education is taught to students of color, regardless of graduation rates or achievement gaps. . . . Right or wrong, fair or not, that opinion and belief is out there, and it's shared by quite a few people that I talk to, who call into my radio show and speak to me offline and who send me emails. It's a shame that this issue has to go there, but this is what happens when we as a community don't openly and honestly discuss issues concerning race and ethnicity.

THOMAS J. MERTZ: Derrell Connor, again, I didn't say you did, I said many supporters of Madison Prep . . . I started by saying it was a fair criticism and I was trying to explain why I have felt it necessary to fact-check and pointing out that there has been a lot of misinformation, along with explicit belittling of people's motives, knowledge, and actions (or inactions) on the other side . . . You may be right that some people have a racist take on Kaleem Caire's credentials (probably are right). For me the issue is that his career has been in the service of those whose explicit agenda is to destroy public education and that from my perspective he has been on the wrong side of every major educational issue for the last decade, doing much more harm than good. Nothing to do with race; everything to do with his actions (and I really don't care about his motives, it is actions and consequences that count).

DERRELL CONNOR: But the problem is, those same people that feel that there's a racial component to this also feel that it isn't just Kaleem, it's ANY Black man or woman in this community that presents an idea such as this. And that's a problem . . . Some don't like Kaleem because of whom he may have associated with on the issue of education. That's fine. But is he wrong on this issue? That's the question.

On the one hand, this example does demonstrate how online realms offer public space to have long, substantial exchanges debating civic proposals.

This conversation is respectful and offers qualities necessary for good deliberation. However, we don't see an exchange about the advantages or disadvantages of Madison Prep. Instead this represents not a dialogue so much as talking points questioning motives for support or opposition. Is the opposition racism or is it concern about political ideology? Is the support about political ideology or is it about solving the problem? This exchange highlights many of the structural obstacles to public talk that we saw in all of our case studies: People's adherence to specific ideologies and identities inhibits their ability to deliberate because it distracts the attention from the problem/solution itself. This very circumstance became debated. On Caire's public Facebook page, a White activist called out two White women who had been criticizing the charter school on Caire's page:

> You are completely opposed to this school and want to argue against it at all costs. That isn't what true communication is about. I want to work toward a solution that will heal this horrific situation that faces the Madison community. There is too much at stake. I thought I was engaging in communication. I see now it is an effort to prove who is right.

The question debated in these Facebook exchanges is not whether the charter school would help resolve the disparities and how the city could afford it. Rather, they cut to the heart of people's motivations in speaking out. Connor wants to bring to light racism implicit in people's comments. Mertz wants to focus the conversation on the agenda behind the school. None of these people is practicing effective deliberation, though all are respectfully conversing. Although there is some "heeding" going on (such as when Mertz acknowledges racism may be at play here), very little willingness to compromise is displayed. All cling to their ideologies – that all charter schools are tools for evil Republicans, that all obstruction to the proposal is evidence of racism or righteousness.

I see what is happening in these exchanges as boundary-work as its core. Mertz is seeking to protect the status quo against would-be interlopers in the field, particularly right-wing operatives who want to hijack public education. This defense plays out in his insistence of a certain communication style and practice – demands for evidence, a declared stance against "misinformation," a valuing of "fact-checks." Connor and other supporters online are challenging not only the education system as is, but also the ways in which people communicate about it, implying their reasons for rejecting the school are not based on practicalities but rather on entrenched biases. These boundary defenses and challenges are born from ideologies and identities that shape the structures of public talk in these progressive cities and can often create obstacles to true deliberation.

OUTCOME FAILURES

The last public hearing on Madison Prep, the one where the Board of Education voted, was the last straw for many of the parents in this study, as I wrote in the opening anecdote of this chapter. More than five hundred people showed up wearing blue "I Support Madison Prep" T-Shirts and spent four hours in testimony in that frosty December night in 2011. Their frustration came through in raised voices at the meeting: "I trust that you are good people. Basic intelligence is common to all. You can get in your heads and intellectualize this issue all you want to and you will have missed the point." After each speaker in support of the school finished, the crowd gave standing ovations. Meanwhile a much smaller number of supporters, many from the teachers' union spoke, calling it an issue about poverty or a problem with the homes and parents, and contending Madison Prep would take money away in a strapped budget for a small population of students. At the end of the meeting, late in the evening, the board members took out their written statements and voted down the school. To one White official with the local YWCA, this kind of response to the Black community's efforts generated intense distrust and stifled any feelings of encouragement or pro-action:

When they really got engaged and they all showed up and they said, "Madison Prep is what we want for our children. This is what our families need." We said, "Mmm, not so much." Whether or not you agree with Madison Prep, and whether or not you think it was a bad, whatever, I think that something people really need to understand that when some of our ... more marginalized folks who are directly affected by this issue actually do show up, the experience they have does not feel good and does not make them want to keep showing up and is not empowering.

Years after the 2011 vote, Madison Prep supporters remained bitter. At the focus groups with parents who have Black children in the schools, people expressed universal cynicism and disdain:

All you hear is the same old: "I have a dream!" It's the same ol' Martin Luther King and Malcolm X speeches. I don't want to come to this meeting because it always is about conversation. I am done with talking. Do something. To hell with this conversation. Quit talking and do something.

Throughout the anecdotes we heard from parents and activists, one major cause of discontent presented itself as a major obstacle to public talk: *outcome failures*. Several Black community leaders in my sample refused to sit on committees and task forces anymore or talk to reporters because "it's all talk. Nothing ever gets done," explained one. Parents yearned for resolution – but a resolution based on addressing the underlying, systemic causes of the disparities: "There is a lot of talk about it but it is not clear about how it can be resolved. How can we come up with some ideas to close the gap? How did it come about? I don't even understand why this is," said one parent. Whether we asked about school hearings, the lack of people of color in power, or media coverage of disparities, people expressed frustration with the inaction and absences.

One major outcome failure was the simplistic media coverage of racial issues. Media scholars have found that journalism – one major vehicle for communicating information about the schools to the public – actually flattens the discussion about educational policy, simplifying the root causes and failing to fully explore any proposed solutions other than for what those resolutions would mean politically. Frames for these news articles fall back on unhelpful, inadequate binaries such as for or against, bad versus good teachers, Black versus White or poor versus rich. Education reporters rarely incorporate academic research as evidence.[20] News reports about educational issues relay persistent racial stereotypes and demonize or scapegoat minorities.[21]

In Madison Prep coverage, logistics and procedural details dominated mainstream news, with most broadcast reports filming from hearings and newspaper writers concentrating on officials and activists for their sources. Consider this headline on the *Wisconsin State Journal's* Facebook page on December 9, 2011, just days before the vote: "Kaleem Caire rips the Madison School Board. Whose side are you on?" The post set up the discussion as a

---

[20] Berliner D. C. and B. J. Biddle, *The Manufactured Crisis: Myths, Fraud, and the Attack on America's Public School* (Cambridge, Mass.: Perseus Books, 1995).

[21] Ronald L. Jackson, *Scripting the Black Masculine Body: Identity, Discourse, and Racial Politics in Popular Media* (Albany: SUNY Press, 2006); Carolyn Martindale, "Coverage of Black Americans in Four Major Newspapers, 1950–1989," *Newspaper Research Journal* 11 (3) (1990): 96–112; Shanara Rose Reid-Brinkley, "Ghetto Kids Gone Good: Race, Representation, and Authority in the Scripting of Inner-City Youths in the Urban Debate League," *Argumentation & Advocacy* 49(2)(2012): 77–99; Catherine R. Squires and Sarah J. Jackson, "Reducing Race: News Themes in the 2008 Primaries," *The International Journal of Press/Politics* 15(4)(2010): 375–400, doi:10.1177/1940161210372962.

battle between sides, recreating a "Black people versus White people" mentality. This dichotomy played out in the comments under the post:

So you want the schools closed? That's what happens if you don't have any teachers. The way they're treated by the Walkerites and then trashed by people, it's no wonder. They do a fantastic job and deserve to be rewarded. Most public employees get paid much less than their private sector counterparts. Plus they get whiny criticisms from jerks who could never take on their jobs themselves.

The commenter, a White woman, accepts the offer to "take sides"; she is on the "side" of the teachers. Here Caire is made to be the aggressor "ripping" the school board – that is, angry Black man – instead of portraying the leader as challenging the board to propose solutions to the disparities. Readers like the woman who commented must accept the winner-loser binary rather than reframing the dialogue around naming the problem and brainstorming alternatives in the wake of the rejection as a community response to achievement disparities.

Finally, another major outcome failure is the stark absence of the Black and Brown stakeholders throughout the ecology, frustrating everyone. Editors find it exasperating they cannot find Black or Brown reporters to join their all-White staffs in Madison. Reporters give up on finding "regular" people of color to talk to them. Parents are discouraged there are not more Black reporters, teachers, school administrators, and politicians. School officials want to see more parents of color at meetings and hearings. Activists want to see more people of color in important policymaking positions and at meetings. These absences generate disconnects that result in policy being made by people lacking all perspectives at the table. One Latina community leader from Madison tried to explain the problem with public talk about race in this way:

All these people who are supposed to be helping close the achievement gap don't really have a racial analysis. So how can we have that conversation? How can we even understand that you need to [have] a person from a different perspective from you in order to have that conversation? … I still hear that when I go to those meetings with those high-level folks, I still hear, "certain parents don't value education and certain parents don't blah blah blah" … I know if I get up, if I stop, and stomp my hand, [then I would] say, "damnit you are talking about me. And it is not true. It's not true to me. It's not true to my neighbors. It's not true to the people I know."

Research studying the problems of community talk has determined that failed outcomes in the past inevitably determine the success of future interactions.[22] This is in part because the bitter taste of failure leads to cynicism, fatigue, and suspicion. A Black activist in Madison added, "For a lot of people in this community there's a lot of mistrust. A lot of distrust."

(DIS-)TRUSTING RELATIONSHIPS

Distrust between and among citizens and civic institutions results from all of these obstacles. When people have a negative experience – such as attending a meeting, hearing a polished presentation, having only a minute or two for feedback, and not influencing the outcome – they develop suspicions about an institution's motivations that color all their future dealings. These negatives become an ingrained and expected part of the narrative between the races. This distrust is so prevalent and visceral it permeated the texts and appeared in interviews in every single one of my cities. It affected my interactions with all my African American, Latino and other participants of color, resulting in miscommunications, and creating wariness and cynicism about my motivations regarding me and my study. For example, toward the end of my study I sat down with Everett Mitchell, who is the communications director for the University of Wisconsin-Madison, an African American, and also a reverend. I knew a lot about him: hailing from Texas, he has degrees in mathematics, theology, and law; was at the forefront of the race discussions in town in the wake of the police shooting of an unarmed Black teen; and had appeared in media talking about race relations. My first comment? I noted his "over-achiever" background. It was a comment I had also made to another participant, a White woman with mastery of dance, law, and social work, and I had meant it as an icebreaker and compliment. Mitchell blinked and we went on with the interview. Later on, once he had established my perspective, he circled back around to the comment as an example of the racial overtones he attributed to comments like it. When I said "over-achiever" he had tacked on: "for a Black man." In another interview, Derrell Connor talked to me about the low expectations White teachers held for Black children and told me an anecdote from his childhood. When he was in kindergarten, the teacher had handed the students a

---

[22] Richard Harwood, "Yes, Our Democracy Is a Mess, and Yes, Our Opportunities Are Real," *Connections: The Kettering Foundation's Annual Newsletter*, 2014; Gillborn, "Education Policy as an Act of White Supremacy: Whiteness, Critical Race Theory and Education Reform."

letter for home about an upcoming field trip. He read the letter immediately and excitedly told his mother when she got to the school. His teacher was taken aback that he could read.

"I'll never forget their faces," he said.

I said, "But I mean that could also be because you were five."

"True," he added, "but what I learned from that experience though through school is that there were certain teachers, not everyone, but there were certain ones that you had to prove that you were capable and prove that you possessed some intelligence before they go, 'Oh OK.' Because they automatically assumed you were behind. Automatically assumed you couldn't read at the grade level. That's the stuff that people are talking about."

Many other Black people – especially parents – refused to meet with me, a White academic. When I asked Rev. Dr. Alex Gee at the end of the interview for some help convincing parents in his networks to talk to me, he balked. "Why should they trust you?" he admonished. I became defensive in spite of all my reading and all my training and all of my best intentions. These cultural disconnects exemplify the difficulties these cities face when all the people sitting at the table have the very best intentions, but White people say racially naïve things or blithely dismiss concerns, and Black people jump to conclusions about motivations.

The Facebook exchange mentioned in a previous chapter highlighted the tensions between not only professional journalists and communities of color regarding media, but also the importance of relationship building. As described earlier, the national network NBC contacted the head of the Boys & Girls Club of Dane County, Michael Johnson, for a story on Madison's disparities. Johnson asked the producer, whom he had never met, to put into writing what the story's focus, as well as to conduct a conference call with community leaders. When the network refused, Johnson declined to be a source. He posted his disdain on his Facebook in May 2014, saying "I can't be part of a blind story." The post drew 23 comments, including several journalists defending NBC's actions and a number of people from Black communities who said, "They talk nice and sometimes they do good. But their interests are not your interests. The media is rarely your friend." The reporters who commented argued about protocol and objectivity and a commitment to the truth of the evolving storyline, failing to understand the significance of the request for Johnson. Johnson noted in our interview that he and local media had spent much time building a trusting relationship – something the national network had not done; the requests he had made were meant to build some of that trust. Those who supported Johnson's rejection cared little for journalists' set of norms and standards that help protect their professionalism in an age of constant information challenge. The short but intense exchange illuminated the significant chasm of understanding between these two communities of information exchangers.[23]

This distrust between information exchangers is also a result of fundamental suspicions between White progressives and Black community members regarding each other's motivations in the Madison Prep debate. Although White online contributors such as bloggers Brenda Konkel and TJ Mertz recognized the need to alleviate disparities, they worried a charter school and school vouchers as tools for doing so played into more nefarious conservative agendas. Rather than debating whether the charter school could work, Mertz spent many blog posts criticizing the possible motivations behind the school. In one post,[24] Mertz worried that the conservative move to support charter schools for Black students was a hidden, racist one of segregation, suggesting the Urban League is either intentionally setting out to destroy public education or is an unwitting pawn. This distrust over motivations prevented White progressives from truly deliberating on the issue.

Along the same line, many Black community members expressed similar concern about White intentions as well, as seen in this post from a Black parent made on Caire's public Facebook wall:

@Harris, You asked "Why does Madison Prep supporters blame teachers and the school board rather than parents of color and their children." Why do you ask? Because, it begins with TRUST. Without TRUST, you have nothing! ... UNTIL you have lived in a home that is NOT middle class, has NOT met your emotional and financial means to thrive, or being a person of color, DON'T compare YOUR upbringing or how your success has benefited you and your children as your reason WHY there is no need for MADISON PREP!!!!!!!!!!! Just like you, the school board and many teachers; all of you have said one thing and have done the exact opposite behind the backs of people of color and their children. Now, tell me who really is the con man and hustler???

This kind of diatribe was common in the sample among Facebook posts on Black activists' pages and infrequently under news articles (though still

---

[23] The conversation also provides a snapshot of how the local media ecology is expanding to include these alternative social-media spaces of public content where new actors can insert themselves and others into the flow of information. The exchange also represented a part of the ecology that allowed negotiation of who and what that ecology should contain.

[24] http://madisonamps.org/2011/09/23/is-it-all-about-the-kids-and-what-that-might-mean-take-one-in-relation-to-ulgm-and-madison-prep/.

occasionally present). This important statement demonstrates how conversation beaks down when public comments make general, racist charges born from White privilege. The author evokes the concept "trust" as a missing ingredient in this public dialogue specifically. She makes some strong points before then she too accuses the man as being representative of all White people who "hustle" and "lie" and "con" Black people – which will always shut down deliberation.

CONCLUSIONS: FIELD INERTIA AND BOUNDARY WORK

Throughout the case studies, the theme of distrust arose repeatedly as individuals made statements meant to make themselves more visible in the field, but were often seen as malevolent challenges. The result is that each individual speaking out works not to advance the dialogue, but rather to improve his or her position in the field – and sometimes, frankly, to stymie others' field mobility. In other words, the missed connections, poor communication habits, and outcome failures that inhibit effective public talk also maintain the status quo. These keep people in their existing field positions – some highly networked with many others isolated or marginalized. Bourdieu equates our aesthetic, cultural, semantic choices with the system of power,[25] and it is through the practice of these choices – what Bourdieu might call "habitus" – that boundaries are drawn between social groups.[26] The contexts that are given, say in a news article, and the narratives that are used, create cultural products that operate as sites for boundary struggles within the field where individuals and groups jockey for position.[27] Power dynamics (that is the dominant group's privileged positionality) can inhibit any upward mobility on the part of subordinate groups and individuals. These must be played out as a struggle, as one group competing against others to uphold its superiority is connected

[25] Pierre Bourdieu, *Distinction: A Social Critique of the Judgement of Taste* (Cambridge, Mass.: Harvard University Press, 1984).

[26] Pierre Bourdieu and Jean-Claude Passeron, *Reproduction in Education, Society, and Culture* (Beverly Hills, Calif.: Sage Publications, 1972); Bourdieu, *Distinction*; Michele Lamont and Virag Molnar, "The Study of Boundaries in the Social Sciences," *Annual Review of Sociology* 28 (2002): 167–195.

[27] Somers M. R., "Reclaiming the Epistemological 'Other': Narrative and the Social Constitution of Identity," in *Social Theory and the Politics of Identity*, by C. Calhoun (Cambridge, Mass.: Blackwell, 1994), 37–99; Lamont and Molnar, "The Study of Boundaries in the Social Sciences"; Michele Lamont, *Money, Morals, and Manners: The Culture of the French and American Upper-Middle Class* (Chicago: University of Chicago Press, 1992).

directly with one's core identity. To maintain social and collective identities, actors practice "in-group" vs "outgroup" categorization and segregation, leading to a tendency toward preferential treatment and discrimination as a way to protect against dilution.[28]

We certainly saw this struggle between journalists and Black activists and others who want more from the journalists than the journalists were willing or able to give. For Benson, Bourdieu, and others who have examined journalism as a field, they note how reporters' practices and ideologies – what goes into their professionalism – extend the systems in place as a way to understand why change is so difficult in the newsroom. Once a field is formed, it assumes a sociocultural "inertia" that inhibits its evolution over time because people get stuck in their ways.[29] I have seen this over and over in the newsrooms I studied and throughout the interviews I held. "Journalists are caught up in structural processes which exert constraints on them such that their choices are totally preconstrained."[30] Bourdieu argues that competition within the journalistic field – and reporters' tendency to obsessively observe each other, and also to base their decisions of coverage on what others in the field are doing – leads to uniformity of content.[31] So it doesn't occur to journalists to allow parents to speak out anonymously or to compromise more on deadlines. The institutional and organizational expectations are also tied to financial and other realities that demand copy at a certain time, of a certain style and substance. Furthermore, the journalists' routines are interlinked with the other mainstream institutions such as the schools and government. So when *Ann Arbor News*[32]

---

[28] Hogg M. A., *Social Identification* (London: Routledge, 1988); H. Tajfel and J. C. Turner, "The Social Identity Theory of Intergroup Behavior," by SWG Worchel (Chicago: Nelson-Hall, 1985), 7–24; Lamont and Molnar, "The Study of Boundaries in the Social Sciences."

[29] Rodney Benson, *Shaping Immigration News: A French-American Comparison* (Cambridge University Press, 2013); Walter W. Powell, "Expanding the Scope of Institutional Analysis," in *The New Institutionalism in Organizational Analysis*, by Walter W. Powell and P. J. DiMaggio (Chicago: University of Chicago Press, 1991), 183–203; Mark Schneider, "Does Culture Have Inertia?" Newsletter (Sociology of Culture Section of the American Sociological Association, 2001).

[30] Pierre Bourdieu, "The Political Field, the Social Science Field and the Journalistic Field," in *Bourdieu and the Journalistic Field*, by Rodney Benson and Erik Neveu (Cambridge: Polity, 1995), 45.

[31] Pierre Bourdieu, *On Television* (New York: New Press, 1999), 73. See also Pablo J. Boczkowski, *News at Work: Imitation in an Age of Information Abundance* (Chicago: University of Chicago Press, 2010).

[32] The *Ann Arbor News* actually became AnnArbor.com in 2009. Its print product ended, and the majority of its 272 employees were laid off. In 2013, it became MLive.com and the newspaper was revived Sundays and Thursdays as *The Ann Arbor News*.

publishes the "top high school scholars" and fails to include any Black students because reporters simply use the information they get from school guidance counselors, the outcome generates more missed connections, as this Black activist from Ann Arbor said, "So, again, we kind of throw up our hands. And so I don't look for support, necessarily, from the *Ann Arbor News*." Here, as in many, many other comments from parents and activists throughout my case studies, we witness how newsrooms' historical, entrenched routines lead to distrust about motivation and frequent missed connections.

Bourdieu details the formation of social class as determining an actor's position in a particular field. He maps actors' social spaces made up of their cultural (i.e., education level) and their economic capital, and notes people in proximate locations on that map tend to interact more, form associations, and share common traits. Although Bourdieu dealt mostly in money and prestige, for the purposes of this book we can think of information capital as a form of symbolic capital determined by one's place in the field. Several factors contribute to a person's amount of information capital: their job description, their connection to an information institution such as a news organization, their background, their activism, and their job flexibility. A person who feels as if he is an expert in a topic is more likely to participate online as well as someone who has been trained in journalistic practices. Also those who are White and progressive will be more apt to speak out, knowing they will be reinforced by others, and my case studies support that. So, if I extend this conceptualization to what's happening in the journalistic field, I think about the informational capital of Black people and other groups who are typically marginalized within mainstream communication flows. Furthermore, their absence from positions of authorship historically – in my major study site of Madison there was not a single Black reporter at the time of my data collection covering Madison Prep – contributes to the annihilation of them from the public conversation completely. The bottom line then is that if the dynamics are right in a field, people have the potential to change positions, but a field's structure makes those shifts difficult.

Deliberation scholars on race have also suggested that perhaps wanting everyone to talk together is not always the best idea. They note some topics in some discussion groups may merely irritate already inflamed discourse such that it creates more conflict instead of more understanding and productive deliberation. In public deliberation, Petrocik has demonstrated how the presence of distinct groups such as Democrats and

Republicans (or for our purposes, White people and Black people) creates the perception that each side "owns" some issues.[33] This can have the effect of disengaging folks from within both camps who might disagree with the dominant narrative of their "side." Making this situation somewhat more complex, scholars have shown how when talking about race, people often (and here I mean White people mostly) can speak around racial reasoning with euphemisms or in other ways that don't mention race at all – at least superficially. White people will go out of their way to wax eloquently about the universal good in lieu of racial references in order to avoid being seen as racist. I view this kind of deliberative duplicity – intentional but also unintentional or at least, well-meaning – as a significant obstacle to public talk on achievement disparities in local communities. Furthermore, even when the arguments made by White people are valid, research has shown that Black people will scrutinize the message for racism regardless of its presence and that both races approach issues such as achievement disparities from radically different perspectives. This dichotomy existed throughout my cities, representing real obstacles to public talk.

In this chapter we saw how missed connections, ideological and identity structures, and outcome failures comprised challenges for meaningful deliberation in public spaces such as journalism. We saw how journalistic routines are meant to protect their professionalism – and profession – but how they also perpetuate absences in the media. We saw how the public dialogue in our towns set up winner-loser and other kinds of binaries that simplify the discussion and generate acrimony. And we saw how the absence of alternative voices in mainstream information flows (at meetings, in newsrooms, in stories, in leadership, etc.) help ensure a dominating ideology with little effective challenge within the information-exchange field. Trusting relationships cannot materialize when personal, physical-world interactions are desired but digital ones prevail, when different communicative values create suspicions of motivations, or when citizens "want steak" but are only being offered "mashed potatoes," as one Black parent suggested in a focus group. As the key actors in this information-exchange field police the boundaries of their networks, they work to preserve the White sense of self that ruled Madison. And the result is that marginalization, feelings of injustice, and real inequities persist. As one example, Ms. Jones, one of the Black parents with whom I

---

[33] Petrocik J., "Issue Ownership in Presidential Elections," *American Journal of Political Science* 54 (1996): 825–850.

began this chapter, moved out of Madison, back to Brooklyn, N.Y. with her son.

"I am never going back to Madison," she said.

A permanently missed connection, I thought. Ms. Jones had left "the room" and would not be re-entering it.

"Has it gotten any better?" she asked me just before we ended the phone call.

5

Legitimation Strategies in Public Discourse About Race

Had things gotten any better in Madison, Wisc.? The question from the parent who had moved to New York nagged at me as I continued to interview people about public discourse on racial achievement disparities in my cities. It was a full year after the Madison school board voted down the Madison Prep charter school proposal when I had my interview with John Matthews, the head of the teachers' union in Madison. During our two-hour talk at a local coffee shop, we were routinely interrupted as he chatted with people stopping by. This seemed fitting, given his lengthy descriptions of his extensive networks. Prior to Madison Prep, it had been a rough couple of years for Matthews, who had led Madison Teachers Inc. (MTI) for forty years and suffered a catastrophic defeat at the hands of Wisconsin Gov. Scott Walker. Walker stripped public unions of their bargaining power through the passage of Act 10 in early 2011.[1] At the same time, Kaleem Caire proposed the Madison Prep charter school just as Matthews was itching for a fight he could win. Entering the twilight of his career, Matthews remained as committed to the progressive, pro-teacher dogma as when he had arrived as a young, feisty champion of public education and defender of Madison's (mostly White) public-school teachers in the 1960s. In our conversation, he lamented Walker's maligning of education, teachers, and the unions. Although he acknowledged vast achievement disparities existed between White people and everyone

---

[1] Just a few years after the passage of Act 10, union membership was down 40 percent from their 2010 numbers, http://host.madison.com/wsj/news/local/govt-and-politics/union-membership-down-nearly-percent-since-act/article_60c1bb7e-3ae3-57d0-b4b3-a9aa46f0e59f.html.

else, Matthews believed them to be "100 percent" the product of poverty, pure and simple – and as such, not the responsibility of the schools. Thus, Madison Prep – with its nonunion staff and its $10 million proposed use of public school money – would take resources away from the school district to try to solve something it could not. When he first heard of Caire's proposal, Matthews felt a keen sense of wariness at what it meant for the teachers he represented and for the union (MTI). He wrote to me in an email after our interview: "MTI is responsible to its members. This means an obligation to first look at a proposal's impact on MTI members to determine whether that impact is positive or negative." His scrutiny also was very strategic as he considered what such a school would mean for his embattled bargaining status with the district – his political capital.

Matthews was peerless when it came to his power to network in Madison. He insisted to me that he didn't regularly read the local newspapers (though he quoted from them three times during the interview), and held bloggers, Facebook, Twitter, and anything else digital in high disdain. He spent 14- to 15-hour days ("and one day on the weekend") networking – calling people on the phone, visiting with them in their office, and going to meetings, events, and press conferences. He read a couple of progressive and union-related blogs suggested to him by his teacher union reps. He checked his gut against the interests (and progressive ideology) of the union to determine any information's credibility. He knew all the city's power players, and named them throughout the interview. He spent a few minutes of every meeting gaining what some might call "information capital" – asking about their background, finding connections, and creating good will; he even did this with me. He always had a union rep at the school board meetings. His influence reigned in private spaces. "You don't want to cross the union," he said to me at one point, already smiling and holding out his hand as someone else came up to the table to shake it.

During mid-2011, the organizers of the Madison Prep proposal held several meetings to win Matthews' and the union's approval. The major sticking point was the Urban League's insistence that staff such as social workers and others be trained to help this particular population – and be preferably of color. The Urban League didn't want to be hemmed in by union rules (or the mostly White teacher pool). Matthews wanted these employees to be union members, worried that hiring nonunion staff would set a precedent and also mean those employees would not be protected. In the end, said Matthews, this "stubbornness" of Caire's in not capitulating on the amount of public funding or union representation of the staff did the plan in. For many, it appeared that very little of the actual deliberation over this charter school happened in the public realm, where it should have happened, some argued. Persuasion happened in the hallways at events and in coffee shops around town. Minds were made up before the meeting. And the information networks made up of mostly White progressives of the city dominated talk, both privately and publicly – or so it seemed to Madison Prep supporters.

This chapter examines the strategies used to overcome those challenges when having discussions involving race. Every person we interviewed approached their public – and private – talk about achievement disparities with deep intention, considering the most effective way their words could be heard and the power elite to be persuaded. This chapter seeks to answer the question: How are stakeholders – including school officials and administrators, journalists, bloggers, union representatives, teachers, activists, parents, and others – using public and private information channels to build tactical relationships, improve social capital, achieve levels of trust, and become empowered to participate in community life? Many of these strategies were successful while others failed – doomed perhaps from their very beginnings. Why is that? By identifying people's strategies, we can continue the investigation into isolating the contributors of polemic talk and work toward more effective deliberation, better amplification of marginalized voices, and better news coverage of racial topics such as achievement disparities. That's my hope.

Furthermore, we can understand what happened with Madison Prep's particular information flow in terms of field theory, specifically with an understanding of doxa, habitus, and social capital. I will explore these three field terms and apply them to how Matthews and others talked about how they did what they did during the time of Madison Prep. Then, I will consider the notion of legitimation strategies as a way to attain authority in the field through these understandings. The bulk of the chapter will dissect which legitimation strategies people used in my cases in order to appreciate what these tactics indicated about their field positions and possibilities for movement within the information network. Upon first glance at this public dialogue, it seems obvious that some attempts at legitimation triumphed at the expense of others. But looking deeper, it is evident how social media and other new-media platforms helped to buoy some voices and techniques of information exchange in a way that boosted visibility and encouraged public talk – outcomes that will be explored more in the concluding chapter. Techniques of strategies included: repetition across and within platforms, the making of dynamic dialogues online, and the taking advantage of the fluidity of public and private networks.

HABITUS AS AN EXPRESSION OF DOXA, SOCIAL CAPITAL, AND INFORMATION EXCHANGE

To answer these questions about legitimation strategies, we return to the concept of habitus as a structuring principle that guides the action (and nonaction) taken in this field. Meant to be theorized in conjunction with doxa and social capital, habitus is a foundational construct for Bourdieu in theory of practice, referred to in metaphors such as the rules of a game[2] as well as a "way of being, a habitual state (especially of the body) and, in particular, a predisposition, tendency, propensity or inclination."[3] Habitus is not exactly the same thing as the word in the title of this chapter, "strategies." The concept is more ingrained into a person operating as a structuring force. According to Bourdieu, "The *habitus* is a spontaneity without consciousness or will."[4] And we know that strategy, on the other hand, implies a more conscious, active motivation on the part of an actor. Nonetheless, Bourdieu considers habitus to be a type of strategy, and in a footnote describes habitus as a most successful one because it takes little thinking and manipulation on the part of the actor.[5] Furthermore, habitus links to an agent's (and field's) historical background, a key ingredient to the construct – a characteristic that Bourdieu argued set the concept apart from the word "habit."[6] Importantly, habitus with one's social position in the field *and* their social capital manifests a set of particular practices.

Next we consider doxa. Bourdieu described doxa as representing the dominant ideology and therefore "as a universal point of view."[7] In applying doxa to the newsroom, Ida Schultz described it as a "set of professional beliefs which tend to appear as evident, natural and self-explaining norms of journalistic practice."[8] It is what helps reporters

[2] Pierre Bourdieu et al. *The Logic of Practice* (Stanford, Calif.: Stanford University Press, 1992), 64.
[3] Pierre Bourdieu, *Outline of a Theory of Practice* (New York: Cambridge University Press, 1977), 214.
[4] Ibid., 56.
[5] Ibid., 62, 292.
[6] Pierre Bourdieu, *Sociology in Question* (London; Thousand Oaks, Calif: Sage Publications Ltd, 1994), 86.
[7] Pierre Bourdieu, *Practical Reason: On the Theory of Action* (New York: Polity, 1998), 57.
[8] Ida Schultz, "The Journalistic Gut Feeling," *Journalism Practice* 1(2)(May 2007): 194, doi:10.1080/17512780701275507.

routinize and order what would otherwise be the chaos of the world's daily stories. This kind of hegemonic value system tends to be unspoken but widely believed and generally undisputed and self-reinforcing.[9] I saw evidence of doxa overlaying everyone's habitus throughout these cases. One reporter in Ann Arbor, Mich., for example, appreciated that power differentials were at work among his sources, but the idea of treating the parent of color unlike the way he dealt with a public official would defy entrenched journalistic convention. Others in Madison recognized the doxa of the city, as in this comment from Ananda Mirilli, the school board candidate and social justice director for the local YWCA whose story was covered in the previous chapter. Here she senses the doxa layering her conversations in Madison:

It is almost like they grew up with this religion ... School has forever been this central point, this equalizer – this place for equity, this place for social mobility for folks. [But] ... You grow up with this strong value of holding this piece and part of what [is] holding this place is what you believe. And now you have to believe in something else that is different to what you believed in for such a long time.

In most of the interviews with those in power I heard this kind of "patriotism" that essentially absolved the schools from responsibility for either the cause of the disparities or any possible relief.[10] Mirilli traveled throughout the city, presenting data about the racial disparities in the schools and encountering much resistance and defensiveness. She described to me how she strategized these presentations:

I try for the most part to be nonthreatening – to be not blaming or not accusatory. Just to give you a practical demonstration: At this last racial justice summit, I had a session on restorative justice as dismantling the school-to-prison pipeline. And I knew there were a lot of educators in the room. One of the slides was data from last year for suspensions broken down by race and ethnicity. ... In middle school last year, we had 1,400 African American students and we had 1,449 suspensions

---

[9] Schultz, "The Journalistic Gut Feeling"; Cecile Deer, "Doxa," in *Pierre Bourdieu: Key Concepts*, by Michael Grenfell (Durham, UK: Acumen, 2008), 119–130; Bourdieu, *Practical Reason: On the Theory of Action*; Bourdieu, *Outline of a Theory of Practice*.

[10] To be clear, the superintendents we talked to were very keen on closing racial achievement gaps in their districts and did not hold the view that schools were absolved. These districts were all part of the Minority Student Achievement Network, including those in Madison, Evanston, Chapel Hill, Cambridge, and Ann Arbor. They had developed, researched, proposed, and lobbied for many, many programs over the years (such as Evanston's move to reduce barriers into advanced classes for Black and Brown students). Indeed, their very involvement in MSAN demonstrated this priority. However, all faced (often intractable) obstacles, especially from powerful people when they tried to disrupt the status quo.

for nondrug or no weapons . . . So I'm like "You know, now this is nationwide this happens. Zero tolerance is nationwide. Disparity is happening everywhere. Small towns, little towns, rural areas, urban areas, east/west coast. In Madison we have this as well." . . . And so I showed the numbers, and I held it there because I knew some folks in the room needed some time to process that information.

In this strategy, she demonstrated a healthy respect of the power of the doxa, which can determine whether someone is easily able to process the contrary information. To challenge their proschool perspective is to challenge their identity (their guiding, centering doxa). And doxa informs the habitus; it serves as a foundational aspect of the habitus.

As part of exercising one's doxa via habitus, there is the spending and accumulation of social and other kinds of capital. I am using capital in the Bourdieuian tradition in assigning value to both symbolic (like connections and relationships) and tactile (money) assets that can boost privilege or, in their absence, suffocate one's chances of field mobility.[11] Like Mirilli in Madison, the superintendent in Cambridge, Mass., set out to build social capital among his district's different communities, especially Black and Brown groups as well as those in low-income brackets. First and foremost, he told us:

I had to make connections with people in the community who were credible . . . They're not used to talking to a superintendent. They don't have any idea what a superintendent does other than cold or snow days. So . . . I'm an unknown person. And so having a person who is known to them, and credible and trustworthy to them was critical in getting groups to the inner centers.

As this superintendent and others in interviews noted, a consistent community presence – sponsoring festivals, forming parent groups, engaging constantly – was a way of building trust. The Cambridge superintendent added that aggregating mass amounts of data both quantitative and qualitative in the form of personal experience is a must, but that it must be conveyed in a way that connects the problem to everyone:

Understand that people do not change for my reasons; they change for their own . . . If their lives are going to get happier or easier or more productive or more satisfied, . . . that's when people change. Not when they're talked into it by someone who happens to have a governmental . . . title.

Thus, any social-capital building must be done so in a way that establishes not only a connection with individuals, but also prompts the

---

[11] Robert Moore, "Capital," in *Pierre Bourdieu: Key Concepts*, by Michael Grenfell (Durham, U.K.: Polity, 2008), 101–117.

individual to see a way to self-advancement in the field by way of the association. In Madison, MTI Executive Director John Matthews' entire networking strategy set him up to achieve political, social, and information capital in the K–12 public school field. Every meeting he held, every time he asked about someone's kids or relayed the behind-the-scenes conversation he'd just had, he was asserting his dominance as an information king and acquiring more information he could use.

An anecdote from our interview illustrates this point: After Act 10, MTI and other public unions lost their bargaining power, and it was mandated unions could negotiate only one-year contracts. Matthews asked the new superintendent (Jennifer Cheatham) to negotiate three one-year contracts. She said no. He went to the school board members individually and got three to agree to it. He needed a fourth. He met that fourth – a good friend, someone who had campaigned with him – in a coffee shop and the conversation quickly got heated. He ran into a former school board president on the way out of the coffee shop and asked her to help convince the member of the need for three one-year contracts. That didn't work either. "It was clear the superintendent had gotten to them." He called his "troops" – who responded because Matthews was almost single-handedly responsible for getting them more resources – and got people to attend the meeting, which was on the budget. Each person spoke for a few seconds about the budget and then was instructed to "just give your speech." He ended up with two one-year contracts and listed this in the victory category. Here, though, we can see how when Act 10 was passed and his political capital took a huge hit, so did his ability to maneuver within the field. Even his social and informational capital was affected (e.g., even his friend declined to back his request).

Information exchanges have the power to preserve the authority these institutions have to reign over our cities. Habitus prop up the status quo and work with doxa and social capital to create a reality where some voices dominate a community instead of others. For Bourdieu, the habitus enables these institutions to "attain full realization."[12] Reporters in these cities reified the main institutions – schools, the local government – in their sourcing choices and frames. Consider this comment by an MLive reporter in Ann Arbor, Mich., in response to someone tagged "mmppcc" who asked "Who decided it was the job of public schools to solve America's inequality problem?"

---

[12] Bourdieu, *The Logic of Practice*, 57–58.

Box 5.1. An interlude: Public talk in Evanston, Ill., about race

One public official – an African American – called Evanston, Ill., a physically beautiful city with "drive-by diversity" for its superficial appearance of rich integration but a reality of segregation in daily life. On the shores of Lake Michigan, Evanston is a liberal-leaning town that is just north of Chicago, hosts Northwestern University, and prides itself on its civil rights history. In interviews, more than one person referred to it as the "People's Republic of Evanston." Many residents cite its diversity as one of the reasons they chose to settle there. With a population of 75,658, about 65.6 percent identify as White, 18.1 percent Black, 9 percent Latino and 8.6 percent Asian. Like our other cities, the city is highly educated with 66 percent of residents holding a bachelor's degree or higher, compared to 34.7 percent of the population in Cook County.

Two school districts run Evanston schools: District 65 oversees K–8 education and has seven elected members; District 202 administers the high school with eight elected board members. The districts are both a majority minority; in the high school, just 43 percent of the student population is White, 31 percent Black, 16.6 percent Hispanic, 3.9 percent Asian. Large achievement disparities exist in both districts with gaps of more than 50 percentage points by some metrics. The district de-tracked classes by eliminating freshman-year honors classes, hired Glenn Singleton to hold "courageous conversations" about race, and created a number of other initiatives, including a two-way immersion program, literacy goals, African-centered curriculum in some schools, and city partnership of social services to help at-risk children. The school board has been widely praised for its aggressive combating of achievement disparities and transparency with performance data.

Nonetheless, some of our interviewees lamented the city's seeming inability to have "honest conversations," which are "frequently avoided" or peppered with "code words." Like with other cities, Evanston harbors several obstacles to public talk about racial disparities. The first is zero-sum thinking within the community with some White parents feeling: "if we're bringing new opportunities

Box 5.1. (cont.)

and advantages to some kids, then we must be taking away resources and opportunities from other kids, which would be their kids." Parents of honors students worried that the high school was "dumbing down" the curriculum. A second obstacle has been the discord between Evanston's professed love of its diversity and the general population's lack of interrogation of its inequities. A third impediment has been lack of engagement with all parent communities. One official noted an exceptionalism that permeates the community, where White progressives in the city think Evanston is different from other places in terms of race relations, but is not.

In truth, Evanston seemed more progressive than many of our other cities in terms of its outreach. We found several news stories addressing, for example, the pervasive segregation. Nearly everyone interviewed singled out the *Evanston Roundtable* as providing insightful, deeply analytical coverage about the school district sparking public dialogue. Publishing bimonthly since 1998, the *RoundTable* is distributed to 18,000 homes and community drop-offs. The paper's coverage of the achievement gap has primarily focused on the metrics used to measure college readiness, and it even partnered with a Northwestern University professor to conduct a deep dive into the testing scores and develop a better way to measure student abilities. In addition, the *Evanston Now* is an online newspaper that allows readers to submit their own blogs. The *Chicago Tribune* covers Evanston as part of its suburban beat. Finally, Evanston's proximity to the large media market of Chicago has meant a fair amount of national media attention, particularly for the de-tracking initiative in the high school.

Furthermore, a movement in the city called "Evanston Own It" encouraged residents to have a greater stake in all neighborhoods. And both the school districts and city officials were working actively to identify more effective dialogic strategies. For example, some spoke of holding frequent roundtables with citizens in different kinds of formats – eschewing the more typical formal hearings. Others talked about casual listening sessions when officials head into the community for informal gatherings with citizens.

Perhaps no one decided it was the public schools' job to solve the inequity problem, but a burden does fall on the shoulders of public educators. What do you suggest the country do to make life more equitable for everyone? www.mlive.com/news/ann-arbor/index.ssf/2015/03/ann_arbor_schools_narrowing_ac.html.

Here the reporter reminded readers of the district and county's responsibility to societal problems, in part by linking back to one of her own stories. Bloggers, such as this one in Chapel Hill, N.C., noted how they will sometimes jump into the comments to redirect conversations: "Once in a while it just seems like it went too far afield and I come in and refocus." This constant information work helps maintain the boundaries of institutions and their status quo – which help keep that dominant doxa in play – while also boosting the authors' influence as authority figures in these networks. These practices also determine the content and direction of the information flow in the overall media ecology.

LEGITIMATION STRATEGIES

One way that actors in an information-exchange field such as education journalism maintain those boundaries is by practicing legitimation strategies. Legitimation strategies are enacted as instruments of control to reinforce or change positions in a network.[13] The kinds of legitimation strategies that reporters perform reflect a doxic value system.[14] Gans formalized how reporters abide by an implicit, ideological value system in the United States that exudes: responsible capitalism, small-town pastoralism, altruistic democracy, individualism, moderatism, leadership, ethnocentrism, and a certain social order.[15] Another system of doxa structuring newsrooms is journalistic professionalism. Bourdieu and others have described "doxa" as ubiquitous in newsrooms, innate and dominating.

In order to create, enact, and extend these social orders through narrative, journalists practice strategies of legitimation, which "provide the 'explanations' and justifications of the salient elements of the institutional tradition ... [and] justifies the institutional order by giving a normative

[13] Karl Maton, "Languages of Legitimation: The Structuring Significance for Intellectual Fields of Strategic Knowledge Claims," *British Journal of Sociology of Education* 21(2) (2000): 149.

[14] See Schultz, "The Journalistic Gut Feeling." She also thinks about reportorial norms and standards as indicative of field dynamics.

[15] Herbert Gans, *Deciding What's News: A Study of CBS Evening News, NBC Nightly News, Newsweek, and Time* (Chicago: Northwestern Press, 1979).

dignity to its practical imperatives."[16] Habermas, Berger and Luckmann, van Leeuwen, and others have suggested that all communication reflects legitimation through vocabulary, framing, and other exercising of language.[17] When someone is considered legitimate, they embody an authority to influence people in their relationships, decisions, and other actions. Much research had documented how journalists seek to assert their authority over and over through such legitimation tactics as quoting experts, bearing witness, being self-reflexivity, storytelling via narrative, and using such semantics as "said," "according to," and "confirmed."[18] Through coverage of political elites, journalists improve their own position and career trajectory by working in collaboration with officials who have the power to make or break their access. Reporters engage in paradigm repair work and other methods to elevate their content above the fray and single out themselves as the true – and only – storytellers.[19] van Leeuwen showed how legitimation strategies occur through narrative work, and introduced four categories to describe these strategies. The first, authorization, includes references to an institution, law (impersonal authority), expert authority, and other modes including tradition (or customs) and conformity. In applying his schemata to education coverage, van Leeuwen noted the techniques for authorization include "specific utterances and clauses (such as terms like "expert") and citation of legalities." The second category, moral evaluation, references value systems through "statements, abstractions, and analogies that offer 'common-sense' reasoning for ensuring consensus." Producers of public content, such as journalists and bloggers – and the sources they reference – offer a "systemized morality that comes through in the text and "teaches" those

[16] Berger P. and T. Luckmann, *The Social Construction of Reality* (Harmondsworth: Penguin, 1966), 111.

[17] Jurgen Habermas, *Legitimation Crisis* (London: Heinemann, 1976); Berger and Luckmann, *The Social Construction of Reality*; Theo van Leeuwen, "Legitimation in Discourse and Communication," *Discourse & Communication* 1(1)(February 1, 2007): 91–112, doi:10.1177/1750481307071986.

[18] Stuart Allan, *News Culture* (Berkshire, England: Open University Press, 1999); Barbie Zelizer, *Covering the Body: The Kennedy Assassination, the Media, and the Shaping of Collective Memory* (Chicago: University of Chicago Press, 1993).

[19] Matt Carlson, "Blogs and Journalistic Authority: The Role of Blogs in US Election Day 2004 Coverage," *Journalism Studies* 8(2)(2007): 264–279; Peter Dahlgren, "Introduction," in *Journalism and Popular Culture* (London: Sage, 1992), 1–23; David Eason, "'On Journalistic Authority': The Janet Cooke Scandal," in *Media, Myths, and Narratives: Television and the Press* (Newbury Park, CA: Sage, 1988), 205–227; Barbie Zelizer, "Journalists as Interpretive Communities," *Critical Studies in Mass Communication* 10(1993): 219–237.

of us reading what to think." The third, rationalization, includes two types: Instrumental rationalization entails laid-out purposes, goals, uses, and effects within the text to guide the reader, and theoretical rationalization suggests a "natural order for an expressed ideology." According to van Leeuwen, common techniques for these legitimation devices include "asserting a kind of 'just the way things are' tone, declarations of purpose based on moralization, explanatory passages and definitions." Finally, mythopoesis, or moral-laden narratives, provides an avenue to convey legitimation through "narratives whose outcomes reward legitimate actions and punish non-legitimate actions."[20] In these categorical descriptions we can appreciate how doxa informs, habitus relates, and capital is a given. van Leeuwen's typology was an incredibly useful analytic framework for my copious data, as you will see in the next section.

When some perspective is considered legitimated, alternative viewpoints have a harder time gaining visibility, complicating facts can be obscured, alternative ideologies tend to be demonized, countercultures rarely get covered (except as "other"), and power elites become voices of reason – all in the name of a good moral. Analyzing a racially charged political drama, Ettema wrote that "the press gives its readers guidance in *how* to think about issues as well as how to act upon them, and in doing so, the press helps to 'contain,' in Carey's term, the domain of the political within the cultural." He argued that the press enacted a mass-mediated ritual of social control through its coverage, allowing politicians, reporters, and others with access to the public discourse the opportunity to legitimate specific stories over others.

Some have begun tracking how citizens who utilize social media and other digital platforms to mass communicate gain authority though legitimizing storytelling. In light of digital technologies that allow for mass self-communication, bloggers can redefine what is legitimate content. Some have begun doing so by avoiding a detached reportorial style and instead providing stories of personal experience.[21] As a result, some audiences rate bloggers as being more credible than journalists.[22] Indeed

---

[20] Leeuwen, "Legitimation in Discourse and Communication."

[21] Matheson D., "Weblogs and the Epistemology of News: Some Trends in Online Journalism," *New Media & Society* 6(4)(2004): 443–468.

[22] Tom Johnson and Barbara Kaye, "Wag the Blog: How Reliance on Traditional Media and the Internet Influence Credibility Perceptions of Weblogs among Blog Users," *Journalism & Mass Communication Quarterly* 81(2004): 622–644; Tom Johnson and Barbara Kaye, "Believing the Blogs of War? How Blog Users Compare on Credibility and Characteristics in 2003 and 2007," *Media, War & Conflict* 3(3)(2010): 315–333.

one study found blogs are starting to help set the agenda on some issues.[23] And these blogs offer values: justice, honesty, courage, redemption, freedom, industriousness, independence, and democracy are popular themes among the bloggers studied by researchers.[24] Commenters, too, are testing the boundaries of information authority by questioning the "facts" of a story and dominant storylines of reporters as well as developing their own norms.[25]

Legitimation Strategies of Journalists

Journalists have worked hard over the last century to establish themselves as *the* authoritative storytellers in public realms. As I started to write this book, I wondered whether White reporters used different strategies in covering racially charged issues, given the distrust that pervaded Black communities toward the media. I was also curious whether new digital networks and the ability to interact directly with sources forced changes in strategy. But no, in the cities I analyzed, reporters relied on traditional legitimation strategies – particularly techniques of authorization, rationalization, and mythopoesis. This makes sense if only because when we feel uncomfortable or uncertain, we tend to fall back on what we know and what is familiar. Also, in my 13 years as a reporter, I never considered changing my strategies even when covering issues about race because it would have gone against my training. When I felt in doubt about my authority over a particular topic or within a kind of community I was not a part of, I relied on this training to assert my legitimacy to tell the story; my outsider status lent me credibility, or so I believed at the time. But let's see not only what the reporters had to say about how the racial disparities in our cities were covered, but also what community leaders, parents, bloggers, and others were doing to amplify their voices in the information flows of these media ecologies.

---

[23] Angeline Gautami Fernando, L. Suganthi, and Bharadhwaj Sivakumaran, "If You Blog, Will They Follow? Using Online Media to Set the Agenda for Consumer Concerns on 'Greenwashed' Environmental Claims," *Journal of Advertising* 43(2)(2014): 167–180.

[24] Mary Meares and Khalil Islam-Zwart, "'The Real Story': Blogs as a Mechanism for Employee Voice" (International Communication Association Annual Meeting, Dresden, Germany, 2006).

[25] Sue Robinson, "Redrawing Borders from Within: Commenting on News Stories as Boundary Work," in *Boundaries of Journalism*, by Matt Carlson and Seth C. Lewis (New York: Routledge, 2015), 152–168.

Authorization, Rationalization, Mythopoesis

Many of the mainstream news articles that covered achievement disparities cited and referenced members of the dominant institutions in the cities studied. This routine reified the power structure in place and also legitimized reporters' connections to these authoritative bodies.[26] A common tactic by reporters included citing statistics and drawing from government reports as forms of *expert authorization* that helped position the journalist's content as a credible – even as it reinforced the White-dominated institutions that produced both those reports *and* the disparities.[27] A Cambridge, Mass., reporter, for example, called herself a "lay person" whose job as a journalist was "to simplify these things." She saw her role as the liaison between the officials (and "their jargon") and the people. School board members and superintendents were by far the most cited source in the stories of all of the cases throughout the country. Many of the reporters – and the evidence in all the media texts bear this out – reported using these officials as their first (and sometimes only) foundational sources of information. At times, reliance on these sources meant obscuring important parts of the story. For example, another reporter – this one in Michigan – said that little historical context of the

---

[26] Matt DeFour, "Nichols Seeks to Unseat Silveira on School Board," *Wisconsin State Journal*, February 28, 2012, http://host.madison.com/wsj/news/local/govt-and-politics/e lections/nichols-seeks-to-unseat-silveira-on-school-board/article_3f090dec-61ab-11e1-b 970-001871e3ce6c.html; Paul Fanlund, "Madison360: On School 'gap' Issue, There's Also a Gap between Leaders," *The Capital Times*, February 20, 2012, http://host.madi son.com/ct/news/local/madison_360/madison-on-school-gap-issue-there-s-also-a-gap/ar ticle_b09fc24e-5b47-11e1-9e63-001871e3ce6c.html; Pat Schneider, "Grass Roots: Will Dan Nerad's Retirement Help His Plan to Close the Achievement Gap?)," *The Capital Times*, March 27, 2012, http://host.madison.com/ct/news/local/grassroots/grass-roots-will-dan-nerad-s-retirement-help-his-plan/article_ab29112a-7790-11e1-8a6a-001871e3 ce6c.html.

[27] Nathan Comp, "Tepid Response to Nerad's Plan to Close Achievement Gap in Madison School District," *Isthmus*, February 6, 2012, www.thedailypage.com/daily/article.php? article=35889; Matt DeFour, "School Board Rips Nerad's Diversity Proposal," *Wisconsin State Journal*, January 9, 2012, http://host.madison.com/wsj/news/local/educa tion/local_schools/article_b6193661-f1b0-574b-a88c-b34b0568f23c.html; Matt DeFour, "Nerad Unveils $12.4 Million Plan to Close School Achievement Gap," *Wisconsin State Journal*, February 7, 2012, http://host.madison.com/wsj/news/local/education/local_ schools/nerad-unveils-million-plan-to-close-school-achievement-gap/article_8e3e9140-51 23-11e1-94a9-001871e3ce6c.html; Nathan Comp, "Madison Prep Backers Seek School Board Re-Vote," *Isthmus*, January 14, 2012, www.thedailypage.com/daily/article.php? article=35705; Cogan Schneier, "Tests Find Readings Key Area for Achievement Gaps," *Badger Herald*, March 28, 2012, http://badgerherald.com/news/2012/03/28/tests_find_ readings_.php.

achievement gaps made it into the stories because no school officials wanted to talk about the failures of the past. Furthermore, reporters tended to choose those comments from officials that characterized the officials' personal authority in the city as the overseer of the community's children: " 'We have some very important issues on the table currently, so we have to stay focused on the 26,000 students we're serving,' [school board member Ed Hughes] said. 'I don't know if the timing is right for Madison Prep."[28] Such comments demonstrated the kind of synergetic relationship that has been described as an indexed power system based on reciprocal relationships. The reporters help these officials maintain their field position and, in the process, demonstrate their access to and their acceptance of the authoritative structure in place.[29]

In their articles, reporters routinely call on tradition, conformity, and the impersonal authority of an institution. Consider this one piece about questions surrounding the Madison Prep budget:

... two major fundraising events, co-hosted by Burke, were held in the fall at the Maple Bluff and Nakoma country clubs. The Madison Prep fundraising campaign hasn't sought a go-ahead from the United Way of Dane County's Capital Fund Raising Committee, which analyzes and coordinates major local capital fundraising campaigns.[30]

The United Way in Madison operated as a quasi-institution, demanding that all fundraising in the city be coordinated through it – a status its description in the article implies. While no formal requirement exists, most nonprofits have traditionally acquiesced. To not have the United Way as a campaign backer meant facing closed doors from the limited number of big donors in the small community. Here the reporter uses this lack of compliance as an example of the project's opaqueness (along with the title of the article, "Madison Prep founders won't say much about private financing plan"). The result casts the organizers as outside the system, as not a "player" in the establishment and serves to de-legitimate the project.

---

[28] Comp, "Madison Prep Backers Seek School Board Re-Vote."

[29] W. Lance Bennett, Regina G Lawrence, and Steven Livingston, *When the Press Fails: Political Power and the News Media from Iraq to Katrina* (Chicago, Ill.; University of Chicago Press, 2008).

[30] Pat Schneider, "Grass Roots: Madison Prep Founders Won't Say Much about Private Financing Plan," *The Capital Times*, January 8, 2012, http://host.madison.com/ct/news/local/grassroots/grass-roots-madison-prep-founders-won-t-say-much-about/article_13becb72-3965-11e1-b72f-0019bb2963f4.html.

Some Madison reporters boasted of their ubiquitous presence, mentioning their connections to the power elites: "The first time I heard from Nelson Cummings was about a year and a half ago when he called me up in response to something I'd written about race and Madison ... I called Cummings on Saturday ... "[31] In another piece, an editor inserted himself into the public deliberation, calling on a school board official to agree with him.[32] In their blogs associated with their beats, the reporters boosted the legitimacy of their work.[33] These reporters institutionalize themselves, and in doing so, add to the weight of the structure supporting the status quo.

Meanwhile, the majority of the mainstream news articles on Madison Prep referred to the project's primary Black organizer Kaleem Caire not as an expert, but as a "charismatic champion"[34] experimenting with a "laboratory."[35] This reference marginalized his credentials, which included his position as president of the Urban League and his years working with President Obama on the "Race to the Top" education policy. In all coverage of Madison Prep, only those Black and Brown citizens who were part of White institutions were granted "expert" status, such as Professor Gloria Ladson-Billings at the University of Wisconsin-Madison.[36] This was reinforced in the interviews as reporters talked about what represented a credible source. All the reporters interviewed articulated very specific – and uniform – understandings of "good" sources.

---

[31] Chris Rickert, "Don't Let Failed Prep School End Dialogue," *Wisconsin State Journal*, June 5, 2012, http://host.madison.com/news/local/chris_rickert/chris-rickert-don-t-let-f ailed-prep-school-end-dialogue/article_91f2249e-aea4-11e1-8095-0019bb2963f4.html.

[32] Paul Fanlund, "Next School Head May Need to Walk on Water," *The Capital Times*, June 25, 2012, http://host.madison.com/ct/news/local/madison_360/madison-next-sch ool-head-may-need-to-walk-on-water/article_9d9cf244-bcb7-11e1-b2ef-0014abcf887 a.html.

[33] Pat Schneider, "Grass Roots: Dan Nerad Wants You to Help Bridge the Achievement Gap," *The Capital Times*, February 7, 2012, http://host.madison.com/ct/news/local/grass roots/grass-roots-dan-nerad-wants-you-to-help-bridge-the/article_6f177c46-51cd-11e1-8aec-0019bb2963f4.html; Jack Craver, "Madison Politiscope: Madison Prep, Unions Overshadow School Board Races," *The Capital Times*, February 8, 2012, http://host.m adison.com/ct/news/local/govt-and-politics/politiscope/madison-politiscope-madison-pr ep-unions-overshadow-school-board-races/article_be1bf564-51c4-11e1-90b3-001871e 3ce6c.html.

[34] Schneider, "Tests Find Readings Key Area for Achievement Gaps."

[35] Comp, "Madison Prep Backers Seek School Board Re-Vote."

[36] Susan Troller, "Chalkboard: Madison Prep Gets Closer but Big Questions Remain," *The Capital Times*, October 7, 2011, http://host.madison.com/ct/news/local/education/blog/ chalkboard-madison-prep-gets-closer-but-big-questions-remain/article_bc33f60a-f06e-11e0-a62f-001cc4c03286.html.

They expressed skepticism about nonprofits and activists: "Everybody's got an angle. Everybody is trying to get his or her story out, essentially," said one White reporter. They found sources mainly through press releases, planned events, connections with officials such as school principals or activists, and by talking to people like parents who contact them. They considered themselves "impartial observers": "I have to disassociate as much as possible any organizations or groups," said another. They very rarely turned to Facebook or other social-media platforms for anything other than finding sources or posting a question to their own network. To be credible, one must have credentials, be willing to be named, and be visible to these reporters.

In seeking people deemed "credible" and "expert," reporters bypassed neighborhoods and community centers and attended meetings instead. There, they would find people already motivated to provide a name as they spoke before the school board, for example. Said one reporter: "I do feel like a lot of what we have written ... includes the same names. That happens in every subject that you cover. [With race,] I wouldn't even know how to begin" to find different sources who were still credible. Another reporter said, "It's really difficult to find parents to speak on the record." So they talked to the superintendent and called the contact on the press release. To overcome those obstacles, journalists employed impersonal authorization that comes from staying among the power elite and their data.

The ubiquitous strategy of impersonal authorization produced administrative, process-based stories. This presented another common strategy for journalists – that of instrumental rationalization, which reporters use to help orient the reader. By framing the story around the *instrumental rationalizations* of the institution, the journalist reminds readers the natural social order in place will resolve the conflict "logically" in a formal procedure. However this strategy also meant White reporters missed deeper dives into the racial aspects of the debate. For example, one Madison reporter suggested he fell back on reports, meeting stories, financial pieces, and political-game coverage so as "to maintain impartiality on a sensitive issue ... I mean that was kind of one of my weaknesses as covering the beat as I was a lot more up in the power structure." Rather than focusing on the causes of the disparities themselves, the reporter concentrated on the school board and its actions or the meeting happenings to "orient" the reader for the debate, he said in an interview. But the result was that the school board became a prominent rationalizer in the narrative and its actions as the ordering of society.

Furthermore, reporters positioned the board and other power players in a grand narrative as "protagonists" and those challenging the system as "antagonists" – a common strategy by reporters that van Leeuwen would label *mythopoesis*. The dominant mainstream story told a moral tale about societal structure, where any change must be made within the existing hierarchy of power.[37] Every anecdote and detail about the issue was framed in terms of all of the major bodies of power involved, as in this news story: "The controversial charter school has been a hot topic in the community, setting up the two school board contests as a perceived battle between the Urban League and the teachers union, which opposed the school."[38] Audience members were even asked to choose a side in the narrative, as in this December 2011 *Wisconsin State Journal* Facebook post promoting an article: "Kaleem Caire rips the Madison School Board. Whose side are you on?" Within this he-said/she-said framing, reporters set up two of the major storylines at the heart of the issue, as stated in this column by one editor: "... that leads to what our other moral responsibility is, and that is to educate our students the best we can. It is really a perfect storm, because we have more children in need now than we've ever had before with less funding."[39] This storyline tension arose over and over again.[40] As van Leeuwen argued, these moral tales offer a prescription for a specific social

---

[37] *The Capital Times*, "Vote for Mary Burke for School Board," *The Capital Times*, March 28, 2012, http://host.madison.com/ct/news/opinion/editorial/vote-for-mary-burke-for-school-board/article_134acd31-0183-58cb-8ced-a81e7fabb281.html; Ruth Conniff, "Crunch Time for Madison Prep Charter School," *Isthmus*, September 29, 2012, www.thedailypage.com/isthmus/article.php?article=34790; DeFour, "Nichols Seeks to Unseat Silveira on School Board"; Michael Kujak, "Experts Debate Ways to Reduce City Achievement Gap," *Badger Herald*, May 7, 2012, http://badgerherald.com/news/2012/05/07/experts_debate_ways_.php; Pat Schneider, "Grass Roots: Race Talk Fuels Tension in Madison Prep Debate," *The Capital Times, Madison.com*, January 12, 2012, http://host.madison.com/news/local/grassroots/grass-roots-race-talk-fuels-tension-in-madison-prep-debate/article_3b5e43fc-3ccf-11e1-b398-0019bb2963f4.html.

[38] DeFour, "Nichols Seeks to Unseat Silveira on School Board."

[39] Paul Fanlund, "For Our Schools, Is Blame the Only Certain Outcome?" *The Capital Times*, March 29, 2012, http://host.madison.com/news/local/madison_360/madison-for-our-schools-is-blame-the-only-certain-outcome/article_af318e80-a6b3-11e1-affa-001a4bcf887a.html.

[40] Matt DeFour, "Madison Prep Charter School to Get First Part of Grant," *Wisconsin State Journal*, September 9, 2012, http://host.madison.com/news/local/education/local_schools/madison-prep-charter-school-to-get-first-part-of-grant/article_2ee1034a-da68-11e0-ae3d-001cc4c002e0.html; Jacob Kaczmarowski, "Wisconsin Claims Highest High School Graduation Rate in Country," *Badger Herald*, March 20, 2012, http://badgerherald.com/news/2012/03/20/wisconsin_claims_hig.php; Staff, "MMSD Gathers Input on Preliminary Plan to Close the Achievement Gap," *The Madison Times*, March 14, 2012, www.themadisontimes.com/news_details.php?news_id=1833.

order. In these stories, we see how the educational system stands as the dominant power that must be engaged with and its representatives the most influential characters.

Meanwhile, whole stories about the people affected by the disparities in the school system went untold. Only two of the 30 Madison journalists we interviewed attempted to go to events in neighborhoods with more diverse citizens. All candidly expressed difficulty in covering race issues as White reporters. Said one reporter:

The core truth is we are White people writing about Black people and you are aware of all of these assumptions being made. I think the intentions have always been good, but if you say something wrong . . . any progress you have made is gone.

So they played it safe. Their strategies in covering race included: going to meetings where they knew people would be willing to attach their names to comments; talking to people who understood reporter deadlines and the journalistic need for sound bites and acceptable storylines; and adhering to procedural routines that could be done quickly. They were constrained by time and deadlines, access to the communities, and traditional conceptions of expert credibility.

Legitimation Strategies of Citizens

At this point I turned to the content production by nonjournalists. Did citizens strategize in different ways in online spaces? Interestingly citizens aligned themselves according to the "sides" that journalists had laid out for them – those seeking an alternative to the status quo (the "other" whose voices tended to be marginalized in public debate) and those trying to protect the establishment (that is, those who typically were speaking from comfortable positions within the system). White, Black, and Brown activists and community leaders all employed theoretical rationalization and moral evaluation to make their points in online spaces, in contrast to the reporters (whose doxic tenets usually prohibited them from engaging in such methods). However, in Madison, highly networked White progressives also mimicked journalistic strategies of impersonal authorization – aligning with "objectivity" values and avoiding talk of race and focusing on what was "best" and "fair" for the majority as well as the institutions (such as the schools). Meanwhile, those supporting the school called on much more personalized, emotional stories that lay bare notions of race, privileged communal health, and practiced grassroots networking. The next sections detail these strategies.

White Progressives

White progressives wrote almost all of the blogs about education or race issues that circulated widely in Madison and the other cities, and, in the wake of Act 10's passage, felt the same assault on their ideology and position in the community as the teachers' union.[41] After Act 10, Madison progressives circled the wagons. And when the Urban League tried to propose a school without some union positions, some saw an opportunity to protect the values they failed to preserve just months prior. In understanding the power at work in such coverage, one cannot negate the history and context, socially, culturally, and politically.

Like the reporters, the White progressives who wrote against Madison Prep cited statistics from government sites, linked to news articles and blogs, and found academic reports that disparaged charter schools in a kind of impersonal authorization.[42] For example, in one March 2012 Facebook post one White progressive, who ran a nonprofit housing center in town and wrote a blog called Forward Lookout, reported how the vast majority of homeless in the county were minority (70%) and implied this related to education disparities. In the comments, another White progressive blogger, who had just won election to the school board at the time of his post in March 2012, added "40% of African American 10th graders in MMSD entered their current school after the third [week of school]. Yes, that has much to do with achievement issues." Each of these frequent contributors read each other, cited each other, and referred to each other's points throughout the media ecology. They frequently promoted their own expertise, suggesting that their jobs or their blogs mean they "know more." Consider, for example, one Madison White progressive who wrote a blog and had a talk show. In his writings and the interview, he referred to his historian background, aligned himself with "facts," and valued "objectivity." He told us: "That's where my skills come in sometimes: What are the questions that are asked? What is the size of sample? How is change over time calculated? Or plotted?" He called his blog "a form of journalism" in the interview. Similarly, bloggers in all of the other cities – Ann Arbor, Mich., Cambridge, Mass., Evanston, Ill., and Chapel

---

[41] Several people of color in Madison wrote blogs or guest columns in more niche spaces that did not achieve prominence in the mainstream information-exchange flow.

[42] To be clear, not all of those against Madison Prep were White or progressive and not all those who supported the school were Black. However, those who were frequently commenting in public were part of an established, vocal group of progressives who showed up repeatedly in my sample.

Hill, N.C. – also described their intention to be credible by linking to reports and data. One blogger started to blog to address gaps she saw in reporting, and then began contributing to a more institutionalized media platform. Another did not link much in her posts, but her background efforts were highly networked with – and informed by – her association with Harvard as well as with the Department of Education for Massachusetts.

In their theoretical rationalization strategies, these progressives labeled charter schools as "alternative" and exuded skepticism about anything they feared diminished public schools (and teachers and unions). In one example, one White blogger described the information coming out of the Madison Prep movement as being "PR unleashed" in a Facebook post, suggesting the information about the proposal circulated was irrational and aggressive. Another continued this strategy in a Facebook post:

Madison Prep wants another vote in February. Smells like an elections stunt to me. I really wish instead of cramming their ideas down our throats, we could back up and Urban League would lead an open, transparent and inclusive discussion . . .

In characterizing the Urban League as a charlatan with hidden motives, this blogger aligned herself on the side of democracy, as someone protecting the will of the people from those who wish to stifle the process of deliberation.

Many other White commenters employed theoretical rationalization mixed with moral evaluations based on "facts" that were not backed up in any authoritative manner. Take for instance this comment on the Facebook page of Channel 3000, a major local news outlet:

Kids from disadvantaged homes are going to underperform. They tend to be kids of color. Unfortunate? Yes. But we can't ask schools to take the place of parents and families who devote themselves to supporting and nurturing their children. My kids' schools pay aid[e]s to help students with projects that most do at home, with the support of their parents. Wouldn't it be nice if those parents put in the time I did to support my kids? And sadly, I can tell you factually that in my daughter's 4th grade classroom, these are the Afro-American boys. No amount of tax money can compensate for a home life that is not supportive of education.

This comment articulates a particularly nasty stereotype that Black and Brown families do not care about education, a gross defamation described here as a "fact." Posts such as these make declarative statements without links or quotation marks but form an argument that is persuasive through moralization. In Ann Arbor, commentary on news articles echoed these same themes as in this much-condensed post: "Some more feel-good attempts at closing the gap. It all boils down to fixing the family structure." These comments – common throughout the dataset – illustrated how people's strategies reflect a commitment to a system that works for White children without consideration for why the system may be not working for others. The narrative that the problem's roots were in Black or Brown communities themselves negated the opportunity for any change to the schools.

Those Challenging the Status Quo

Those in support of Madison Prep and all the subsequent measures to resolve K–12 racial disparities recognized the political struggles around public funding for schools between the progressives and the conservative actions by state lawmakers, and tried their best to react using theoretical rationalization and moral evaluation. In this Facebook post on the wall of a Black leader, one Black woman wrote:

It is very unfortunate that it is difficult for some to see pass [sic] their own interests. When does it become about making sure that all children get to graduate. This is so not about [Gov.] walker … This is about poor and minority children only graduating at 50% … 1 in every 2.

She tried to shift the focus of the narrative away from teacher bashing and the union battle. Using theoretical rationalization combined with moral evaluation, she also employed impersonal authorization by citing education statistics and reminding audiences of the American commitment to public education. Supporters of the charter school were challenging not just the system in power but also the very ideology – doxa –privileging the status quo.

However, the lack of a cohesive, agreed-upon message in favor of the charter school made this task difficult in public information networks. And the pro–Madison Prep community was not as networked as those in opposition. One result of this dynamic meant that those not in Black communities but in support of the charter school found themselves activating personal experience as a legitimation strategy – seeking credibility not just with audiences but also with people of color. Consider the long list of associations with Black people and organizations that this White man felt the need to display under a public Facebook status update of a Black activist:

I am certainly not an expert and never will be, but I have been studying the education of our minority children for a number of years now … I have been a member of Mt. Zion Baptist Church for over 5 years now ... I work with teens, helping to teach them Sunday School ... I have been associated with the Southside Raiders youth football program for 3 years now and was the 5th grade head coach last year ... I have been added to the planning team for the South Madison Promise Zone...

Many of those in support of the charter school called on personal authorization as a way to insert themselves into the narrative. Comments like the one above attempted to demonstrate that the need for such an alternative solution was real because he had *witnessed* that need. This kind of bearing witness reflected grassroots community values rather than more macro democratic ones.

Throughout this sample, those in support of the school reclaimed the storyline put forth by journalists and those writing in opposition. Consider one activist, a 60-year-old White single mom and psychologist who had been involved in race issues in California and moved to Madison for its good, diverse schools. Her commentary could be found under news articles and blogs, and on various Facebook pages of everyone from Black activists to White progressives to news organizations. In an interview, she said her only intentional strategy was to "make people aware that there are real people behind their words, that we are talking about children." For example, a reporter shared on his Facebook page a blog post about a school board candidate's speech, eliciting a dialogue between a group of half a dozen progressive activists, most of whom were at the event and had taken notes. They each told their "story" of what happened, portraying different characters from the Madison Prep debate, relaying dialogue in quotation marks, challenging the "fact" of whether the candidate was changing her story about her position on the charter school, and offering motivations for her words. That this dialogue took place on the major reporter's Facebook page – with no intervention by the reporter – is significant.[43] It attracted this White Madison Prep supporter, who responded to the commenting exchanges about the candidate, Nichelle Nichols:

Nichelle ... may well be one of the most direct and honest people I have ever known. Her position on Madison Prep is the same every place she speaks. She is an advocate for closing the achievement gap and creating a positive academic and social environment in the schools for all students ... IF YOU HAD talked to her ... you would know that.

---

[43] DeFour asked the candidate to respond to the Facebook conversation and posted her note to him several days later.

This woman's post contained no quotation marks, links or other mechanisms of authority – only the implication that she had talked to the candidate herself. She said in an interview that she felt "compelled" to state her mind online, and wrote in passionate, emotive statements "based only on my many years of experience ... grounded in tomes of research and statistics." Her main strategy, not just in this post but in dozens of other ones, involved moral evaluation, as in the last line of her post: "Be respectful ... the children ... are watching."

In these online conversations, citizens engage on issues of race on a much deeper level than in the journalistic copy. One important difference between these public comments and what is found in journalism in the Madison information flow is a constant reference to the more systemic forces at work in regards to racial disparities. One striking conversation on a Black community leader's Facebook page was spurred when the activist posted about hearing from his children and others how disconnected they felt. Eighty-six comments were exchanged as participants debated the causes of the gap and weighed the possible solutions in a deliberative, measured manner. When someone posted a comment that was deemed too sharp, that person apologized and the discussion continued. Many disagreed with the post's tone regarding teaching, suggesting it implied that the majority of teachers were incompetent in instructing Black children. Others argued that it wasn't about individual teachers, but a system that institutionalized low expectations for children of color. A civil, deliberative conversation unfolded on the page of this African American's public Facebook page with dozens of citizens weighing in, thoughtfully and respectfully. Commenters heeded to doxic differences, and the effectiveness of the dialogue helped the community leader earn more social, informational capital in the process.

In other exchanges, community leaders, activists, and engaged citizens could use digital forums to confront directly the arguments made for and against the school, often igniting a raw yet important dialogue about race in the city. Let's revisit the November 2011 exchange between Mertz (the White blogger) and Connor (the Black community leader) that happened on a public Facebook wall:

There are folks in this community that feel that the White liberal establishment in Madison believe that they and they alone know and should decide how education is taught to students of color, regardless of graduation rates or achievement gaps. So along comes Kaleem Caire and the Urban League, who present an idea to help address the issue. And while it's met with skepticism by some who have legitimate questions, there are others who have the attitude of "who does this Black man think he is, telling US how we should educate students or how our way isn't the only way?"

He here uses theoretical rationalization to lay bare the feelings that many in the city felt but were not willing to say in the public hearings at the school. The White progressive replied:

I was trying to explain why I have felt it necessary to fact-check and pointing out that there has been a lot of misinformation ... You may be right that some people have a racist take on Kaleem Caire's credentials ... for me the issue is that his career has been in the service of those whose explicit agenda is to destroy public education and that from my perspective he has been on the wrong side of every major educational issue for the last decade, doing much more harm than good. Nothing to do with race; everything to do with his actions ...

By offering a "color blind" argument strategy, Mertz argues his opposition is purely political. He portrays supporters of the Madison Prep charter school as people either knowingly or unknowingly becoming pawns for the far right, weaving a tale of good characters ("heroes of the schools") and perpetrators ("enemies of public education"). Throughout his commentary throughout the Madison ecology, the White activist assigns these characters motives and describes their actions. But Connor shoots back, unwilling to let his deeper point be undermined:

But the problem is, those same people that feel that there's a racial component to this also feel that it isn't just Kaleem, it's ANY Black man or woman in this community that presents an idea such as this ...

In his interview, Connor told me he used social media to call out Madison's hidden biases and that reporting data-filled sound bites – though useful at times – was not as effective. He said:

Data is important ... We need an unbiased view of where we are. But I also think too that not only do we need to be honest about the data itself, but we need to say things that sometimes are going to make people uncomfortable.

In his prolific public commentary, Connor sometimes contradicted the original post. He asks people to stop villainizing Caire, the proposer of the school, and instead focus on the problem. He set out to reclaim the storyline and restate the morals.

In a follow-up post after the no vote on Madison Prep in December 2011, a school board member who also blogged wrote a mea culpa piece that reflected a rationalization strategy intended to evolve parts of the dominant narrative. It included the sentence, "Many African Americans who are not newcomers to Madison perceive a pandemic of poisonous social forces pulling their children down, particularly their boys, and, despite best intentions, our Madison public schools have been virtually powerless to stop it." Here he debunks several common memes circulating – that the Black people having trouble are from out of town (that is, they are "other," not Madison, and therefore do not deserve taxpayer dollars) and that the schools should not be responsible for resolving racial achievement disparities among K-12 students. This rationalization strategy was backed up by anecdotes from the hearings and combined with a moral evaluation of the situation: "We should have found a way to make it work. We should have found a way to make it work and we just didn't." Here we see the value system of the White establishment shifting through the writing in the blog. This is a major outcome that I will discuss in the conclusion.

TECHNIQUES FOR STRATEGY

van Leeuwen's categorization – though helpful in thinking about strategy as a field manipulator – doesn't account for how the content appeared or whether digital technologies played any role in the search for legitimation. Thinking back to the typology of roles in the networked media ecology, I searched for commonalities in all the case studies that would shed light on how these content-producing actors were working the network to manipulate more attention for themselves or their position on the issue at hand. Why did Madison's White union representative – a man who authored no content publicly – become an influencer in the information flow around the charter school's proposal while others who were more prolific in digital spaces failed to achieve any authority in the media? The answer had to do with the ways in which these people were networked both online and offline with the powerful, dominant institutions – political, education, media – in the cities. Thus, these networks – informed as they are by these White-constructed institutions – reflected a racial dynamic. Successful influencers effectively combined methods for getting their message out, taking full advantage of different kinds of information. Furthermore, someone already established such as the union representative could tap into traditional networks in a way an interloper – someone challenging the field and its doxa – could not. In this section I explore *techniques of strategy* by identifying those bids for a field position change and understanding how digital networks might have facilitated those movements. Across the thousands of articles, comments, and exchanges in the five cities, I found three consistently used techniques: repetition across and within platforms, the making of dynamic dialogues, and the taking advantage of the fluidity of public and private networks, particularly in the sense of border crossing.

Repetition across and within Platforms

First, the sheer number of different platforms for the public discussion on racial achievement disparities – from physical-world hearings and meetings to virtual forums such as Facebook and Twitter – meant certain influencers (especially authors I have dubbed "community bridges" and "niche networkers") could appear over and over throughout the information-exchange field. These influencers tended to be those motivated to share and publicize a certain perspective across platforms. Consequently, repeated content could be found throughout the ecology. For example, one White teacher posted some version of this comment ten times on the *Wisconsin State Journal's* public Facebook page over the course of several months:

Teachers work hard and much more than 40 hours. They still are not rich, unlike the lies the rightwing spreads around. The ironic thing about this school was that they wanted minority teachers, so this means minority teachers would be treated worse. Sort of like Jim Crow.

The online interactivity allows an actor to "work" the network according to audience segmentation, achieving forms of information capital through the legitimation strategies employed and also becoming more connected. Digital networks provide immediate access to a wide variety of spaces for message spamming and several of the more prolific actors studied exercised this technique, often in savvy ways. The progressive blogger TJ Mertz was particularly adept at choosing his content and technique carefully by fitting each message to the appropriate platform. For example, on his own personal Facebook page (public) and several progressive forums, Mertz tended to be more adamant in his stance that the district-funded charter school was a bad idea (moral evaluation), but in more general forums such as a newspaper website or on pro-Madison Prep activist Facebook pages, his criticism was more muted. Here, he linked more to data and framed himself as an education historian merely trying to glean the best approach to resolving the gaps (instrumental rationalization). His difference in technique did not go unnoticed by others in the field. In interviews, some people spoke of Mertz' chameleon actions in a negative light and called them "manipulative." This suggests that those interested in becoming more prominent in a field must take care to not only appreciate different audiences in different platforms but to remain consistent not only in content but perhaps also in technique of strategy. At least one blogger in almost all the other cities was similarly ubiquitous, working the communicative networks. However, it should be noted that Mertz and several of our other White progressive bloggers – all "community bridges" and "niche networkers" – advanced in the field, winning local elections and attaining more power. Also, "individual institutional producers" such as reporters very rarely traversed platforms, preferring to stick to the institution's websites or other controlled spaces such as their own blogs and Facebook pages. When they did appear on other people's Facebook pages, for example, the ongoing dialogue shifted abruptly; people who had been challenging the status quo (often issue amplifiers) tended to drop out of the conversation while those who were reifying the dominant structures proliferated.

Making Dialogues Dynamic

Second, digital technologies enhanced content, making it dynamic in a way that is impossible in mere text or in discrete public settings. Actors liberally took advantage of their ability to link words and phrases, post URLs from other spaces and times in the ecology, decorate wording with fonts and colors, emphasize expressions with emoticons, and otherwise add meaning to content. This added dimension to the legitimation strategies so that the rhetorical argument includes a speech-text hybrid that could incorporate visual imagery, emotive tone, and even portals to evidence on a different site. For example, commenters to an Ann Arbor, Mich., story about a field trip exclusively for Black students in 2010, put their words in all capitals to tell alternative stories about the narrative:

To me the most disturbing part of this story is the following reported exchange between Mr. Madison and the students: April 29: Madison, upon learning of this, went to the classroom and proceeded to yell at the kids. Yes, YELL. There was no "discussion." Per my son: "Do you have a problem with me taking children of my race on a special field trip?" Little Muslim girl, who mustered the courage to speak: "Well, as a matter of fact, I do[.]" Madison cut her off and loudly yelled: "I SAID DO YOU HAVE A PROBLEM WITH WHAT I DID????" [S]o, we have the principal, the man in charge, making it clear that "his" people are the Black students and all the other students are second class in "his" school.

Others in this thread tagged other commenters, bringing those who had long left the conversation back in and prolonging the dialogue. Some commenters used the interactive function of the commenting section: "Posted below is the Non-Discrimination Policy of the AAPS, taken straight from their website. I'd be very curious to hear how Mr. Madison and the AAPS Administration would rationalize how the Lunch Bunch club adheres to this policy." These dynamic recountings paired with this linking evidence made their point in a more credible manner, or at least such was the tactic.[44]

Taking Advantage of the Fluidity of Public/Private Networks

Finally, actors traveled easily and often between public and private, online and offline networks such that these worlds merged in terms of information exchange in this field. Not a single major actor interviewed worked solely in one dimension: No key influencer had relationships that only appeared online;. Even those actors who professed disdain of social media, such as the union leader, John Matthews, were still highly connected via listservs, newsletters, email, and mobile devices. A Black community leader, local minister, and University of Wisconsin-Madison official, Everett Mitchell, noted how he strategized his public comments, combining offline and online worlds:

I have to create a tapestry of information that works among the people that are here, my boss, the chancellor. Let them know what's going on, what issues are happening. Because you have to use that to support when you live in a sound bite community, that they will pull the craziest things out of your words and so you have to really make sure that your infrastructure understands what you're saying, who you are, before you go out to make sound bites. Before I take any media comments, or before I take anything to the media, I fully brief both my congregation as well as my bosses here so they know what's going to come out in the media about that. So ... they're never caught off guard.

Here, Mitchell talks about preempting the public conversation he is about to have by tapping into his personal information networks and letting them know his real meaning behind the sound bites he would give to the world. This is an interesting strategy of public information exchange because it notes how actors "work" their various networks to gain and reinforce their own position in the field, lest other actors try to manipulate (consciously or unconsciously) their words. Furthermore, the presence of a known, trusted host, such as Kaleem Caire or TJ Mertz, mitigated any sense of public ness. Personal Facebook walls were viewed as "safer" and

---

[44] All of these comments were in: David Jesse, "Field Trip for Black Students Sparks Controversy at Ann Arbor Elementary School," *The Ann Arbor News*, May 3, 2010, www.annarbor.com/news/black-student-only-field-trip-sparks-controversy-at-ann-arbor-elementary-school/.

people seemed to behave themselves more than when they were in institutional spaces such under a news article or the district website.

CONCLUSIONS

If we are to understand the ways in which the local media ecology is being reconstituted in a digitally networked environment, we must appreciate the roles of the actors within that ecology. For every John Matthews – an "institutional producer" whose presence anchors the network to a particular doxa and who can dictate how capital flows in the system at one level – we have a Mertz, a "niche networker" striving to improve his position in the field and using social media to do so. What I observed in these cases is that "niche networkers" and "community bridges" actively seek out new associations for themselves. These actors are dynamic in the field; that is, they work to improve their field position, to expand it. And they do this through the content strategies van Leeuwen identified – with different field actors choosing different strategies – and also through a number of techniques. These techniques help extend their digital social networks – linking to articles, participating in a variety of commenting forums and social-media realms. They also traverse between virtual and physical worlds, enhancing both using emails, listservs, digital tagging of people, and then more traditional media such as phones and newspapers and meetings. Elements of both worlds inform these strategies, or at least are present in them, and these elements spur new connections, build capital in new ways, and help enhance (but also in many cases, diminish) one's position in the field. People who are not in the system strive to make an impact with personal authorization; those already sanctioned by the system use impersonal authorization because they are backed up by an entire paradigm (doxa, ideology, habitus, structure, institution). With this backing, operating from this kind of position, a well-networked individual doesn't need to spend time on personal authorization, which is the act of justifying one's own legitimation in the role. Instead, they want to reproduce the system and so cull from systemic sourcing

Furthermore, we can see from the content analyses which ones – or rather which combination of ones – are most popular among which actors; using our network maps, we can infer then which ones are most successful by appreciating who are the biggest influencers in the field. But we must also scrutinize what platforms they are authoring on. So, although Caire is technically our biggest influencer according to the maps and the math, he is the biggest influencer because he appears in other people's content more than anyone else (which makes sense given his position as the one proposing the school). But remember he lost the school (and eventually, within a year, his position in the field). On the other hand, another major influencer, TJ Mertz, really had no position to speak of – at least institutionally – but authored across platforms, utilizing a large variety of sources, techniques, and strategies; by the end of this story, Mertz was elected to the school board. It should be noted that Mertz mirrored the status quo – White, male, and pro-schools and pro-government as institutions; he also called himself "progressive" and was a part of the local, formal Progressive Dane party. In the end, Caire dropped out of visibility while Mertz won a seat on the school board.[45]

This data showed how reporting deeply on race issues would disrupt the narrative born from journalists' authorization and instrumental strategies. This is part of the foundation of inertia that dogs any public communication about race: issues of political and institutional identity. Law professor John Powell suggests that White supremacy and institutional racism comes from an entrenched White identity that has enacted American policy of enlightenment principles for centuries. To challenge that system is to challenge the majority's sense of the White American self. Journalism is part and parcel of this system. We can see from the values and strategies in this content and in these interviews how committed to this journalistic sense of self these community reporters and editors were during this conversation. When journalists were asked why they didn't take the Madison Prep debate as an opportunity to explore racial issues in the schools, they talked about traditional sourcing mandates (everyone needs to be named or they can't be in the news), or deadline and other logistical issues (they know the usual players will be available to talk in a way that best fits the story). They use school board and other government meetings as story props, but these settings of story reify the power structure in the community, essentially pushing any other voices to the margins. With the meeting as the central narrative fulcrum, reporters cite officials and those who have already self-selected to speak (or who have been recruited by the unions or activists to add presence to a meeting). Other citizens would be superfluous to the storyline; they have no role in that narrative. Journalists grant expert status to school board members and other people whose credentials come from institutional hierarchy – as demonstrated by the ubiquitous presence of informal authoritarian

---

[45] A few years later Caire reemerged as he fundraised successfully for an early childhood education program, which opened in 2016.

legitimation strategies. To challenge the status quo – to really explore racial disparities, change standards to make people more willing to talk, or build in the time for communal storytelling – would pose a threat to their way of being. To not have named sources or to accept personal, informal experience as expert, for example, creates credibility challenges in an environment where their authority as society's storytellers is already compromised.

This brings us to whether interactive spaces online might extend opportunities to counter these systems of power. Should I be more optimistic? Many in Madison's Black communities argued for the charter school as an alternative to the public schools using a combination of legitimation strategies. For them, the rationalization of Madison Prep lay in the moral principle that community takes care of its own. But even as their stories found their way into the discourse, those against the school inevitably juxtaposed their position against those of the institution (as opposed to being evaluated on their own terms). If you were in favor of the charter school, you were against the public school system. Those who opposed the charter school also used links to databases and news articles and other impersonal authorization techniques. To de-legitimate the Madison Prep position, the school's opponents successfully called into question its supporters' motivations, using institutionally sanctioned facts and suggesting that Madison Prep was a puppet for wealthy conservatives seeking to privatize education. This de-legitimation strategy served to play into the progressive political agenda that dominated the city as well as resurrect an age-old racist concept that Black people cannot think for themselves.

This is not to say that people who opposed the charter school were either indirectly racist or intentionally supporting a racist system. Nor is it to say that those against Madison Prep didn't have a real argument regarding its role as part of a conservative trend against public schooling. Likewise, this is not about whether those supporting the school were realistic in considering spending millions from an already strapped public school budget. Rather, this exploration centers on how the narrative strategies that were employed and the values relayed in communicating about this topic reflected existing power dynamics in this city through common stories articulated over and over in these kinds of American conversations. The White progressives closed ranks, exercising a medley of legitimation strategies that ultimately served to support the existing social order. The Madison Prep supporters attempted to find a foothold in the dialogue. The resulting story relayed narrative tension threaded with competing values of fiscal frugality versus the future of children, parental versus institutional responsibility, and individual needs versus the larger community. The school did not pass and those supporting the proposal felt a sense of defeatism with many growing cynical. Our circle of White progressive bloggers reinforced the arguments of the journalists while Black community leaders found spaces for new kinds of evidence to be presented. In fact, it did not seem to matter which platform the author was writing in – Facebook, blogs, or even news articles – or whether the nature of their content offered a new argument. Rather, the role of the person in the field, according to his or her networks, dictated how alternative the new material might be. If the person's social, civic, or professional networks aligned him with policymakers, the content reified the status quo. If the person's networks included people who existed on the fringes of the field, we saw much different discussion in those spaces. But these places were siloed, meaning little (though, not zero) cross-pollination occurred. When a supporter of Madison Prep entered these spaces that were of the dominant ideological domain, they tended to be trolled or drowned in defensiveness. Furthermore, when groups of people don't accept the strategies others use in deliberation, there is a failure to have the kind of heeding necessary for meaningful engagement. So, if these people value moral statements while their deliberative partners employ rationalizations, or these people find data compelling as evidence but their partners privilege personal stories, silos of talk develop in which people do not recognize the information relayed as credible in terms of evidence, or worthy of inclusion. The result is a situation of disrespect and distrust.

As I was writing this book in March 2015, a biracial teenager named Anthony (Tony) Terrell Robinson who had just graduated high school took some mushrooms and was having a bad trip. A few hours later, unarmed, he was shot and killed by a Madison police officer. Protests erupted. Vigils were held. Investigations ensued. A year later (while I was *still* writing the book), the city remained in crisis. The police officer who killed Robinson had not been indicted.[46] And even by 2016, the Madison Common Council (basically the city council) refused to elect a Black man as its council president.[47] The campus – my campus – at the University of

[46] Nico Savidge, "No charges against officer," *Wisconsin State Journal*, May 13, 2015, http://host.madison.com/wsj/news/local/crime_and_courts/madison-police-officer-matt-kenny-cleared-in-shooting-of-tony/article_428b0cf9-da97-5951-9936-2f699547ba3f.html.

[47] Robert Chappell, "'Missed Opportunity': People of Color Shut Out of Common Council Leadership," Madison365, May 12, 2016, http://madison365.com/index.php/2016/05/12/missed-opportunity-councils-change-of-heart-means-no-people-of-color-in-leadership/.

Wisconsin-Madison became embroiled in racial strife as hate-filled incidents occurred with regularity and students demanded change.[48] In late October 2016, two men dressed as President Obama and Secretary of State Hillary Clinton brazenly fashioned a noose and put it around Obama's neck while in the stands at a UW football game. The event was followed by initially tepid responses by the university administration and uproar in social platforms. Thinking about what we know about how actors operate within fields, how power and authority over information manifest from not only exercised privileges but also histories of networked relationships, I admit I was not all that optimistic for real structural change.

Nonetheless, the very fact that this Madison Prep story entered the mainstream discourse – a direct result of Black communities' assertive online efforts – opened up narrative space for a community-wide conversation about these achievement gaps over the next few years. In the wake of this challenge, the power elites were forced to consider an alternative social practice and its potential implications for the community. Five years after the Madison Prep vote, Madison still had significant racial strife. But much had changed around information exchange, and that change was not insignificant. A renewed social movement called Justified Anger occurred with public forums on race and collaborations with local media. One major Madison Prep supporter won election to the school board. An entire new media platform called Madison365 entered the field, highlighting diverse voices and countering mainstream narratives. *The Capital Times* news organization dedicated time and resources – in the form of cosponsored community events as well as money to the Justified Anger initiative – to improving public dialogue around race relations in town. The *Wisconsin State Journal* dedicated two reporters to a multipart series on homelessness. *Madison Magazine* hired an executive editor who was also a member of the Ho Chunk Nation, a major Native American tribe in the state. And after each display of racism, White, Black, Brown, and other people of color started important conversations on hash tags and in their Facebook feeds, calling for change and contributing to a real social movement. The next, concluding chapter, investigates these changes as "outcomes and opportunities." And the answer to that question that I began this chapter with – "Had things gotten any better in Madison?" – is answered in the affirmative.

---

[48] Sue Robinson, "Why Is This Progressive College Town So Racist?" *The Progressive*, May 13, 2016, www.progressive.org/news/2016/05/188723/why-progressive-college-town-so-racist.

6

Outcomes and Opportunities in Community Trust Building

It was late 2013, and the publication of the *Race to Equity* report had just shown Madison to be the worst in the nation in terms of racial disparities between Black people and White people. The new Madison superintendent of schools, Jennifer Cheatham, who hailed from Chicago, had made tackling suspension rates and the systemic racial inequities in the district a priority. Across town, Paul Fanlund, editor of *The Capital Times*, received a call from a former managing editor, Phil Haslanger, who had left the paper during a series of buyouts to become a minister and was active in local politics. Now he had a proposition for his former boss: meet with Rev. Dr. Alexander Gee, another local minister who led a mostly Black church, and listen to his thoughts on racism in Madison. A few weeks after the phone call, Gee penned a front-page column, "Justified Anger: Rev. Alex Gee says Madison is failing its African-American community,"[1] which lamented the slow progress of race relations in the supposedly progressive utopia and challenged "the entire community to become concerned and involved." Another column followed Gee's piece – this one by the leader of the Boys & Girls' Club of Dane County, Michael Johnson,[2] as well as a series of videos that featured six prominent Black citizens

---

[1] Alex Gee, "Justified Anger: Rev. Alex Gee Says Madison Is Failing Its African-American Community," *The Capital Times*, December 18, 2013, http://host.madison.com/news/lo cal/city-life/justified-anger-rev-alex-gee-says-madison-is-failing-its/article_14f6126c-fc1c-55aa-a6a3-6c3d00a4424c.html.

[2] Michael Johnson, "Driven to Act: How I Got through Racial Hazing and How What I Learned Can Help Madison," *The Capital Times*, February 12, 2014, http://host.madison .com/news/local/driven-to-act-how-i-got-through-racial-hazing-and/article_e7852daa-0f f1-5429-a6f2-61a41fe97970.html.

(including Caire and his wife) talking about how difficult it was to be Black in Madison.[3] Fanlund told me the goal was to facilitate progress "in a way that keeps these issues in front of people, allows people who are so inclined to understand them fully, understand what options are out there, more fully, and to be provocative in thinking about these issues." These columns unleashed a wave of defensiveness, handwringing, and White guilt. They also marked the beginning of a movement, "Justified Anger," led by Gee. More than eight hundred people attended its first meeting – a mix of races and ages. Fanlund dedicated a website called TogetherApart,[4] cohosted forums around the city, and eventually handed Justified Anger a check for $150,000.[5] In other words, by the time I was starting to write this manuscript in early 2015, a good chunk of Madison was electing to "stay in the room," as Kaleem Caire had hoped way back when he started the Madison Prep movement four years before.

And then came March 2015. A 19-year-old recent high school graduate named Anthony (Tony) Terrell Robinson – in the middle of a bad drug-induced trip – was acting erratically on Madison's east side. A White police officer named Matt Kenny arrived on the scene first, and he forced entry into the house. Kenny said he was immediately knocked to the ground by Robinson, at which point the police officer shot him seven times in the span of three seconds.[6] Robinson, who was biracial, was unarmed. He died at the scene. The city erupted. The Black Lives Matter movement joined the city's Young Gifted & Black Coalition[7] (which included allies from LGBTQ, Hispanic, and other groups in town) to lead protests for weeks, including mass student walkouts of the local schools. And in the media, the cycle of vitriol began anew. Coverage was predominantly about whether the protests would be peaceful or disruptive and violent – and obscured the message of those speaking

---

[3] Paul Fanlund, "Paul Fanlund: A Gathering of Black Voices Is Helping Chart Our Path on Race Relations," *The Capital Times*, January 20, 2014, http://host.madison.com/ct/news/ local/writers/paul_fanlund/paul-fanlund-a-gathering-of-black-voices-is-helping-chart/arti cle_dob5c6ca-88a7-5597-b253-6b221441coda.html.

[4] This website is now called "Race in Madison", http://host.madison.com/ct/topics/race-in-madison/.

[5] Paul Fanlund, "Paul Fanlund: Evjue Grant to Justified Anger Meant as Antidote for 'our Divided City'," *The Capital Times*, June 1, 2015, http://host.madison.com/ct/news/local/ writers/paul_fanlund/paul-fanlund-evjue-grant-to-justified-anger-meant-as-antidote/arti cle_a57d658a-f45f-5762-b9ff-016e729e208b.html.

[6] A full accounting of what happened can be found in this *The Guardian* story on March 13, 2015: www.theguardian.com/world/2015/mar/13/tony-terrell-robinson-madison-wiscon sin-police-shooting-how-it-happened.

[7] www.ygbcoalition.org.

out. Comments bubbled with unhelpful diatribes about the sanctity of law enforcement and the "problems" in "the" Black community.

One reporter gained the ear of those protesting; her writings stood out for their thoughtfulness and holistic, thematic, nonepisodic coverage. She was Zoe Sullivan, a White freelancer for the London-based *The Guardian*. A Madison native, Sullivan traveled the world, freelancing for international organizations, before coming home about six months prior to the shooting. She showed up at the protests regularly, and stayed for hours. She wrote eleven stories over the course of two-and-a-half months, some long, in-depth pieces and all considered to be fair by those involved with the communities of color, according to my interviews: "Because she was present, consistently – at night, in the cold, day after day," said one local activist who helped organize some of the rallies.

Her stories offered a more nuanced explanation than other mainstream media at the time. For example, one piece about the tension leading up to the decision on whether charges would be filed against the officer highlighted the calls for peace by the family of Robinson, and prominently described the Young Gifted & Black Coalition, which led the protests, with their mission. The story also offered gradation such as describing Robinson as "a biracial youth" rather than as simply Black.[8] Reflecting on her coverage, Sullivan said in an interview with me:

I feel like so much that gets written about race ends up being very divisive. There is a tendency to make things very black and white and the police versus the community of color. I think that dynamic is in a way very real but it is also not a very helpful one. And so talking about structural stuff in Madison was an attempt to say that this was not about one cop and one kid. What I was trying to do was to look at some of the deeper issues without making it personal.

During this time, Henry Sanders, an African American Madison politician, lamented the lack of "good" media coverage about the protests. In our interview, he said:

When the Tony Robinson shooting happened, I remember that everyone was upset about how a few people were speaking for the community. And I remember thinking to myself, "well that's true. What can we do to make sure that everyone's voices are heard in these dynamics?" So that's what planted a seed of saying, "what can we do to solve that problem?"

---

[8]   Zoe Sullivan, "Family of Tony Robinson Urge Calm with Decision on Charges for Officer Imminent," *The Guardian*, May 11, 2015, www.theguardian.com/us-news/2015/may/11/family-tony-robinson-calm-decision-charges-police.

Sanders called his friend David Dahmer, a White editor who had just ended a decades-long stint at *Madison Times*, a newspaper for the Black communities. The two brought in White public-relations specialist and a former *Madison Magazine* columnist Robert Chappell and they founded the nonprofit Madison365 in August 2015. The site promised: "Madison365 uses excellent journalism to start conversations, find real and lasting solutions, build community, invite action and encourage emerging leaders in Greater Madison's communities of color, and to foster dialogue between members of diverse communities." A Kickstarter campaign netted $10,000 and an extensive network attracted dozens of people willing to write and report for free.[9] The stories ranged from an early "Things I Do for White people"[10] column that listed how the author crossed the street, didn't laugh too loud, and took other actions to keep from appearing to be "Scary Black Man" to an in-depth piece called "Harsh Truth: The White Wing Media."[11] But it also featured positive pieces about community happenings, highlighted movers and shakers, and included tabs on sports, health, and arts. The editors forged partnerships with entities across Madison such as the mainstream online Channel 3000 and its partner *Madison Magazine*, which agreed to run Madison365 pieces and vice versa. Quickly, the number of monthly unique visitors exploded from ten thousand in August to more than three hundred thousand at the anniversary of Robinson's death in March 2016.

I begin this concluding chapter with these anecdotes about *The Capital Times*, Tony Robinson, and Madison365 in Madison as a way to explore the *outcomes* of the obstacles and strategies of communicating in public spaces, such as journalism, in relation to what they mean for *opportunities* for people facilitating such conversations. What does successful discourse look like and how might online and offline networks as well as a careful consideration of field dynamics and identity constructs resolve the kind of vitriol our cases revealed? To answer this question, this chapter interrogates the structural conditions, referred to and described in detail throughout this book, as an integral consideration in any effective strategy. Identity constructs in particular must be honored and appeased when

---

[9] At least at first. Later, Madison365 paid its writers.

[10] Joel Daniels, "Things I Do for White People," *Madison365*, August 31, 2015, http://madison365.com/index.php/2015/08/31/things-i-do-for-white-people/.

[11] Madison365 staff, "BEST OF 2015: Harsh Truth – The White Wing Media," *Madison365*, December 30, 2015, http://madison365.com/index.php/2015/12/30/best-of-2015-harsh-truth-the-white-wing-media/.

making calls for change. This chapter expands our material beyond the five case-study cities to include interviews with international experts on racial dialogue, such as Glenn Singleton, author of influential *Courageous Conversations About Race: A Field Guide to Achieving Equity in Schools*, and Shakil Choudhury who wrote *Deep Diversity: Overcoming Us Vs. Them*. This chapter calls for a renewed commitment to objectivity – but one free of power hierarchies that so plague the way the tenet is practiced in mainstream media. Scholar Stephen Ward described this "active objectivity" in this way: A "pragmatic objectivity starts from the idea that journalism is an active, interpretive, cultural activity."[12] And I call on what we have learned from the networks in these cities to appreciate how key community brokers of information might traverse both digital and physical realms to create more inclusive dialogue. And, we learn from what worked in our cities. This concluding chapter documents the evolution of our cities, revealing opportunities for improvement through the narratives of this public talk about race. The superintendents and other school officials we talked to had all tried numerous initiatives to improve dialogue around race in their districts with varying success; thus, I cull from what worked to inform this chapter. Finally, I detail recommendations for communication practitioners in progressive or liberal communities.

In these progressive cities, we saw how information authority resulted from having privilege and how trust – and intense distrust – manifested as people wielded their power and adhered strictly to their ingrained doxa, or their sense of identity. In the introduction to this book, I noted how we can apply Bourdieuian field theory to explain why marginalized voices have difficulty being heard and how those "facilitating" public discourse on race issues reify existing exclusive structures. In particular, I laid out how journalists work in networks of information exchange that exclude some citizens consistently. Chapter 2 showcased a typology explaining "signatures of the new media ecology": institutional producers, individual institutional producers, alternative sites, network facilitators, community bridges, niche networkers, and issues amplifiers. In the maps, we could see the relationships between information-exchange actors, how they are

---

[12] Stephen J. A. Ward, "Inventing Objectivity: New Philosophical Foundations," in *Journalism Ethics: A Philosophical Approach*, by C. Meyers (New York: Oxford University Press, 2010), 146. See also Sue Robinson and Kathleen B. Culver, "When White Reporters Cover Race: News Media, Objectivity and Community (Dis)trust," *Journalism* (2016), http://journals.sagepub.com/doi/abs/10.1177/1464884916663599

linked – and who is not linked or poorly linked. As we watched the information circulate in the ecology in Chapter 3, we could identify how power affected its course and what those communicative actions meant for the authors. Understanding how effective that circulation is for some people – those well positioned in the field – I was not surprised to see how prolific bloggers or posters in almost all of the cities we studied ultimately gained political capital and advanced in the power structure, at least in part because of their postings. Several won election to local school or municipal boards. But in more marginal spaces, we could see how dialogue stopped at the presence of unequal power displays in some forums (such as when a school board member showed up in a Facebook conversation to comment) and blogs that died. Credentials, reports, and other common associations with "expertise" sometimes served to exclude voices rather than carve space for everyone.

The problems – and there are many – with this evolving ecology is even as it gives opportunities for new amplification of all voices who are connected digitally, it also encourages silos of public talk. Chapter 4 explored what inhibited good discussion in my cases. It typically came down to who held power in the field and how people were trying to challenge that power. Ingrained journalistic conventions, such as the ways in which "objectivity" was practiced, represented impossible barriers for those interviewed. Distrust with mainstream media ruled. All of this resulted in consistent missed connections, intractable and debilitating habits, and failed outcomes plaguing public talk in these cases.

A number of strategies were enacted to overcome these obstacles and in Chapter 5, I documented how people attempted to gain legitimacy through building information capital in this conversation. Prolific content producers such as TJ Mertz and Kaleem Caire swept past media to communicate via Facebook, Twitter, and blogs. These authors carefully strategized their public exchanges, thinking about how best to move the information flow in a certain direction and to achieve influence in the field as a whole. Social media allowed people to privilege nontraditional legitimation strategies such as experiential storytelling, but they had to be properly networked for that work to be noticed. Using reports, links, and research-based evidence in vast networks that straddled both the digital and physical worlds, others found their content shared profusely – as long as it adhered to the dominant values of the city.

Through all of these chapters, we watched as power over information in these media ecologies ebbed and flowed according to people's position in the communication field and their adherence to the place's ideology of progressive politics in particular. However, even those who considered themselves liberal experienced trouble amplifying their voice when they were not networked in the most advantageous manner. A key finding here centers on how we can identify prominent influencers ("niche networkers" and "community bridges") to link otherwise disparate communities of dialogue around these issues of race. The problem was that so few of these bridges actually served as liaisons in any mainstream vehicle such as journalism. Rather, people like Kaleem Caire or TJ Mertz, became icons who *represented* entire communities – ones that were actually quite diverse in their perspectives – without amplifying the voices they were connected to. They became punctuation points instead of bridges. This chapter shows how the way in which the actors in this field are networked and the way in which the information flows through the ecology change how the content appears, and what values, ideologies, and collective identities come into play.

DOMINANT IDEOLOGIES AND HIERARCHAL NETWORKS

In December 2011, Kaleem Caire knew he didn't have the votes for his charter school, Madison Prep. As we detailed in Chapter 4, the Board of Education in Madison, Wisc., denied the license with little debate just before Christmas in 2011. Rather than engaging with the material in circulation – at least publicly – the board cited teacher union issues and policy protocol in its decision. At the final vote on the school, Board of Education members drew statements from their pockets and read aloud from prepared remarks. Most opposition stemmed from either the idea of diverting millions of dollars of taxpayer money for a small subset of the student population or that supporting a school without full union staff was against the law. A motion to continue the conversation failed. The BOE did authorize the district superintendent to find a new plan to address the gap. But when it appeared six months later, Superintendent Dan Nerad's thick report read like an academic journal article. Again, it failed to engage the board, which eventually passed a vastly scaled-back plan. In the years that followed, posts on Facebook, in blogs, and in the commenting sections of news articles revealed unresolved tension around how best to address achievement disparities, with some articulating significant discontent about the process of the public deliberation that occurred. Caire and his predecessors at the Urban League continued to try to raise money for Madison Prep to open privately, but failed. With the "no" vote of the Board of Education for Madison Prep, the movement for a K–12 racial achievement gap solution seemed stalled.

It was at this point that I entered as a White academic looking to understand what transpired. Once impressed with my community's progressive ways, I grew more and more frustrated and embarrassed as I talked to people outside my normal academic and social networks, began working with a number of nonprofit organizations, and attended racial justice workshops and conferences. I had to grapple with my own hesitancy to support Madison Prep – Wasn't it segregation? Wouldn't it sidetrack us from fixing the public schools? – and wondered whether my reluctance wasn't also steeped in my belief that liberals know best when it came to public education. My veil of complacency and ignorance lifted ever so slowly, and I realized the amount of work I and my adopted city had ahead for true racial understanding – never mind equity. I set about to write my own version of this communication story and began participating in online forums, advising Black media and student journalists on campus, and becoming a voice in local media on diversity issues.[13] In so doing, the irony was not lost on me that I – a former reporter, a journalism professor, a newsroom consultant, and especially a White writer – was a part of the very hierarchal networks I was researching and trying to change.

In the work at hand examining the overall media ecology, silos of public talk occur, characterizing the information flow in startling ways. At the top, we have legacy media organizations and the people working for them connected to policymakers and each other; I called these "institutional producers" and "individual institutional producers." Next, we have a burgeoning group operating with varying degrees of success in terms of reaching community members; these are the "alternative sites" and "network facilitators." Many are former journalists, operating under the traditional paradigm and with those normative notions of "expertise" and "authority" in community. Many of them collaborate with media organizations as well. Right under this level we have the "niche networkers" and "community bridges" such as bloggers, prolific Facebook posters, and others producing content, such as activists, politicians, companies, and others who wish to bypass traditional journalism and build niche audiences. And then we have an entire micro level of citizens

---

[13] Such as appearing on the Joy Cardin show (Wisconsin Public Radio) in December 2015 to talk about race issues on campus.

who are sharing, commenting, linking and also, yes, "reporting" as "issue amplifiers."

My worry as I look at this emergent ecology is this: these levels parallel each other, rather than bisect. In Chapter 2 I offer visual maps of this in a "whole" information network, where you can see the disparate communities of public information exchange happening. It's important to understand not only who the major content players are, but also how they are all connected and why, as well as whom their audiences are. New entrepreneurial ventures, special-interest bloggers, sharing activists, and others are important for the field's evolution and have grand potential for a more informed citizenry, no doubt. But very few of the policymakers interviewed even knew about many of these players. Many of the journalists declined to read the comments under their stories. Reporters went to government meetings to find citizens to talk because they knew they would get their names, meeting their deadlines and their standards. Both journalists and power brokers we interviewed cited traditional media and each other as major influencers. Meanwhile, regular citizens harbored immense distrust for both the media and policymakers and declined to participate in those spheres, preferring to "talk" in niche forums such as a friend's Facebook page.

Furthermore, all five of the cities studied experienced steep losses in their newsrooms with news organization sell-offs, merging of staffs, rampant layoffs, and elimination of beats such as education. The loss of journalists who cover these issues corresponded to a significant rise in polemic conversations in these places. In all of the cities, activists have stepped in to fill the void – intentionally so. This is problematic because many of these activists' histories with those in charge involved aggressive tactics such as raw accusations and what some in power thought of as obstructionist tendencies. They tended to be strident in their viewpoints and were perceived as not being willing to compromise. This all-or-nothing approach combined with the often publicly aired animosity between activists and city or school officials created cynicism for other citizens who were inclined to engage and even pushed them to be more polarizing in their own commentary. Indeed, these findings join other research in showing how extreme representation in public talk begets more fragmentation and polarization destructive to deliberation.[14] In addition, when only "insiders" such as politicians or experts or activists who specialize in

---

[14] Michael Xenos, "New Mediated Deliberation: Blog and Press Coverage of the Alito Nomination," *Journal of Computer-Mediated Communication* 13(2008): 485–503.

the topic and have unyielding agendas come to the table without mediators like journalists, the resulting talk can exclude "ordinary" citizens. The public dialogue becomes filled with acronyms and assertions of expertise, which exclude possible participants. As Pfister[15] lamented about science journalism, "citizens must learn the vocabulary of climate science, know the points of stasis in the controversy and be able to judge public arguments about it in order to have a robust role ... The conversation must move to a more public idiom." This is true as well in the education field, where acronyms were thrown around liberally, where many in these cities had advanced degrees, and where the voices of those without easy access to databases or such specialized knowledge get drowned out. Feelings of intimidation and ignorance are too high a price for many citizens to pay for participation, so they disengage. Journalists can help mitigate these negatives, but they have to be present and engaged. Industry downturns have made this almost impossible in the mid-sized regional mainstream publications studied.

So what happens once activists and others take to social media? The media ecology expands, but in compartmentalized ways. What we saw in this research demonstrated how offline hierarchies structured online networks.[16] In his *Rise of the Network Society*, Castells described how society is moving toward a three-tiered "space of flows" that resembles to me a kind of fluid field characterized by interlinked networks.[17] For Castells:

both nodes and hubs are hierarchally organized according to their relative weight in the network. Indeed in some instances, some places may be switched off the network, their disconnection resulting in instant decline, and thus in economic, social and physical deterioration. The characteristics of nodes are dependent upon the type of functions performed by a given network.[18]

When activists took over the role of public communication about racial disparities in our case cities via digital-publishing platforms, their actions and reception in the community reflected the networked hierarchies in place.

---

[15] Damien Smith Pfister, *Networked Media, Networked Rhetoric: Attention and Deliberation in the Early Blogosphere* (University Park, Penn.: Penn State University Press, 2014), 142. Habermas also made this point.

[16] Hindman and others have demonstrated this. See Matthew Hindman, *The Myth of Digital Democracy* (Princeton, N.J.: Princeton University Press, 2008).

[17] Manuel Castells, *The Rise of the Network Society: The Information Age: Economy, Society, and Culture Volume I* (Malden, Mass. Wiley-Blackwell, 2009), 413.

[18] Ibid.

People in our cities were extremely sensitive to how these power dynamics played out in public deliberative spaces such as school hearings, Facebook walls, or even in news articles. One editor for the *Madison Times* noted the sense of disdain that followed the Madison Prep rejection by the BOE:

Connor said that African Americans feel like they haven't been heard in this whole conversation. "People have been made to feel like, 'don't worry about it . . . we got it . . . we know what your problem is'," Connor said. "I saw a sample of that at the Dec. 19 vote for Madison Prep and that really set me off when I saw some of the board members with a condescending attitude."[19]

When the Madison school board members declined to engage at all with the hundreds of Madison Prep supporters who showed up the hearing on the night of the vote, in an instant they set trust relations back between those in power and those in the Black and Brown communities. As of 2017 – five years later – the relationship between the schools and these communities remained tense. But to have changed this process and engaged in a discussion about why a charter school might be one solution would have required a public introspection that would have been politically disastrous when Republicans were on the offensive in their defunding of public education. It is very difficult to change doxa given the inertia of any field, especially without advantageous positionality.

My case-study cities' commitment to the progressive political ideology – a dogma founded to question and reform public institutions – actually inhibited debate about K–12 racial achievement disparities in the schools. Those highly networked were compelled to keep the status quo to avoid a loss of power while those without sufficient networks to influence the information flow had to strategize their challenges. Many in information-exchange positions of power – such as bloggers, journalists, activists, and politicians who used public venues of communication – found themselves caught up in the dominant doxa of this stilted progressivism. Field theory explains this tendency, especially thinking about doxa as what helps structure an embedded field. Several studies point toward the institutional tendency of journalists and others to work to maintain their position within the news field. For example, in this data, a news story's importance was as much about its relational position within the larger news ecology (Who else ran it? Where did it run?) as it was about the sources named or which

---

[19] David Dahmer, "Town Hall Meeting Opens up Discussion on THE Issue in Madison," *The Madison Times*, March 14, 2012, www.themadisontimes.com/news_details.php?news_id=1838.

reporters wrote it. This also proved to be true for the blogs in this information flow of our cities. Blogs that adhered to the dominant doxa tended to be linked and shared more often in better networked circles where policymakers were present, thereby gaining influence for both the author and his or her ideas in the field. And content that challenged the status quo circulated in more closed networks.

We can see how this positionality in context affected outcomes within an ecology using the example of *The Capital Times* Editor Paul Fanlund. Between 2013 and 2016, Fanlund became an influencer who represented an institutional actor and yet also a bridge to mainstream information networks. He was not only an "individual institutional producer" but also embodied an "institutional producer." Throughout the various communicative flashpoints around race in Madison from Madison Prep to the Tony Robinson shooting, Fanlund published columns, sought out reporters of color (hiring two interns and one full-time journalist who were African American), and worked to "shine a bright light" (as he described it) onto issues of race. He worked behind the scenes, meeting with activists, cosponsored discussion sessions, and helped fund local initiatives on the topic. *The Capital Times'* efforts to change the conversation about race in Madison – even amidst its significant resource hits during this time period – succeeded.

When he came under criticism, he said he tried to listen, to be introspective. For example, after one of Fanlund's cohosted forums, a *Wisconsin State Journal* reporter took a comment out of context from a prominent Black activist in an article and came under fire. Fanlund wrote a follow-up column to explore the tension. The incident received kudos in a 2016 media textbook on covering race with the authors praising Fanlund for "staying in the room" when things got tense.[20]

But the attacks continued, especially from the new start-up Madison365. From its inception, Madison365 took on the mainstream press in a blatant challenge to its authority and in a bid to improve its position in the information-exchange field around issues of race – boundary work in essence. In both private and public, Madison365's founders lambasted Fanlund for what they perceived to be a "patronizing" attitude, described him as "just discovering" the social-justice problems in the city, and said that despite his talk, he had done little to change things (hiring just one Black reporter, for example). In a February 2016 radio show, founder

---

[20] Keith M. Woods, "Talking Across Difference," in *Cross-Cultural Journalism: Communicating Strategically About Diversity* (New York: Routledge, 2016), 19–36.

Henry Sanders and host Darrell Connors called out Fanlund for a column[21] in which he wrote:

Other Madison media began paying oodles more attention to racial topics while seldom crediting the *CapTimes* for accelerating the conversation. When I kvetched a bit, Black leaders instructed me – in so many words – to get over it. Racial disparities, they lectured, are finally top-of-mind in Madison and that's what matters, not your petty competitive sensibilities.

Connor and Sanders took issue with the idea that he was solely responsible for the ongoing discussions in Madison and that he wanted "credit" for something he should have been doing all along. They ignored the larger point of the article, which was Fanlund admitting his attitude – which he himself called "petty" – was part of the problem and unhelpful. Fanlund began getting emails and phone calls, filled with the same criticism. It was as if none of the news organization's intense efforts seemed wanted or desired, it seemed to him. Why continue the efforts – especially in an environment of continued financial pressures and competing news topics?

This display of tension demonstrates how even the most well-meaning progressive actors in our network cannot simply open a bridge and watch the information flow unencumbered through the networks. Deep histories of distrust will characterize whatever efforts are made and prime any reaction – especially when those actions are taken by the institutional players that helped create the problem. Thus, it matters what role one has been playing in the mediated ecological scaffolding. Importantly, the new Madison365 was focused on advancing its position in the field, especially around issues of race. Battling *The Capital Times*, a century-old, progressive-oriented news organization, was a strategic move to do that. However, constant attacks against "institutional producers" who are trying to change will only propel the actors to instinctually entrench further into their dominant field position. The larger mission – to allow for more amplification of marginalized voices in the progressive city – goes unfulfilled and everyone loses. For *The Capital Times'* part, Fanlund sensed his authority on race issues was waning and his instinct was to preserve the institutional authority in other realms. Refusing to engage

---

[21] Paul Fanlund, "Paul Fanlund: What's Holding Us Back on Racial Progress?" *The Capital Times*, February 1, 2016, http://host.madison.com/ct/news/opinion/column/paul_fan lund/paul-fanlund-what-s-holding-us-back-on-racial-progress/article_c6597d53-b5e3-5 b21-b290-e2a74d72e69f.html.

will not make the boundary challenge disappear, but only exacerbate the attention it receives.

I understood the exasperation that Fanlund was feeling. Frustration churned in me at Madison365 that they seemed so intent on girding their closest allies. And yet, this was the process of my own privilege emerging and my defensiveness rising along with Fanlund's – born from all of those years in the newsroom, trying to do what was right, trying to make a difference, trying to be a champion for the voiceless. I had come to realize that the whole "Shining White Knight"[22] complex could be just as destructive when considered from a field-theory lens: such well-meaning but hierarchal support serves to prop up one's own authority rather than make room for new actors. Who doesn't want credit for putting in the time and effort to do what's right? But it's the credit that helps reify the system.

In an email to Fanlund after I heard the radio show, I urged him, "Stay in the room, Paul. Please."

He assured me he would be "staying in the room."

CHANGING STRUCTURES OF INFORMATION EXCHANGE

In 2009, freelance writer Nancy Oates was watching a political situation unfold in her town: a Chapel Hill councilman had resigned to move to New York *after* his successful campaign had just wrapped up. She found herself dismayed at the lack of public outrage. "I couldn't get anybody else really interested in it so I thought 'let me start my own blog and start writing about some of these things'." The blog *Chapel Hill Watch* was born.[23] By November 2015, Oates, who is White, had run for Chapel Hill Town Council, in part on a "diversity" platform that focused on equity in housing and wages but also touched on education achievement disparities. She won.

Over in Cambridge, Mass., Emily Dexter was busy writing *Public School Notes: Essays, Reports, and Grassroots Information about the Cambridge Public Schools* – a prolific blog mentioned by most of those interviewed in Cambridge as being a major influencer in the city's media

---

[22] This is the idea that well-meaning White people swoop in as a savior for marginalized communities, without appreciating and working to resolve institutional and structural racism – perpetuated by White people themselves – or interrogating their own racial journey and privileges that contribute to the problems.

[23] http://chapelhillwatch.com/.

ecology on education issues.[24] Dexter, who is also White, has a doctorate from Harvard Graduate School of Education, worked in literacy and youth development, and considered herself an activist. She wrote using data and reports from the Department of Education, the Harvard Schott Foundation and other highly respected establishments, and committed herself to posting "a lot on this just because I'm interested in getting information out." In late 2015, Dexter also ran for – and won – political office and became a Cambridge School Committee member.

Like TJ Mertz – and his Advocating on Madison Public Schools (AMPS) in Wisconsin[25] – Oates and Dexter effectively worked their cities' information networks to gain the necessary political capital to achieve office. They reported utilizing both private communication such as listservs and emails as well as public postings on social media to build relationships, highlight their message, and extend their influence. All three were White progressive politicians with formal credentials as well as deep experience with communicating publicly about their issues. Their information production was not only a stated part of their public service, but also a way for them to exercise their activism. Reporters in each of these cities named their blogs as a source of information for articles on racial disparity. In these ways, all three were able to parlay their information production throughout their media ecologies into furthering their own political ambitions and improving their position of power in their chosen fields. One effective strategy for these bloggers involved peppering the ecology with content and messaging, adapting what they said and how they said it according to the venue and audience. This of course is a huge advantage with digital technologies, but it also helped that the bloggers were well connected through their credentials and their social, political, civic, and professional networks.

Others had the same opportunities in these cities, but for those challenging the status quo, they found themselves playing defense. This post from Kaleem Caire, responding to a complaint that organizers had only asked Black men to stand up at an event he hosted, exemplifies the pushback and constant need for explanation: "I think you missed the point of my asking men to stand. The point was that we need to do more to get young men to participate in such events. All, let's focus on purpose and not the people." Engaged citizens in the cities may have been well networked in communities of color, but had to be aggressive in getting selected for a task force or elected to public office. Once in place, they said they tended to be

---

[24] www.publicschoolnotes.wordpress.com.
[25] http://madisonamps.org.

dubbed the "race" person and became pigeonholed. This meant they had difficulties building social, civic, and political capital on other (nonrace) issues that the progressive bloggers could do with ease.

Those who were successful at challenging the dominant doxa in our cities overcame these hurdles by "finding our champions" as Susan Baskett, a Black Ann Arbor school board member, said. Baskett took to heart what a professor in the University of Michigan's education department had told her during her first campaign:

I said, "ok, why have we not solved this issue?" And he looked at me and said, "It's not that we don't know how. It's not that we don't know who. It's the lack of political will." And as a board member, potential board member, do I, will I have the guts, if you will, to have the political will to solve the issue?

She and the other Black board member fostered fellow board members as allies instead of as opponents: "There's a lot of pushback when you start talking about race. Particularly, race disparity. But now, . . . we've grown from adversarial about it to really leaning on each other to do our thing." Such leadership cohesion helped build trust throughout the communities, which advances progress on the issues.

For many information producers – but not all – social media spaces played a large role in prompting and perpetuating a strong dialogue, reaching people mainstream outlets failed to touch. All of our progressive cities prided themselves on their commitment to community. This political – and personal – identity construction pervaded all of our ecologies. Many of the niche networkers, community bridges, and issue amplifiers we talked to considered their actions in these public spaces to be civic engagement, to be helping democracy at a fundamental level. Said one White progressive blogger in Madison:

The sharing of info is something that is important for me to do so that my fellow staff members and other people who read my stuff can go to one source where I have 15 articles that I'll put in a blog post, and I will have gotten them from ten different sources. Then other people don't have to search as much and then I also get to throw in my two cents in . . . It's almost like public therapy as far as all the things that have gone on. Trying to do my part to also speak up about what I feel is right and wrong with the world.

These alternative outlets for citizens spurred more coverage in mainstream media than might otherwise have been – especially in Madison. Here, attention by the press – both local and national – meant the "problem" of racial disparities was sanctioned for public talk in news organizations as well as on social media, spurring forums and more posts. Old information reemerged, new discussion groups were organized, and various entities such as the City of Madison formed subcommittees and produced action plans as a result of the networked information flow.

Ultimately this kind of aggregation of commentary and willingness to come together in online spaces to discuss race will strengthen community ties. As Young stated: "The unity that motivates politics is the facticity of people being thrown together ... a polity consists of people who live together, who are stuck with another."[26] I and other researchers have noted how online communities can develop into so-called "Third Places" akin to coffee shops or bars where informal gatherings offer rich interaction between citizens in familiar spaces.[27] Though no shortage of vitriol could be found throughout our ecologies, the vast majority of that acrimony could be found in virtual places associated with institutions – that is, news organizations or school district websites. The best deliberation occurred in more individually managed, though still public, spaces that fostered a more intimate setting for "followers" or "friends." After one particularly deliberative Facebook exchange about racial achievement disparities in Madison, one commenter wrote:

Amen to dialogue, and amen to a happy Thanksgiving. This post/comment thread has been exceptional because there are so many viewpoints expressed here about issues near and dear to everyone's very being, and yet every single commenter has been civil and respectful to everyone else AND to their ideas and opinions.

A feeling of respect pervaded the thread with commenters noting when they were offended, actual apologies being issued, and – most importantly – the offense being let go so that the dialogue could continue. These communities worked because of the trust built around the individual sponsoring the page, as if the person was hosting a party and people wanted to respect the host and the spirit of the gathering.

---

[26] Iris Marion Young, "Communication and the Other: Beyond Deliberative Democracy," in *Democracy and Difference: Contesting the Boundaries of the Political*, by S. Benhabib (Princeton, N.J.: Princeton University Press, 1996), 126.

[27] Sue Robinson and Cathy DeShano, "Citizen Journalists and Their Third Places," *Journalism Studies* 12(5)(2011): 642–657, doi:10.1080/1461670X.2011.557559; Ray Oldenburg, *The Great Good Place: Cafes, Coffee Shops, Bookstores, Bars, Hair Salons, and Other Hangouts at the Heart of a Community* (Berkeley, Calif.: Marlowe & Company, 1999); Charles Soukup, "Computer-Mediated Communication as a Virtual Third Place: Building Oldenburg's Great Good Places on the World Wide Web," *New Media & Society* 8(3)(2006): 421–440, doi:10.1177/1461444806061953; Erickson I., "Geography and Community: New Forms of Interaction among People and Places," *American Behavioral Scientist* 53(8)(2010): 1194–1207, doi:10.1177/ 000276 4209356250.

The online space also nurtured an expansive sense of restoration and encouraged – in some – a process of personal evolution in thinking and attitudes. For example the social-media space offered a unique place for one Madison school board member, Ed Hughes, to explore a change of heart on the Madison Prep charter-school proposal following the 2011 vote:

> I can't help feeling that the vote came out the way it did not because of faulty analysis, but because of too much emphasis on analysis. The proposal certainly raised a host of issues, but too often we viewed those issues as excuses for saying no rather than as challenges to be solved. More, we saw the notes but missed the music. We simply weren't able to appreciate and appropriately value all the emotional capital arrayed in the school's support . . .[28]

In other words, Hughes has a eureka moment on his blog. And others who had fought viciously in offline public spaces against the school turned to social-media spaces to mend fences: "My prayer is that whatever the vote is on Monday that all of you energized intelligent people continue to fight for all of our kids as they all deserve a high quality education and the foundation for a successful and productive adulthood," wrote one White progressive activist on Caire's Facebook page after the vote. This online mea culpa and desire to unite the torn community helped establish an offline policy environment that eventually led to the hiring of a new superintendent – a White woman with a biracial son and a stated commitment to social justice issues – and a scrapping of the no-tolerance discipline policy that had disproportionately affected students of color.

SOME RECOMMENDATIONS

After a long day of meetings, school visits, and public hearings, Cambridge Public Schools Superintendent Jeffrey M. Young was finally driving home, reflecting on the day's revelations. To start the day, the school board had held a public hearing at 9 a.m. to discuss a controversial proposal where citizens were given three minutes to voice their concerns. Young found himself asking a series of questions about the participation he saw: "Who do you think is available at 9 in the morning to show up at the city hall to make a speech? . . . Who is not intimidated by the city hall, by speaking in the city hall chambers? Who doesn't mind speaking into a

---

[28] Ed Hughes, "We Blew It on Madison Prep," Blog, *Ed Hughes School Blog* (December 23, 2011), https://edhughesschoolblog.wordpress.com/2011/12/23/we-blew-it-on-madison-prep/.

microphone? Who speaks English? Who wants to be on cable television when they're making their speech?" he said in our interview. After that hearing, he arrived at a scheduled walkthrough of one of the less advantaged schools where he met the entire seventh grade: nine African American boys who were learning in science that hot and cold water make warm water. Finally, he drove to a school in a more affluent neighborhood near Harvard Square. There, he was invited up on stage with the 60 seventh graders who were presenting the finale of their oral history project for which they had interviewed major Cambridge luminaries and dressed up like historical figures to tell the history of Cambridge. Young ruminated on the evening festivities to us:

Beautiful. Exactly what seventh grade is supposed to be doing. Right? History. Research. Working in groups. Public speaking. Real, authentic audience. The auditorium is standing room only. All the parents are in there cheering and screaming their kids on. They all have video cameras, taking movies of their kids on stage who have absolutely done a splendid job. So I'm driving home that night, and I'm thinking about the three parts of my day. The public hearings, the nine Black boys and the 60 kids and the oral history project. And I'm thinking, what's wrong with this picture? How can I come to work tomorrow and say "this is OK"? And of course, the answer was, I couldn't. The complete inequity of the experience took my breath away, yet made me more sure than ever that we had to change.

He immediately implemented a new kind of public interaction – meetings in the public housing projects, seeking out and finding parents who would not be able to attend a morning hearing or an evening event. Small groups. Food. Community centers, not City Hall. Translators. Child care. No entourage of officials. Just talking with people. Not at them. No three-minute time limits. Not even any microphones. It was a start of a conversation. I was impressed as Young talked about the results: more input, better policymaking.

Then we talked to Denise Simmons, a Black Cambridge city councilor who was in the middle of a (successful) campaign for mayor. For Simmons, officials like herself and the journalists covering them needed to go beyond potluck dinners with child care. Consider the work of facilitating conversation about disparities in a more holistic manner. One must commit "soul and body to understanding the communities you want to reach," she said.

Anybody, regardless of what you do, should steep themselves in cultural competency. I don't think anyone can write about someone they don't understand enough. If you're in any direct service of the community, you should be steeped in cultural competency. For years, Cambridge used to struggle with, "why does this meeting start at six o'clock and no one is here?" Six o'clock for some people just means quarter to six. Six o'clock to other people might mean six fifteen. But if you don't understand the social/cultural nuances of the constituents you serve, you're going to make judgments ... When we have a school department, where 60 percent of its kids are kids of color, if we don't have a room with 60 percent people of color, we've not done the work.

It's not enough to take the strides to include other people. It's also about embracing a concept of community as a diverse, multiperspectival, fickle, complex organism that cannot always be structured into a potluck dinner. Furthermore, such a community thrives only once representation is not only achieved but also enacted and people are listened to. Improving dialogues about racial achievement disparities must center on making connections in all constituent communities and building trust among their members. Over and over, the advice to emerge from the interviews was "be courageous" and "stay in the room." But how do we do this when so many participants will hear things that cut at their very identity and prompt defensiveness, shutting down conversation and deliberation? The answer emerges in understanding how to work around and within those constructs through key strategies that reconceptualize – and recommit – to fundamental principles at the heart of progressive ideology. Turn failed outcomes into successful policy.

First, appreciate the messiness of what true inclusion will mean in public community dialogues. For Shakil Choudhury, author of *Deep Diversity: Overcoming Us vs. Them* and an international consultant on racial dialogues, this means pointing out how instinctual implicit bias is and asking people to embrace the emotion of the topic – both from others and within themselves.

We approach this as though this was a rational topic. And so we expect people to understand the stats and kind of just engage in it. But nothing about our identities is rational. Everything about our identities evokes a deeply emotional place and as weird as it sounds, everyone, White people react to issues of race ... and don't want to talk about it. Cause at some level, being wrong, being bad, being rejected means we're out of the tribe. Right? And that's what we're trying to have a conversation about is people who are outside the tribe, people who aren't in yet. We are wired to react this way.

Acknowledging these competing instincts can lead to a deeper appreciation for others' perspectives – even when those perspectives come off as, well, a bit racist. A big part of establishing the right conditions for public communication around racial disparities is being sensitive to this "us versus them" mentality through how the problem is framed. Author

Glenn Singleton in *Courageous Conversations* counsels the school officials he works with to focus on semantics, among other strategies:

Most people will not advance to a conversation about Whiteness and power, you
know? There are words that the society is more ready to take on like "unconscious
bias" but that is very different than a phrase like "White privilege."

Indeed, Alexis McGill Johnson, executive director of the Perception
Institute that connects research with reality around implicit bias, travels
around the country convincing activists not to lead with the concept
"institutional racism":

Part of the challenge of leading with disparities, or leading with structure, is
that it shuts people's brains down because of historical weariness. Because of
the overwhelming sense of the challenge, right? And the other piece to that is
that oftentimes when we drive these conversations, the fear that the White
person may feel implicated, how they feel implicated, in the construction of the
problem ... not so much in the construction of the solution, but in the
problem ... is also challenging because most do hold very high standards of
themselves around race and egalitarian values. And that's really important to
affirm.

She called this the "sweet spot" of racial dialogues:

It's trying to come into a space and say, "you're not a bad apple. You are a good
person." What we want to do is acknowledge the fact that these disparities exist,
but not because you yourself are a bad person. But this is how the systems work in
relationship to it. And honestly, part of how we have that conversation is by
showing the science without talking about race.

Another approach involves placing race – and each of our own racial
confrontations – at the forefront, exposing these irrational reflexes when
they rear. Make oneself vulnerable, insists Choudhury. This holds especially for the journalist or official leading the dialogue:

I've got to put my mistakes, my vulnerabilities, front and center. Because when the
person at the front of the room is being vulnerable, that gives permission to
everyone else, if they want to choose it, to be vulnerable. And I find that the
bulk of people are really open ... And guess what, this links to this theory here
which shows that we've got all this discrimination. Which means that I was part of
that. And here's how I know I was actively part of that. That gets a conversation
going. It also puts people into the same boat ... But then people also need to do the
other part of the work, which is understand that as much as we're all in this boat
together, parts of this journey are just not the same .... And so everyone needs to
be able to recognize that, [and] that power plays a part.

This self-vulnerability can create space for a deeper dialogue about structural racism, but it must be paired with a sensitivity to language as the conversation unfolds and misunderstandings inevitable transpire.

This might entail starting from a place of narrative and storytelling, a place of sharing. Telling stories of humanity and demonstrating the flawed nature of everyone helps people feel less defensive in such conversations. Singleton points out what he called a "powerful" *New York Times Magazine* article in which the reporter began with a personal anecdote of his own racial journey. Kathy Cramer, a political scientist at the University of Wisconsin-Madison, traveled across Wisconsin to better understand community dialogues about race, and found that personal storytelling – the sharing of individual experiences – helped people understand an "other's" perspective.[29] Meanwhile, data brandished from reports and other formal sources tended to stall dialogue, creating a chasm between those comfortable with this type of evidence and those who valued a different, more informal kind of evidence. Our interviews supported this finding. In our focus groups, for example, parent after parent talked about not feeling welcome at public hearings in which people much more credentialed and much more practiced in public speaking, wanted to be right rather than to be heard. They had stories to tell and experiences to share, but three-minute turns at the microphone could not do these pieces of evidence justice. Furthermore, the fact that all of our cities were populated by so many academics with higher degrees created an uneven deliberative ground for conversation, and people without such education felt their contributions were not as valued and disengaged.

For journalists, writes Rodney Benson, a true commitment to facilitating community forums means giving people space to contribute stories in safe settings. In order to achieve the "ideals of in[-]depth, multiperspectival, and critical news," journalists must exhibit a "willingness to move off center-stage, to give up some of their long-held monopoly over access to the public sphere in order to make room for other voices."[30] Journalists, who are storytellers at heart, play a key role in the ecology in encouraging the sharing of people's experiences as a way to foster deliberation.

These foundational premises point to a series of recommendations:

---

[29] Katherine Cramer Walsh, *Talking about Race: Community Dialogues and the Politics of Difference* (Chicago: University of Chicago Press, 2007).

[30] Rodney Benson, *Shaping Immigration News: A French-American Comparison* (New York: Cambridge University Press, 2013), 211.

- self-introspection as a public-dialogue facilitator (or "First, do the work yourself")
- wide inclusion of all citizens from all communities ("Be inclusive in spirit and in action")
- appreciate and challenge identity constructions that inhibit participation
- collaborate and network online and offline via community liaisons

First, Do the Work Yourself

"Doing the work" begins with basic principles that guide any relationship: embrace complexity and contradictions. Try not to get defensive. Try not to assume ulterior motives. Take people at their words. Listen and try not to talk too much, especially if you are someone who might have more degrees or more money than others in the room. Check your privilege. Expand your networks beyond mainstream information flows. Read ethnic media regularly, become friends with people outside your normal circles, be more *aware* of all experiences in your community. And most importantly, stay in the room, reminded Enid Rey, who as executive director of school choice for the Hartford, Conn. District must convince White parents to send their children to inner city schools. As a person of color herself, she often has to negotiate euphemisms and outright racist attitudes in her job. "It takes courage to have that conversation, to be honest about some of the challenges. And so, you have to have a willingness to stick with it."[31]

In the meeting room on the top floor of the Madison YWCA where I was attending a three-day workshop on social-justice training in 2013, I began to sweat. It had been a long process of White-privilege exercises that anyone who has done any of this work will know well: amassing pennies of privilege[32] or taking steps forward to demonstrate where my privilege revealed itself, such as in my Daughters of the American Revolution heritage or the generations of professors in my family, the family's home

---

[31] I found Rey after I heard her on a National Public Radio *This American Life* program called "The Problem We All Live With" about racial integration: www.thisamericanlife .org/radio-archives/episode/563/the-problem-we-all-live-with-part-two.

[32] This is an exercise where in the middle of the table sits a bowl of pennies. As a facilitator reads off a list of privilege characteristics such as "I inherited or will inherit property" or "At least one of my parents graduated college," each participant takes a penny or refrains from taking a penny. At the end of the exercise, one literally can visualize how wealth accumulates through actions completely out of his or her own control.

and land ownership, and my privilege networks. The seminars were not about my 13-year reporting career per se; indeed, we didn't touch on journalism criticisms at all, much to my relief. Yet, my thoughts began to drift to all the stories I had written as a business reporter about "The American Dream" and the fervent commitment I had to the notion that hard work and dedication were all it took to achieve success in the United States. Fully faced with the implications of the hundreds of years of slavery followed by Jim Crow and discrimination,[33] I began to see how complicit I had been in perpetuating problematic dialogue myself – and how I continued to reify these systems in my own teaching of journalists at the University of Wisconsin-Madison. I felt ill at these realizations. It was only an hour until the end of the session and I was tempted to leave early.

Still, I forced myself to stay in the room.

The idea that journalists "stay in a room" where people are going to demand participation cuts at the heart of traditional notions of detachment reporting and objectivity. A generation of newsroom protocol – one I trained under – mandates that reporters remain free of conflicts of interest: Don't cover issues you are involved with. Don't put political signs up in your yard or bumper stickers on your car. Don't attend rallies unless you are writing a story. Absolutely keep yourself out of the story. In fact, one White ally of the Black community in Madison, insisted objectivity remained an essential characteristic of journalism about issues involving race.

If anything, the coverage of race should be ruthlessly objective so that the audience can see issues of race in the factual context. The more bloodless it is, the better it is. It is an incredibly emotional issue and both Black and Whites have their biases and so, gathering and communicating these facts in the midst of the emotions is one of the most critical things a journalist can do.

This seemed to go against all I was hearing about the importance of embracing my own subjectivity as pivotal to getting the full story. Objectivity for me, I realized, had been easy – to stand apart and not engage do not take a ton of effort. It reminded me of a snippet of Benson's thinking around journalists and field theory:

---

[33] So many books aided my personal journey. Besides the ones I have already mentioned in this chapter by Singleton, Cramer, and Choudhury, I highly recommend *Warmth of Other Suns: The Epic Story of America's Great Migration* by Isabel Wilkerson, *Just Mercy: A Story of Justice and Redemption* by Bryan Stevenson, *The New Jim Crow: Mass Incarceration in the Age of Colorblindness* by Michelle Alexander, *Black Like Me* by John Howard Griffin, and anything by Ta-Nehisi Coates.

Limitations or blindspots in news coverage related to class habitus of reporters may be the most difficult to amend. These kinds of suggestions inspire defensiveness. Most journalists feel that their professionalism helps them overcome any tendency toward special treatment, negative or positive . . .

Benson went on to argue for journalists to back away from these limiting principles that ultimately restrict coverage because of routines of sourcing that inhibit trust-building in communities. He added that one way to achieve more multiperspective news would be to "self-consciously recruit journalists with diverse habitus . . . and to loosen up news genre restrictions so that they have greater freedom to express their class-based perspectives."[34]

Professionalism as a journalist demands both. Little difference exists between being aware of your subjectivity as a reporter or as a school district facilitator, becoming an active citizen in local communities so you know and build trust among all citizens, and using data to expose systematic biases in a way that will connect all communities. It is *both* true that constant self-evaluation and individual action have to be undertaken throughout the reporting of a story *and* that a detached, clinical appreciation for the true causes and effects of racial disparities such as K–12 achievement and opportunity gaps is necessary. Indeed, the second demands the first. Whether we are talking about a reporter or a school official, their mandates are the same: to amplify the voices of all stakeholders and foster inclusive deliberation. Those who care to generate good community dialogue are responsible for creating the proper environment for that conversation. Even reporters must understand their own complicity in creating a public dialogue that excludes entire groups of people and work to improve those circumstances through active involvement. With this revelation, I began to see how closely tied the journalism fundamentals are to the principles of social-justice work: use data in combination with human stories, foster connections through experiential sharing, and remember that the first loyalty is not to the individual citizen but to the good of the community as a whole.

This individual action can take many forms. Singleton, an African American, refuses to even talk to reporters who have not done some internal work around their own privileges. North Carolina Rep. Graig Meyer, a White former director of a mentoring program in Chapel Hill aimed at closing achievement gaps, analyzed the vitriolic public dialogue around the issue. He learned the patterns of discontent and identified

---

[34] Benson, *Shaping Immigration News*, 212.

places of productive talk so that he could reframe subsequent exchanges. Be "ruthlessly transparent," as the Evanston (Ill.) superintendents were in their policy decisions. "Find your champions" and reach out to community partners like those universities in town and leverage some relationships, as the Ann Arbor school board members did.

And when we start to feel uncomfortable? Focus on the ultimate goal: helping citizens deliberate in an effective and inclusive manner, said Singleton. He urges journalists to think holistically and big-picture whenever they want to cover an issue with a racial component. "What is it that you are trying to uncover?," he said in our interview. "You know, what is the story that you are trying to tell? And we go from that place." In other words, recommit yourself to your fundamental missions as a progressive or as a reporter. Without such action, little inclusivity will materialize, said Donte Hilliard, a national expert in social-justice education, cultural studies, and strategic organizational development: "You can have really great intention, but if you're not willing to actually get your hands dirty and take some risks and seek to transform the condition that create these inequities, then it's actually just a feel-good measure."

Be Inclusive in Spirit and in Action

Many have argued for hiring more journalists of color.[35] In our interviews, editors talked about wanting to do this, but come up against seemingly intractable difficulties: "We have tried," they say, "but no one wants to come here" or "we can't find anyone with the necessary credentials." It is certainly difficult to recruit someone of color to come work in a place of isolation. Editors attempt to post in social-media spaces frequented by non-White reporters but remain perplexed when their initiatives fail. Understanding this through a network perspective might offer some relief: First, organizations must establish trust among would-be professionals as well as among audiences and potential sources. Offline appearances – going to the conference and setting up a booth, visiting

---

[35] van Dijk T. A., *Racism and the Press* (London: Routledge, 1991); Hemant Shah and Michael Thornton, *Newspaper Coverage of Interethnic Conflict: Competing Visions of America* (Thousand Oaks, CA: Sage, 2004). It should be noted that some have suggested that hiring more journalists of color is not effective: First, it leads to more marginalization for those reporters who get pigeonholed in the newsroom covering only race issues; second, it can unintentionally lift the onus off White reporters to engage more deeply in better reporting; and third, when reporters of color are trained in the same traditional mindsets, such hiring does little good in changing coverage, say some.

journalism schools with a diverse population – should accompany online efforts to lend credibility to the organization's stated goals. Second, tap major influencers within the communities they wish to employ, ask for email introductions, post on their websites and Facebook pages, and create training partnerships. Third, pay well for people of color whose cultural expertise is a specialty and who must be compensated for helping to populate a newsroom in isolation. Fourth, promote your people of color until they hold positions in every tier of your organization.[36]

Beyond hiring more reporters from underrepresented groups, those in charge of facilitating public dialogue around issues of race should involve people of color throughout the process. School districts might consider hiring people from the neighborhoods they want to reach to help recruit attendees to important hearings. Reporters might organize forums, online and otherwise, via the "community bridges" who have networked communities in non-White spaces. Consider quotas for sourcing and commentary, which builds trust.[37] Designate spots on your boards and meetings that must be filled with people of color.

Even accept exclusivity or consider closed sessions during community dialogues to ensure as much participation as possible. As we saw in Chapter 3, when the Urban League attempted to host a Madison Prep meeting for those with Black children in the school district to discuss their personal experiences, local journalists criticized the move as against the First Amendment and those against the proposal used it as another piece of evidence of how Caire was trying to "get one over" on the Madison public. As a former reporter who has been kicked out of her share of what should have been public meetings, I understand and share the outrage. How are mainstream audiences supposed to understand the dire need for the proposal and truly weigh the pros and cons of the charter school if they cannot hear all of the information? Yet, we must also take into account the intense distrust these communities hold toward media, and the reality that without some protections and assurances, some people simply won't

---

[36] Research shows that one of the biggest reasons reporters of color leave a newsroom is the lack of promotion: Tracie Powell, "Why Young Journalists of Color Leave the News Industry." All Digitocracy. August 11, 2015, http://alldigitocracy.org/why-young-journalists-of-color-leave-the-news-industry/; Jan Wicks LeBlanc et al., *Media Management: A Casebook Approach* (New York: Routledge, 2014).

[37] Melissa S. Williams, *Voice, Trust, and Memory: Marginalized Groups and the Failings of Liberal Representation* (Princeton, N.J.: Princeton University Press, 1998); Jane Mansbridge, "Should Blacks Represent Blacks and Women Represent Women? A Contingent 'Yes'," *The Journal of Politics*, 61(3)(1999): 628–657, doi:10.2307/2647821.

participate. Democracies need places for groups who are disadvantaged, to be used for "gathering their forces and deciding in a more protected space in what way or whether to continue the battle" for equality or just outcomes.[38] This "enclave model of democratic deliberation"[39] can help marginalized groups come to consensus in a supporting space before attempts at a more diverse setting are made. I suggest a middle ground. Create an exclusive forum, have someone take notes without attribution, be transparent about its accountability level, and have a sign-up sheet for people who might want to share their contact information for reporters. This might be one way to encourage empowerment in public deliberation while still having that talk become a part of the mainstream information flow.

Such spaces could also include informal places of gathering. A Black alderwoman in Evanston called her strategy to encourage participation "casual listening":

Casual listening means you may show up at a block party and just ask people questions about what do they think about the school system, what do they think about their community, what do they think about what's happening with their kids, are they having good experiences? In a very casual way you engage them in conversation and use that information then to help understand where they are. And then invite them, to participate in other things. It's a one-on-one. It takes a lot of time and a lot of energy but it works. And you'd be surprised how people will open up and talk.

She noted how necessary this kind of exchange was to building trust. "We just have to be ready for the conversation. Communication and trying to establish relationships. See, nothing happens without having a relationship with someone. You can't just force stuff on folks. You have to have a relationship." In order to garner the support for whatever policy needs to be implemented, buy-in must happen early in the process, noted almost all of our superintendents and school board members. This entails specific invitations for input and explicit acknowledgements of other participants/ perspectives, making clear to the others they are seen and heard – a matter of trust building.[40] A Black Ann Arbor school board member executed a kind of "casual listening" during a community input session:

---

[38] Jane Mansbridge, "Using Power/fighting Power: The Polity," in *Democracy and Difference: Contesting the Boundaries of the Political*, by S. Benhabib (Princeton, N.J.: Princeton University Press, 1996), 47.

[39] Ibid., 58.

[40] Iris Marion Young, *Inclusion and Democracy* (Oxford: Oxford University Press, 2000), 58; Charles Taylor, "Multiculturalism and the Politics of Recognition," in *Multiculturalism*, by Amy Gutmann (Princeton, N.J.: Princeton University Press, 1992), 25–74.

One of the good things I did was held a town hall meeting where we did have the community come out, particularly the African American community and had the school district come and articulate the data in a way that they are able to understand it and ask questions. And I found that to be quite helpful for both because the African American community felt heard and had the opportunity to weigh in. We benefited because we, from that, decided to implement eighth-grade algebra from that very discussion as a part of our curriculum and now it's a standing part of the curriculum in Ann Arbor ... It wasn't easier. It wasn't without behind-the-scenes wrangling and frustrations at times, but it ultimately was a beneficial move.

Appreciate – and Challenge – Identity Constructs

When Political Scientist Katherine Cramer, a White woman and Wisconsin native, sat down with rural residents around her state, she was struck by how tied their political actions were to their identity. This identity stemmed from the sense of their home and way of life as being "othered" by urban, well-educated, affluent folks. These feelings resulted in what Cramer dubbed "politics of resentment" that propelled the Republican Gov. Scott Walker to power, despite the fact that his policies were not in their best interests.[41] She wrote: "This book shows that what can look like disagreements about basic political principles can be rooted in something even more fundamental: ideas about who gets what, who has power, what people are like, and who is to blame."[42] What we say in public spaces, how we vote, who and what we support – these all emerge from our notions of ourselves and our role in the world in contrast to others. Politically progressive individuals understand themselves to be champions of humanity, are reform minded, and see their role as people who proactively seek equality and to right wrongs in the world, especially within public institutions.[43] Similarly, journalists adhere to a kind of progressive identity that boasts a watchdog mentality, a voice for the voiceless, and seekers of truth.[44] Those who label themselves under some kind of identity category – progressive, journalist – hold views as part of a collective, as champions for justice in solidarity. So if evidence

[41]   Katherine J. Cramer, *The Politics of Resentment: Rural Consciousness in Wisconsin and the Rise of Scott Walker* (Chicago; London: University of Chicago Press, 2016).

[42]   Ibid., 5.

[43]   Richard Hofstadter, *The Progressive Movement, 1900–1915* (Englewood Cliffs, N.J.: Prentice-Hall, 1963).

[44]   Bill Kovach and Tom Rosenstiel, *The Elements of Journalism: What Newspeople Should Know and the Public Should Expect* (New York: Three Rivers Press, 2014).

arises that the products of these champions have failed to serve all of humanity – achievement gaps, for example, or biased coverage – it makes sense that defensiveness and disbelief are the reaction.

The key, according to those who come up against these reactions, is to work within the identity constructions and tread lightly while doing so, but to recognize them as such. Strict adherence to such identities (doxa) can mask implicit biases that can run unchecked in the name of convention or protocol (habitus). For example, as Chapter 4 illustrated, a commitment to objectivity propelled reporters to reject stories from unnamed sources and privilege those with credentials and power. However, said one White Chapel Hill politician and former school administrator of his experience with journalists:

The context is what really matters. Language, the language of race, the policies, the actions, are often used to mask history, relationships, fears, hopes. And I think reporters that did the best job were able to ask enough questions, listen long enough, talk to the right sources – and sometimes that meant not the official sources – to really understand the context for a conversation and then be able to write stories that reflected that broader context of the history, the culture of the people, the way to the arguments, the relative kind of knowledge of the players.

Interestingly, his idea of context extended beyond the topic's background, the history of race relations in town, and past policy decisions. He wanted reporters to think hard before quoting the most vocal or credentialed people on the topic.

Who are those people? How long have they been in the community? Why did they move to Chapel Hill? Are they people who've lived here for generations or people who came because they wanted their kids to be in a top-flight academic program and they just moved in the last couple years? Those things matter. Don't forget the city's and district's moral values.

In other words, he is saying that journalists need to be cognizant of the field dynamics at work in any given community deliberation, and adjust coverage accordingly.

At some point, said our informants, reporters and others interested in improving these dialogues must begin with the understanding that all of these identities harbor biases that need to be called out. Said an African American city official in Cambridge: "We have to admit that we live in a biased society and we have to admit that we are ourselves biased. Because if we're not willing to do that, then we're not going to be able to do the work. If we're not uncomfortable in having these conversations then we're not doing the work." Then, we must acknowledge that people of color are the ones burdened with the work of educating others on systemically created and perpetuated disparities. "Because what those conversations depend on are the most vulnerable people rehashing their everyday reality, which we often have to desensitize ourselves to in order to get through our lives," commented the national social-justice expert, Donte Hilliard, who also identifies as Black. "Literally, I might have 10 race-based incidents happen to me before I even get to the office. As a person of color, I can't … I have to figure out how to manage that in a way that it doesn't throw my entire day off. And we do. And people of color do better or worse at that on different days, right?" Thus, some people of color doing this work must develop "habitus" practices to help them achieve success not only to advance within their field of information exchange but also to maintain their own identification. Those of us who do not have to do this extra work have the luxury of spending more time figuring out how we can negotiate these biases as a part of the world we created – or not.

Collaborate, Network Online/Offline via Community Liaisons

Chapter 2 included a typology of new and evolving roles that make up the media ecology, reconstituted by social media. These roles – institutional producers, individual institutional producers, alternative sites, network facilitators, niche networkers, community bridges, and issue amplifiers – work together to circulate information. But each actor – some of whom switch between roles, or occupy several roles at the same time – also play different parts in nurturing community. For example, Choudhury argues bridge builders such as journalists and other communication facilitators must encompass levels of both attachment and detachment in their work. He said in an interview, "If we are too attached to the issues [like an activist might be], then we become polarized and get pulled to the sides. Bridge builders hold that space open in the middle, connecting everyone and taking care of the whole when everyone else is taking sides." But these roles and the actors within them are flexible, explaining why the information-exchange field looks different in any given moment after positions have been challenged or acts of maintenance have been performed. Journalists and others can be the constants in these spaces. They can be what Author Eric Liu, founder of Citizen University, described as "nodes of contagion" – those people who operate as powerful actors, or actors who have empowered themselves to "do" democracy and then their actions inspire others.[45]

Communicators must consider not only the space of practice carefully, but also the other roles of the people in that space – and the doxa and habitus that frame and enact these roles. The places of information-exchange – be it the website of a news organization or a conversation thread on Facebook – matters greatly in deliberative productivity. This is primarily because of the roles associated with those spaces. On a news site, actors work hard to maintain their position or to undermine dominant actors; polarization rules, and it is difficult to have real deliberation with so few people willing to respect other people's perspective. In social media platforms, these roles change according to the level of trust with that "friend" or "follower." The evidence from our case studies points to social media as one of several ways to create productive spaces for communities to congregate. Because trusted community members host these spaces, they are perceived as more trustworthy. In field-speak, we can think of social-media places as within community niches, or perhaps even as subfields. The ways in which blogs have emerged as a communicative platform allow a different kind of message to be shared – such as the way Madison school board member Ed Hughes used his blog to publish his change of heart on Madison Prep in the wake of the vote. Scholar Damien Smith Pfister explains this as the nature of the "networked public sphere," which "revalues norms of subjectivity, passion and partiality."[46] This suggests digital technology privileges an argument made with pathos as a way to construct community and engender feelings of community belonging.[47] For Pfister, the ability of blogs to combine the rational with the emotional can influence doxa and also encourage the public sphere to become more inclusive.[48] He goes on to write: "Though experts still lean on their credentials in order to assume a pedagogical stance in teaching citizens about science, networked media create conditions for an emergent Third culture that is far more participatory ... Networked media help

---

[45] See for example: Eric Liu and Nick Hanauer, *The Gardens of Democracy: A New American Story of Citizenship, the Economy, and the Role of Government* (Seattle, Wash.: Sasquatch Books, 2011).

[46] Pfister, *Networked Media, Networked Rhetoric*, 91.

[47] See also Eric A. Havelock, *The Muse Learns to Write: Reflections on Orality and Literacy from Antiquity to the Present* (New Haven, Conn.: Yale University Press, 1988); Walter J. Ong and John Hartley, *Orality and Literacy: 30th Anniversary Edition* (London; New York: Routledge, 2012).

[48] Pfister, *Networked Media, Networked Rhetoric*, 94–97.

activate the deliberate legitimation process."[49] In a space like a Facebook post, a communicator might find the "Third culture" equivalent to Ray Oldenburg's "Third Places," the coffee shops and other informal places that serve as common, nonintimidating spaces for public talk about civic issues. Similarly, scholars Brewer and Miller make a series of recommendations for good public talk, including that the parties find a neutral place for discussion.[50] Facebook might be one of those places. However, the Facebook conversations in this dataset operated primarily as silos of dialogue, with little crossover to mainstream information streams – and thus, external to the information networks of most policymakers in our cities.

This is where our communicators can help. Those journalists and public officials interviewed for this book all used activists and other highly connected actors as *representative* of communities of color, not as links to other networks. This led to feelings of marginalization and contributed to the sense that the community communicators did not care to know about different perspectives. Social media can be used to open channels of communication between "institutional producers" and the citizens who have circulated in largely isolated networks such as "niche networkers" or "issue amplifiers." Ongoing, informal exchange between races – where each can have a constant exposure to the other's perspectives – seemed to help the integrated meeting be more deliberative. People become more tolerant and accepting when they can empathize with the "other" position.[51] The institutions represent the bulk of the mainstream information flow, even as the other actors are activating alternative streams. Connecting these into one large river of networked information entails utilization of various roles. For example, all of our cities were located just outside of large metropolitan areas, with huge universities attached and lots of buy-in for public, in-person communication (at least among the White progressives). In all of the cities, we saw great success with collaboration with the universities as well as physical-world community forums cohosted by an institutional player such as the school district or a news organization and a "niche networker" who acted as a "community

[49] Ibid., 175.

[50] Brewer M. and N. Miller, "Contact and Cooperation: When Do They Work?" in *Eliminating Racism: Profiles in Controversy*, by P. Katz and D. Taylor (New York: Plenum, 1988), 315–328.

[51] Tali Mendelberg and John Oleske, "Race and Public Deliberation," *Political Communication* 17(2000): 188.

Box 6.1. Tips for Public communicators

- Partner with local "champions" or nurture "community corre-spondents" to hear concerns, provide background, and increase community involvement.
- Break from habitual places and times for public hearings and meetings. Hold regular staff meetings outside the office in com-munity spaces.
- Evaluate. Ask outside consultants and community leaders to review your work.
- Hold regular conversations about race in atypical formats such as monthly community book clubs.
- Tell stories instead of producing data dumps every time a new report comes out. Resist the urge to look for experiences that match the data while ignoring others that don't.
- Steep self in training in cultural competency, diversity, privilege, and your own implicit biases.
- Learn the history of inequities in your community and organization.
- Be aware of the ways in which your routines inadvertently leave community members out.
- Engage personally *and* professionally in community. Volunteer. Offer tours of facilities. Surround yourself with diversity in private life. Experience other cultures. Attend events that are not White dominated. Relocate personal/social routines. Attend a different church. Support business with Black and Brown owners.
- Consider people such as activists as bridges rather than punctua-tion points. For example, ask a source to cosponsor a Facebook chat on important local issues.
- Connect with new networks via online platforms: Have neigh-borhood or other niche Facebook pages dedicated to parts of the discussion that are then used as background for broader stories. "Friend" community leaders. Participate in discussions in social-media pages and hashtags. Tag people who open your story up to entire communities of people.
- To encourage broader participation, praise comments that are "good" and then share them with others, tagging community members you think would be interested in the comment.
- Hire more people of color into your organization in various capacities.

Box 6.1. (cont.)

- Use proposals, events, or reports about disparities as an opportunity to look at patterns, structure, and systemic disadvantages. Ask deeper questions that go beyond the numbers.
- Challenge semantics. Complicate easy categories such as "achievement gaps" by being open to other terminology (such as "opportunity gaps" or "disparities" or "education debt"). Note how words such as "minority" or even "diversity" serve to "other" groups.
- Encourage alternative "evidence" such as personal experience. Academic language won't connect with all citizens. Ask directly for people's stories.
- Avoid phrases such as "the Black community," which assume one opinion from a very diverse set of people.
- Account for power differences among your various communities. For example, as a journalist, consider reviewing stories with those sources who are not used to speaking to the press.
- Leave time for informal dialogue. Remember that some find the hearing or interview format intimidating.
- Follow through. Send links to stories, meeting decisions. Thank them for participation. If you did not use them in the story or the proposal that they wanted failed, explain why and acknowledge how their input helped.
- Put reports/documents/memos online with annotations from experts, translations (such as into Spanish), and commentary options. Send links to highly networked citizens of color asking directly for their perspective.
- Note which students/programs/schools/groups you showcase as success stories.
- Boost online engagement. Think of Twitter, Instagram, Snapchat, and Facebook as places to market proposals or stories, ask provocative questions, seek feedback, build relationships, and spark dialogue. Be active on these yourself.
- Encourage alternative input from community members such as short videos or Snapchats.
- Be willing to be uncomfortable.
- Stay in the room.

bridge." In addition to this kind of collaboration, I suggest the digitally reconstituted ecology can be taken advantage of to make similar online connections to reach more people. Most of our reporters were "friends" with activists on Facebook, for example, but few of them participated or even took notice of the rich dialogues happening on those pages. Besides using social media to mine for sources, reporters largely ignored the venue as a possible place to facilitate dialogue themselves. This dataset suggests journalists might collaborate with activists who have large followings in various communities to offer cohosted online discussions.

CONCLUSIONS

When I caught up with Kaleem Caire a year after the Madison Prep vote, Caire philosophized about the changing demographics of his city and the reaction he still receives from White progressives when he challenges them to fix the schools for all the students of color who now are a majority of the schools' population:

Madison is afraid of entering that new world. White people I think are also inherently fearful of losing power. Ones who aren't comfortable with themselves because they've been in positions of authority or seen themselves in positions of authority for so long. What would the world look like if in 10 years, there were many leaders in Madison of color. Would people stand up and say "That's wonderful! I'm so looking forward to that!" "We're scared as shit." So I think there's that fear that's just been here and that's just permeated American society and that guilt that "I shouldn't think these things. It's not right that these kids are struggling the way they are. But I don't know how to help them. If helping them means I have to give something up, then that means I'm admitting somehow that I'm at fault for why they don't have what they need." I think that's a lot of what's at play here.

Missed opportunities limited the ultimate narrative that defined Madison Prep. During this time period, journalism about racial disparities fell into one of two categories. The first – present during the Madison Prep debate for example – was characterized by procedural stories about hearings and meetings. The "problem" of the disparity was paired with the "Madison Prep controversy" that set up an acrimonious duality between major figureheads in town – the Urban League and the school district (and also the teacher unions). Instead of thoughtful description and analysis, these articles offered logistics, quotes from officials, links to government reports, and anecdotes from meetings. Most of these articles are best categorized as "episodic coverage," which some scholars have lamented characterizes much of journalism (as opposed to thematic coverage that goes deeper into an issue's causes and possible solutions). The second – found during the *Race to Equity* and subsequent Justified Anger conversations – did better at describing the problem, but failed to analyze possible causes or critique programs aimed at resolving disparities. Few from Black communities appeared in news pieces; a few Black activists were asked to speak for their entire demographic.

The story frames in the samples from all five cities studied revealed doxic community visions that tended to be optimistic and institutionally structured. One example was a PBS NewsHour documentary in June 2014 following the Madison Prep debate, *Race to Equity* report, and ensuing intense community dialogue. In a short documentary called "To tackle racial disparity in Wisconsin's capital, community leaders start with the very young," PBS NewsHour reporter Hari Sreenivasan told the story of several programs in Madison trying to ease disparities tied to economic woes for people of color through social work in homes with kids and retraining programs aimed at industries with labor shortages. Sreenivasan interviewed Rev. Gee and the new head of the Urban League, Noble Wray (the city's former police chief) as well as the county executive, and a social worker. The two Black "regular" people he interviewed included a mom and a construction worker, both praising the county interventions. At the end, Sreenivasan said, "Both Reverend Gee and Noble Wray are optimistic that addressing the thorny issue of racial disparity here in Wisconsin could become a template for other communities around the country." Yet the reports and dialogue that prompted the video existed in the ecology because the problem had not been solved, and in truth, Madison could not be considered a model for the nation at that time. The programs in place had been in place for years, but disparities persisted. PBS' coverage, like that of the local journalists, abided by traditional values[52] that America ingenuity and hard work will always triumph. If America has a problem, it will not only fix it but become a model to others in doing so, further perpetuating the American identity as superior.

The public conversation could have gone differently. In opening up the boundaries that structure mainstream information flows, journalists – as well as other public communications such as communication officials – are in a unique position to leverage their existing networks. Damien Smith Pfister

---

[52] As laid out by Herbert Gans decades ago in *Deciding What's News: A Study of CBS Evening News, NBC Nightly News, Newsweek, and Time* (Chicago, Ill.: Northwestern Press, 1979).

pointed out that successful deliberation must always entail a mix of strategies: "Democracy's trick is to balance the creative with the familiar, the emotional with the rational, and the public with the expert. In other words, healthy democratic public cultures temper routinized institutional logics with innovative arguments, blur the distinction between reason and emotion, and stimulate conversation between experts and publics."[53] Reporters could have called on Caire and other activists not for singular quotes in their stories but rather as conduits to entire communities, or asked them to hold a focus-group kind of forum to facilitate a conversation among parents.[54] Reporters could have partnered with the major influencers in different communities to sponsor an online chat on their Facebook pages. The school board could have engaged with the public in different kinds of settings and listened to stories in a way that allowed those experiences to enter their deliberations as evidence rather than as mere check points of democratic protocol. School board members might have visited communities following the vote to explain their decisions and talk in more intimate settings about addressing the issue of disparity. Reporters might have followed up in communities after their stories to talk about the issues in a less formal manner. Could haves, should haves, might haves ... none of it matters if professional communicators divorce themselves from the communities they want to engage.

Any strategies need a holistic commitment to being a part of the community. Fundamental journalistic tenets call for storytelling that enables democracy through community forums.[55] In one journal article,[56] my colleague and I called for the practice of "active objectivity," drawn from Scholar Stephen Ward's conceptualization.[57] This interpretive, active, pragmatic objectivity suggests a renewed commitment to the tenant of loyalty to citizens. Other calls for renewed emphasis on trust building between media and communities have also proliferated recently, such as MediaShift's 2016 "The Case for (Community) Engagement)"

---

[53] Pfister, *Networked Media, Networked Rhetoric*, 3.

[54] Actually *The Capital Times* did something like this years after the vote.

[55] See Kovach and Rosenstiel, *The Elements of Journalism*. Or even way back in 1947 with the Hutchins Commission report: Commission on Freedom of the Press, *A Free and Responsible Press*: "A Forum for the Exchange of Comment and Criticism" (p. 23) (Chicago, Ill.: University of Chicago Press), 1947, https://archive.org/stream/freeandre sponsibo29216mbp#page/n37/mode/2up.

[56] Sue Robinson and Kathleen Bartzen Culver, "When White Reporters Cover Race: The News Media, Objectivity & Community (dis-)trust," *Journalism*, 2016. http://journals .sagepub.com/doi/abs/10.1177/1464884916663599?journalCode=joua.

[57] Ward, "Inventing Objectivity: New Philosophical Foundations."

series[58] or American Press Institute's 2016 "The best way to build audience and relevance by listening to and engaging your community."[59] All emphasize interactive relationships with citizens within the community as opposed to passive publication to mass audiences. Stories that bubble from the community, perhaps even in collaboration with citizens, should join the front page. Stories that portray systemic forces and historic inequities as players in present-day problems, such as achievement disparities, need to accompany episodic coverage of meeting and testing reports. But most of all, newsroom leaders, school officials, and other professional communicators who want to facilitate better conversations about race might foster a different culture, one defying the dominant doxa of hierarchal dialogue. Choose sources differently. Choose venues differently. Choose formats for dialogue and community storytelling differently. Choose the rules differently. Be conscious bridge builders who enable connections and make community meaningful.[60]

Of course it is one thing to write this conclusion with these recommendations, and quite another to try to effect change myself. I needed to follow through. In 2014, I began developing a service-learning, skills-based reporting class.[61] Using the data from these case studies as a guide, I created a curriculum to rethink reporting protocols.[62] The class, "Journalism for Racial Justice: Amplifying Marginalized Voices in Local Communities," ran for the first time in the spring of 2016 with 14 students – all but one female, and all but six identified as White. Most were seniors. The class posed the question: "How do we enable marginalized citizens to contribute their voice to public discourse? More specifically: How can professional communicators exercise good citizenship, tell important stories, and help improve society at the grassroots level by amplifying marginalized voices?" The course included a nine-week partnership with three nonprofit organizations in Madison that worked with kids – mostly

---

[58] Ben DeJarnette, "The Case for (Community) Engagement," *MediaShift*, January 12, 2016, http://mediashift.org/2016/01/the-case-for-community-engagement/.

[59] Mónica Guzmán, "How to Build Audiences by Engaging Your Community," *American Press Institute*, May 2, 2016, www.americanpressinstitute.org/publications/reports/strategy-studies/listening-engaging-community/.

[60] I've always been enamored by John Dewey's idea that any "Great Community" must entail a moral, conscious communication that is based within relationships; John Dewey, *The Public and Its Problems* (Athens: Swallow Press, 1954).

[61] Service-learning classes are courses that force students off campus and into volunteer work with nonprofits in the community.

[62] I had the brilliant K. C. Councilor, a graduate student specializing in rhetoric, politics, and culture at the University of Wisconsin-Madison, to help me design the class.

youth of color, some at-risk students. One group helped high-school students create radio programming, one built a website with middle schoolers, and one served as editors for children aged 7–17 for online research essays and stories. In the second week of class, I asked the Morgridge Center for Public Service at the University of Wisconsin-Madison to conduct a social-justice training that forced some self-introspection.[63] We spent a lot of time in the class working through what it meant to be "objective," to have critical distance, to cultivate different sources and for what purpose, to redefine what it meant to be "expert" and "official," and to write with loyalty to citizens as part of communities. We used John Dewey's writings about "The Great Community," enacting experiential, relational communication among citizens, as a framework. We talked to community members – from LGBTQ, Latino, Black, and other typically marginalized communities – about their conceptions of journalists. And we held a panel with journalists to talk about how they approach issues involving race. I even had the students read a little Pierre Bourdieu to understand structure and power in terms of journalism.

Somewhere around the fourth week of class, someone knocked on my office door. It was a student from the class.

"I am having trouble thinking about how to do things differently. I keep getting caught up in what I've been taught before."

We talked about how I was not advocating that we throw away journalistic principles, but rather that we just approach them differently. Be critically distant with the facts, but be close to the community. We talked about how I wanted her to try on journalism in a different model, and not to worry about failure. The process of this was what mattered.

Curious, I asked her how the White privilege training had gone for her, a White senior from a middle-class family in Wisconsin.

"Oh. It was . . . uncomfortable."

"Yes. For me as well," I responded. I remembered how, after the exercise where everyone with privileges took steps forward and everyone without took steps back, that I stood as far forward as the space would allow. And some of my students were as far back as possible.

She added, "But it was important, I think. I'm already thinking differently about my biases and what they mean for this story I want to do."

Mostly I was happy that she had stayed in the room.

---

[63] In truth I could not have pulled off this class without the Morgridge Center, which also provided transportation for the students to the sites off-campus as well as a wonderful project assistant (named Gloria Young) for the course.

Appendix

When I began this project in 2010, I was looking to document a whole media ecology in a local community, intent on understanding how marginalized voices might be amplified in social-media spaces. First, I conducted some preliminary interviews with locals asking about big issues coming up that might spur coverage of marginalized communities. This is when I first heard that a charter school for Black boys would soon be proposed by the Urban League of Greater Madison. I liked that the topic dealt with race but also that it was about K–12 education, which I felt was under-studied in communication circles. I started by hiring a group of graduate students to catalogue all the media in town that might cover such a proposal, including any ethnic media, alternative media, online-only journalism, blogs, public Facebook groups, Twitter hashtags, and websites. We spent a summer on this documentation, which also included interviews with journalists asking about how they got information, where and how they posted it, how they determined credibility, etc.[1]

In addition, I read everything I could by other researchers documenting information flows. One of the most influential to me was a 2010 piece by Chris Anderson, called "Journalistic Networks and the Diffusion of Local News: The Brief, Happy News Life of the 'Francisville Four'," because he had done exactly what I wanted to do – track a news story as it moved

---

[1] During this time I began my own racial journey as a White female, taking a series of workshops at the local YWCA on social justice, attending the White Privilege and other race conferences, and reading Ta-Nehisi Coates, John Powell, Michelle Alexander, and others. I spent a lot of time just listening to the people of color around me while also interrogating my own implicit and explicit biases. This was a humbling and often embarrassing journey, and it is one that I am still on.

through a community and document the information stream with all its flows and hiccups. I cornered him at a conference to interrogate him on the method, something called "network ethnography." Network ethnography is a way to triangulate techniques by first using network analysis to identify places for deeper dives into the data with more qualitative methods such as interviewing and observation.

Once the Urban League brought the proposal to the Madison Board of Education, I hired another team of graduate students to help collect all the content, using Google Alerts and content mining programs. From September 1, 2011 to September 1, 2012, we collected content about the Madison Prep discussion and anything about race in the schools. We coded for: author, sources quoted and those mentioned, URLs linked, kinds of evidence used, and types of people included. We ended up with 6,331 relationship coding entries, from the original 1,287 contents, as units of analysis, which created a *whole network* for analysis. We input this information into UCINET, a network-analysis software that churned out the maps you see in Chapters 2 and 3 and also calculated our top influencers in this whole network. (The NodeXL add-on for MS Excel program is also used for drawing graphs in Chapter 3.) We coded every single piece of content, including every individual comment. Key to the success of this phase of the project was Ho Young Yoon, my graduate student who not only trained me in the software but also served as point person on all the technology and quantitative tests. Another graduate student, Mitchael Schwartz was instrumental in the coding. Our intercoder reliability was 0.925.

Tests on the content showed us who the most influential authors and sources were according to which platform in the social network. Essentially I had an affiliation (two-mode) network with the articles as one node and the actors such as authors making up the second node. This represented a finite group, or a whole network because we collected all of the available material about our topic during the time space. Then, we conducted a snowball sampling of the actors for in-depth interviews through a name-generator survey, which provided fodder for a second (albeit more limited and incomplete) network consisting of the private information network (who gets information from whom privately). While Yoon produced the network maps, I got to work interviewing those top influencers. Another team of graduate students helped me do this interviewing of 71 people – journalists, community leaders, politicians, and school administrators in Madison. We also spoke with engaged citizens who were prolific in social-media spaces. Finally, I conducted three focus groups involving an additional 15 parents. A colleague of color, the fabulous Dr. Shawnika Hull, a bi-racial African American, agreed to facilitate these groups so we could have more frank discussions.

Once I had all the Madison data, we scaled the project to corroborate the themes that emerged. I developed a partnership with Dr. Madeline Hafner and the center she directed, the Minority Student Achievement Network (MSAN), which is a consortium of 25 school districts that have documented achievement disparities. We settled on four additional cities that resembled Madison – highly educated (attached to large research universities), mid-sized, and extremely vocal on this topic: Ann Arbor, Mich., Evanston, Ill., Cambridge, Mass., and Chapel Hill, N.C. With another team of graduate students – the brilliant Meredith Metzler and Caitlin Cieslik-Miskimen as well as two incredibly competent undergraduate students named Tyriek Mack and Alexa Grunwaldt – we collected any content over the last five years about race in the schools, catalogued all the media in town, and identified a couple dozen people in each place to talk to – basically mini-case studies mirroring what we did in Madison, minus the network analysis. From this phase of the data collection, we gathered 2,479 pieces of content and talked to another 49 people. Finally, I also interviewed ten international experts on public dialogues about race to help me craft the recommendations in Chapter 6.

All of the texts – posts, articles, comments, and interview transcripts – were analyzed using Critical Discourse Analysis, which helps a research uncover the power dynamics at work in the text.[2] This is where I analytically connected the data to Bourdieu's version of field theory, which I could use to understand the make-up of the media ecology we had documented. Analyzing the texts for presence and absence of sources, word choices, links, kinds of evidence, chosen quotations, as well as looking particularly for evidence of relationships and associations among the sources could get at the structure I wanted to understand.

When the writing was all done, I hired an SJMC graduate student named Catasha Davis, who is African American, to read over the whole thing. She gave me professional-level feedback and also helped me see where my White privilege was rearing.

---

[2] van Dijk T. A., *Discourse and Context: A Socio-Cognitive Approach* (New York: Cambridge University Press, 2008); Norman Fairclough, *Critical Discourse Analysis: The Critical Study of Language* (Harlow, England; New York: Routledge, 2010); Norman Fairclough, Jane Mulderrig, and Ruth Wodak, "Critical Discourse Analysis," in *Discourse Studies: A Multidisciplinary Introduction*, by T. A. van Dijk (London: Sage, 2011).

All told, this book took me six years and various teams of some 17 graduate students and two undergraduate students. The most important part of this research has been the last phase: turning this data into useable information for journalists, public information officers, and others interested in facilitating better public dialogues about race in local communities. Through a partnership with the nonpartisan Kettering Foundation, I am working with journalists from across the globe on how to rethink tenets such as objectivity in covering issues important to marginalized communities. Through my partnership with MSAN, I am working with school administrators across the country on how to connect with different communities in their district. I also turned the data into a service-learning class called "Journalism for Racial Change: Amplifying Marginalized Voices in Local Community," with the help of graduate student K. C. Councilor. The class runs every two years and sends advanced reporting students out into the communities to empower youth in journalism, and asks students to reconceptualize core journalistic tenets through collaborative-based projects reported from within communities. At the University of Wisconsin, we hold dear something called the "Wisconsin Idea," which is the notion that our teaching, research, and service must extend beyond the borders of campus to improve society at large. Though the Wisconsin Idea has come under fire by political conservatives in the state, many of us still here take the commitment to heart and practice it at every juncture we can. Long live the Wisconsin Idea.

References

Abbott, A. "Linked ecologies: States and universities as environments for professions." *Sociological Theory* 2(3)(2005), 245–274.

Aldridge, D. P. "Of Victorianism, civilizationism, and progressivism: The educational ideas of Anna Julia Cooper and W. E. B. Du Bois, 1892–1940." *History of Education Quarterly* 47(4)(2007), 416–446. Retrieved from https://doi.org/doi.org/10.1111/j.1748-5959.2007.00108.x.

Allan, S. *News Culture* (Berkshire, England: Open University Press, 1999).

Allan, S. *Citizen Witnessing: Revisioning Journalism in Times of Crisis* (Cambridge, England: Polity, 2013).

Altschull, H. J. *Agents of Power: The Media and Public Policy* (White Plains, N. Y.: Pearson, 1994).

Amit, M. & Fried, M. M. "Authority and authority relations in mathematics education: A view from an 8th grade classroom." *Educational Studies in Mathematics* 58(2) (2005), 145–168.

Anderson, B. *Imagined Communities: Reflections on the Origin and Spread of Nationalism* (London; New York: Verso, 2006).

Anderson, C. W. Journalism: Expertise, authority and power in D. Hesmondhalgh & J. Toynbee (eds.), *The Media & Social Theory* (New York: Routledge, 2008), 248–264.

Anderson, C. W. "Journalistic networks and the diffusion of local news: The brief, happy news life of the 'Francisville Four'." *Political Communication* 27(3)(2010), 289–309. Retrieved from https://doi.org/10.1080/10584609.2010.496710.

Anderson, C. W. Media ecosystems: Some notes toward a genealogy of the term and an application of it to journalism research in *Professional journalism, new producers and active audiences in the digital public sphere.* European Science Foundation workshop: "Mapping the Digital News Ecosystem," Barcelona, Spain (2013a).

Anderson, C. W. *Rebuilding the News: Metropolitan Journalism in the Digital Age* (Philadelphia: Temple University Press, 2013b).

Asen, R. *Democracy, Deliberation & Trust* (Harrisburg, Pa.: Penn State Publishers, 2015).

Atton, C. *Alternative Media* (London: Sage Publications, 2001).

Balaji, M. "Racializing pity: The Haiti earthquake and the plight of 'others'." *Critical Studies in Media Communication* 28(1)(2011), 50–67. Retrieved from https://doi.org/10.1080/15295036.2010.545703.

Becker, A. Wisconsin's black-white achievement gap worst in nation despite decades of efforts. WisconsinWatch.org (December 16, 2015). Retrieved from http://wisconsinwatch.org/2015/12/wisconsins-black-white-achievement-gap-worst-in-nation/.

Beckett, C. & Mansell, R. "Crossing boundaries: New media and networked journalism." *Communication, Culture & Critique* 1(2008), 92–104.

Benjamin, K. "Progressivism meets Jim Crow: Curriculum revision and development in Houston, Texas, 1924–1929." *Paedagogica Historica* 39(4) (2003), 457.

Benjamin, K. Suburbanizing Jim Crow. "The impact of school policy on residential segregation in Raleigh." *Journal of Urban History* 38(2)(2012), 225–246. Retrieved from https://doi.org/10.1177/0096144211427114.

Benkler, Y. *The Wealth of Networks: How Social Production Transforms Markets and Freedom* (New Haven, Conn.: Yale University Press, 2006).

Bennett, W. L., Lawrence, R. G., & Livingston, S. *When the Press Fails: Political Power and the News Media from Iraq to Katrina* (Chicago, Ill.: University of Chicago Press, 2008).

Bennett, W. L. & Segerberg, A. "The logic of connective action." *Information, Communication & Society* 15(5)(2012), 739–768.

Benson, R. "News media as a 'Journalistic Field': What Bourdieu adds to new institutionalism, and vice versa." *Political Communication* 23(2)(2006), 187–202. Retrieved from https://doi.org/10.1080/10584600600629802.

Benson, R. *Shaping Immigration News: A French-American Comparison* (New York: Cambridge University Press, 2013).

Berger, P. & Luckmann, T. *The Social Construction of Reality* (Harmondsworth: Penguin, 1966).

Berliner, D. C. & Biddle, B. J. *The Manufactured Crisis: Myths, Fraud, and the Attack on America's Public Schools* (Cambridge, Mass.: Perseus Books, 1995).

Boczkowski, P. J. *News at Work: Imitation in an Age of Information Abundance* (Chicago, Ill.: University of Chicago Press, 2010).

Bonilla-Silva, E. *Racism without Racists: Color-Blind Racism and the Persistence of Racial Inequality in America* (Lanham, Md.: Rowman & Littlefield, 2006).

Bourdieu, P. "Intellectual field and creative project." *Social Science Information* 8 (1969), 189–219.

Bourdieu, P. *Outline of a Theory of Practice* (New York: Cambridge University Press, 1977).

Bourdieu, P. *Distinction: A Social Critique of the Judgement of Taste* (Cambridge, Mass.: Harvard University Press, 1984).

Bourdieu, P. "Social space and symbolic power." *Sociological Theory* 7(1)(1989), 14–25.

Bourdieu P. *The Logic of Practice* (R. Nice, trans.) (Stanford, Calif.: Stanford University Press, 1992).

Bourdieu, P. *The Field of Cultural Production: Essays on Art and Literature* (New York: Columbia University Press, 1993).

Bourdieu, P. Sociology in Question (London; Thousand Oaks, Calif.: (Sage Publications, 1994).

Bourdieu, P. The political field, the social science field and the journalistic field in R. Benson & E. Neveu (eds.), *Bourdieu and the Journalistic Field* (Cambridge: Polity, 1995), 29–47.

Bourdieu, P. *Practical Reason: On the Theory of Action* (Cambridge: Polity, 1998).

Bourdieu, P. *On Television* (New York: New Press, 1999).

Bourdieu, P. & Passeron, J-C. *Reproduction in Education, Society, and Culture* (Beverly Hills, CaLIF.: Sage Publications, 1972).

Bourdieu, P. & Wacquaint, L. *An Invitation to Reflexive Sociology* (Cambridge: Polity, 1992).

boyd. *It's Complicated: The Social Lives of Networked Teens* (New Haven, Conn.: Yale University Press, 2014).

Brewer, M. & Miller, N. Contact and Cooperation: When Do They Work? in P. Katz & D. Taylor (eds.), *Eliminating Racism: Profiles in Controversy* (New York: Plenum, 1988), 315–328.

Bruns, A. *Gatewatching: Collaborative Online News Production* (New York: Peter Lang International Academic Publishers, 2005).

Bryk, A. S., & Scheider, B. *Trust in Schools: A Core Resource for Improvement* (New York: Russell Sage Foundation, 2002).

Capital Times. Vote for Mary Burke for school board. *The Capital Times* (March 28, 2012). Retrieved from http://host.madison.com/ct/news/opinion/editorial /vote-for-mary-burke-for-school-board/article_134acd31-0183-58cb-8ced-a8 1e7fabb281.html.

Carey, J. A cultural approach to communication. *Communication* 2 (1975), 1–22.

Carey, J. W. *Communication as Culture, Revised Edition: Essays on Media and Society* (New York: Routledge, 1992).

Carey, J. W. "The Internet and the end of the national communication system: Uncertain predictions of an uncertain future." *Journalism & Mass Communication Quarterly* 75(1)(1998), 28–34.

Carlson, M. "Blogs and journalistic authority: The role of blogs in US Election Day 2004 coverage." *Journalism Studies* 8(2)(2007), 264–279.

Carlson, M. Introduction: The many boundaries of journalism in M. Carlson and S.C Lewis (eds.), *Boundaries of Journalism: Professionalism, Practices, and Participation* (New York: Routledge, 2015), 1–18.

Carlson, M. *Journalistic Authority: Legitimating News in the Digital Era* (New York: Columbia University Press, 2017).

Carlson, M. & Lewis, S. C. *Boundaries of Journalism: Professionalism, Practices, and Participation* (New York: Routledge, 2015).

Castells, M. *The Rise of the Network Society: The Information Age: Economy, Society, and Culture Volume I* (Malden, Mass.: Wiley-Blackwell, 2009).

Castells, M. *Communication Power* (Oxford: Oxford University Press, 2013).

Channel 3000 Web Staff. Urban League Voices Concern About Meeting On Charter School (September 7, 2011). Retrieved from http://madison south.channel3000.com/news/education/57744-urban-league-voices-con cern-about-meeting-charter-school.

Chappell, R. "Missed Opportunity": People of Color Shut Out of Common Council Leadership. Madison365 (May 12, 2016). Retrieved from http://madi son365.com/index.php/2016/05/12/missed-opportunity-councils-change-of-he art-means-no-people-of-color-in-leadership/.

Commission on Freedom of the Press. A Free and Responsible Press: A General Report on Mass Communication: Newspapers, Radio, Motion Pictures, Magazines, and Books (Chicago, Ill.: The University of Chicago Press, 1947). Retrieved from https://archive.org/details/freeandresponsibo29216mbp.

Comp, N. Madison Prep backers seek school board re-vote. *Isthmus* (January 14, 2012a). Retrieved from www.thedailypage.com/daily/article.php? article=35705.

Comp, N. Tepid response to Nerad's plan to close achievement gap in Madison school district. *Isthmus* (February 6, 2012b). Retrieved from www.thedaily page.com/daily/article.php?article=35889.

Conniff, R. Crunch time for Madison Prep charter school. *Isthmus* (September 29, 2012). Retrieved from www.thedailypage.com/isthmus/article.php? article=34790.

Conniff, R. Community members are at each other's throats after the Madison school board catastrophe. *Isthmus* (2013). Retrieved from www.thedailypage .com/isthmus/article.php?article=39317.

Cook, T. *Governing with the News: The News Media as a Political Institution* (Chicago: University of Chicago Press, 2005).

Cramer, K. J. *The Politics of Resentment: Rural Consciousness in Wisconsin and the Rise of Scott Walker* (Chicago; London: University of Chicago Press, 2016).

Craver, J. Madison Politiscope: Madison Prep, unions overshadow School Board races. *The Capital Times* (February 8, 2012). Retrieved from http://host.madi son.com/ct/news/local/govt-and-politics/politiscope/madison-politiscope-madi son-prep-unions-overshadow-school-board-races/article_be1bf564-51c4-11e1 -90b3-001871e3ce6c.html.

Dahlgren, P. Introduction in Peter Dahlgren and Colin Sparks (eds.), *Journalism and Popular Culture* (London: Sage, 1992), 1–23.

Dahmer, D. Town Hall meeting opens up discussion on THE issue in Madison. *The Madison Times* (March 14, 2012). Retrieved from www.themadisontimes .com/news_details.php?news_id=1838.

Daly, A. & Finnigan, K. "A bridge between worlds: Understanding network structure to understand change strategy." *Journal of Educational Change* 11 (2) (2010), 111–138. Retrieved from https://doi.org/10.1007/s10833-009-910 2-5.

Daniels, J. Things I do for white people. Madison365 (August 31, 2015). Retrieved from http://madison365.com/index.php/2015/08/31/things-i-do-for -white-people/.

Darras, E. Media consecration of the political order in R. Benson and E. Neveu (eds.), *Bourdieu and the Journalistic Field* (Cambridge: Polity, 2005), 156–173.

Davidoff, J. Madland: Why Isthmus wrote about the expulsion of a "white, middle-class honors student." *Isthmus* (April 8, 2014). Retrieved from www.thedailypage.com/daily/article.php?article=42458.

Deer, C. Doxa in M. Grenfell, *Pierre Bourdieu: Key Concepts* (Durham, UK: Acumen, 2008), 119–130.

DeFour, M. Meeting focuses on achievement gap. *Wisconsin State Journal*. (September 8, 2011). Retrieved from http://host.madison.com/news/local/education/local_schools/meeting-focuses-on-achievement-gap/article_d994ec77-fo32-564a-8467-b7b29dd3531a.html.

DeFour, M. School Board rips Nerad's diversity proposal. *Wisconsin State Journal* (January 9, 2012a). Retrieved from http://host.madison.com/wsj/news/local/education/local_schools/article_b6193661-f1b0-574b-a88c-b34b0568f23c.html.

DeFour, M. Nerad unveils $12.4 million plan to close school achievement gap. *Wisconsin State Journal* (February 7, 2012b). Retrieved from http://host.madison.com/wsj/news/local/education/local_schools/nerad-unveils-million-plan-to-close-school-achievement-gap/article_8e3e9140-5123-11e1-94a9-001871e3ce6c.html.

DeFour, M. Nichols seeks to unseat Silveira on School Board. *Wisconsin State Journal* (February 28, 2012c). Retrieved from http://host.madison.com/wsj/news/local/govt-and-politics/elections/nichols-seeks-to-unseat-silveira-on-school-board/article_3f090dec-61ab-11e1-b970-001871e3ce6c.html.

DeFour, M. Madison Prep charter school to get first part of grant. *Wisconsin State Journal* (September 9, 2012d). Retrieved from http://host.madison.com/news/local/education/local_schools/madison-prep-charter-school-to-get-first-part-of-grant/article_2ee1034a-da68-11e0-ae3d-001cc4c002e0.html.

DeFour, M. State Journal analysis: In Madison, poorer schools get less-experienced teachers. *Wisconsin State Journal* (September 16, 2012). Retrieved from http://host.madison.com/news/local/education/local_schools/state-journal-analysis-in-madison-poorer-schools-get-less-experienced/article_10472fa2-ff62-11e1-bcad-001a4bcf887a.html.

DeJarnette, B. The case for (community) engagement. MediaShift (January 12, 2016). Retrieved from http://mediashift.org/2016/01/the-case-for-community-engagement/.

Derby, S. K. (September 6, 2011). Urban League meeting closed, unless it's not. *Wisconsin State Journal*. Retrieved from http://host.madison.com/news/local/education/urban-league-meeting-closed-unless-it-s-not/article_fb0ab360-d876-11e0-8359-001cc4c002e0.html.

Dewey, J. *Democracy and Education* (Simon & Brown, 1916).

Dewey, J. *The Public and Its Problems* (Athens: Swallow Press, 1954).

Dewey, J. Authority and Social Change in J. A. Boydston(ed.), *John Dewey: The Later Works* (Carbondale: Southern Illinois University Press, 1987), vol. 11, 130–145.

Dixson, A. D., Buras, K. L., & Jeffers, E. K. "The color of reform race, education reform, and charter schools in post-Katrina New Orleans." *Qualitative Inquiry* 21 (3)(2015), 288–299. Retrieved from https://doi.org/10.1177/1077800414557826.

Domingo, D. & Le Cam, F. Journalism beyond the boundaries: The Collective Construction of News Narratives in M. Carlson and S. C. Lewis (eds.), *Boundaries of Journalism: Professionalism, Practices, and Participation* (New York: Routledge, 2015), 137–151.

Eason, D. On journalistic authority: The Janet Cooke scandal in James Carey (ed.) *Media, Myths, and Narratives: Television and the press* (Newbury Park, CA: Sage, 1988), 205–227.

Erickson, I. "Geography and community: New forms of interaction among people and places." *American Behavioral Scientist* 53(8) (2010), 1194–1207. Retrieved from https://doi.org/10.1177/000276 4209356250.

Fairclough, N. *Critical Discourse Analysis: The Critical Study of Language* (Harlow, England; New York: Routledge, 2010).

Fairclough, N., Mulderrig, J., & Wodak, R. Critical discourse analysis. In T. A. van Dijk (ed.), *Discourse Studies: A multidisciplinary introduction* (London: Sage, 2011).

Fanlund, P. Madison360: On school "gap" issue, there's also a gap between leaders. *The Capital Times* (February 20, 2012a). Retrieved from http://host .madison.com/ct/news/local/madison_360/madison-on-school-gap-issue-there -s-also-a-gap/article_b09fc24e-5b47-11e1-9e63-001871e3ce6c.html.

Fanlund, P. For our schools, is blame the only certain outcome? *The Capital Times* (March 29, 2012b). Retrieved from http://host.madison.com/news/local/madi son_360/madison-for-our-schools-is-blame-the-only-certain-outcome/arti cle_af318e80-a6b3-11e1-affa-001a4bcf887a.html.

Fanlund, P. Next school head may need to walk on water. *The Capital Times* (June 25, 2012c). Retrieved from http://host.madison.com/ct/news/local/madi son_360/madison-next-school-head-may-need-to-walk-on-water/arti cle_9d9cf244-bcb7-11e1-b2ef-001a4bcf887a.html.

Fanlund, P. Paul Fanlund: A gathering of black voices is helping chart our path on race relations. *The Capital Times* (January 20, 2014). Retrieved from http:// host.madison.com/ct/news/local/writers/paul_fanlund/paul-fanlund-a-gather ing-of-black-voices-is-helping-chart/article_d0b5c6ca-88a7-5597-b253-6b221 441c0da.html.

Fanlund, P. Paul Fanlund: Evjue grant to Justified Anger meant as antidote for "our divided city." *The Capital Times* (June 1, 2015). Retrieved from http://h ost.madison.com/ct/news/local/writers/paul_fanlund/paul-fanlund-evjue-gran t-to-justified-anger-meant-as-antidote/article_a57d658a-f45f-5762-b9ff-016e7 29e208b.html.

Fanlund, P. Paul Fanlund: What's holding us back on racial progress? *The Capital Times* (February 1, 2016). Retrieved from http://host.madison .com/ct/news/opinion/column/paul_fanlund/paul-fanlund-what-s-holding-us-bac k-on-racial-progress/article_c6597d53-b5e3-5b21-b290-e2a74d72e69f.html.

Fernando, A. G., Suganthi, L., & Sivakumaran, B. "If you blog, will they follow? Using online media to set the agenda for consumer Concerns on 'Greenwashed' environmental claims." *Journal of Advertising* 43(2)(2014), 167–180.

Fligstein, N., & McAdam, D. *A Theory of Fields* (New York: Oxford University Press, 2012).

Fraser, N. "Rethinking the public sphere: A contribution to the critique of actually existing democracy." *Social Text* 25/26(1990), 56–80.

Friedland, L. "Communication, community and democracy: Toward a theory of the communicatively integrated community." *Communication Research* 28(4) (2001), 358–391.

Friedland, L., Long, C., Shin, Y. J., & Kim, N. The local public sphere as a networked space in R. Butsch (ed.), *Media and Public Spheres* (New York: Palgrave Macmillan, 2006), 198–209.

Fuller, M. *Media Ecologies: Materialist Energies in Art and Technoculture* (Cambridge, Mass.; London: The MIT Press, 2007).

Gans, H. *Deciding What's News: A Study of CBS Evening News, NBC Nightly News, Newsweek, and Time* (Chicago: Northwestern Press, 1979).

Gee, A. Justified anger: Rev. Alex Gee says Madison is failing its African-American community. *The Capital Times* (December 18, 2013). Retrieved from http://host .madison.com/news/local/city-life/justified-anger-rev-alex-gee-says-madison-is-fail ing-its/article_14f6126c-fc1c-55aa-a6a3-6c3d00a4424c.html.

Gerstl-Pepin, C. I. "Media (mis)representations of education in the 2000 presidential election." *Educational Policy* 16(1) (2002), 37–55.

Giddens, A. *Central Problems in Social Theory: Action, Structure, and Contradiction in Social Analysis* (Berkeley: University of California Press, 1979).

Gieryn, T. F. "Boundary-work and the demarcation of science from non-science: Strains and interests in professional ideologies of scientists." *American Sociological Review* 48(6)(1983), 781–795. Retrieved from https://doi.org/10 .2307/2095325.

Gieryn, T. F. *Cultural Boundaries of Science: Credibility On the Line* (Chicago: University of Chicago Press, 1999).

Gil de Zúñiga, H., Jung, N., & Valenzuela, S. "Social media use for news and individuals' social capital, civic engagement and political participation." *Journal of Computer-Mediated Communication* 17(3)(2012), 319–336. Retrieved from https://doi.org/10.1111/j.1083–6101.2012.01574.x.

Gillborn, D. "Education policy as an act of white supremacy: Whiteness, critical race theory and education reform." *Journal of Education Policy* 20(4)(2005), 485–505.

Giroux, H. A. "Spectacles of race and pedagogies of denial: Anti-Black racist pedagogy under the reign of neoliberalism." *Communication Education* 52 (2003), 191–211.

Gordon, L. D. *Gender and Higher Education in the Progressive Era* (New Haven, Conn.: Yale University Press, 1990).

Guzmán, M. How to build audiences by engaging your community (May 2, 2016). Retrieved from www.americanpressinstitute.org/publications/reports/strategy -studies/listening-engaging-community/.

Habermas, J. *Legitimation Crisis* (London: Heinemann, 1976).

Harwood, R. "Yes, our democracy is a mess, and yes, our opportunities are real." *Connections: The Kettering Foundation's Annual Newsletter* (2014), 8–17.

Hauser, G. A. & Benoit-Barne, C. "Reflections on Rhetoric, Deliberative Democracy, Civil Society, and Trust." *Rhetoric and Public Affairs* 5 (2002), 261–275.

Havelock, E. A. *The Muse Learns to Write: Reflections on Orality and Literacy from Antiquity to the Present* (New Haven, Conn.: Yale University Press, 1988).

Heinrich, A. "What Is 'network Journalism'?" *Media International Australia* 144 (1)(2012), 60–67.

Hermida, A. "Twittering the news: The emergence of ambient journalism." *Journalism Practice* 4(3)(2010), 297–308.

Hermida, A. Nothing but the truth: Redrafting the journalistic boundary of verification in M. Carlson & S. C. Lewis (eds.), *Boundaries of Journalism: Professionalism, Practices, and Participation* (New York: Routledge, 2015), 37–50.

Hindman, M. *The Myth of Digital Democracy* (Princeton, N.J.: Princeton University Press, 2008).

Hofstadter, R. *The Progressive Movement, 1900–1915* (Englewood Cliffs, N.J.: Prentice-Hall, 1963).

Hogg, M. *Social Identification* (London: Routledge, 1988).

Honig, M. & Coburn, C. "Evidence-based decision making in school district central offices: Toward a policy research agenda." *Educational Policy* 22(4) (2008), 578–608.

Howard, P. N. "Network Ethnography and the Hypermedia Organization: New Media, New Organizations, New Methods." *New Media & Society* 4(4)(2002), 550–574. Retrieved from https://doi.org/10.1177/146144402321466813.

Hughes, E. We blew it on Madison Prep [Blog] (December 23, 2011). Retrieved from https://edhughesschoolblog.wordpress.com/2011/12/23/we-blew-it-on-madison-prep/.

Jackson, R. L. *Scripting the Black Masculine Body: Identity, Discourse, and Racial Politics in Popular Media* (Albany, N.Y.: SUNY Press, 2006).

Jesse, D. Field trip for black students sparks controversy at Ann Arbor elementary school. *The Ann Arbor News* (May 3, 2010). Retrieved from www.annarbor.com/news/black-student-only-field-trip-sparks-controversy-at-ann-arbor-elementary-school/.

Johnson, M. Driven to act: How I got through racial hazing and how what I learned can help Madison. *The Capital Times* (February 12, 2014). Retrieved from http://host.madison.com/news/local/driven-to-act-how-i-got-through-racial-hazing-and/article_e7852daa-off1-5429-a6f2-61a41fe97970.html.

Johnson, T. & Kaye, B. "Wag the Blog: How reliance on traditional media and the Internet influence credibility perceptions of weblogs among blog users." *Journalism & Mass Communication Quarterly* 81 (2004), 622–644.

Johnson, T. & Kaye, B. "Believing the blogs of war? How blog users compare on credibility and characteristics in 2003 and 2007." *Media, War & Conflict* 3(3) (2010), 315–333.

Kaczmarowski, J. Wisconsin claims highest high school graduation rate in country. *The Badger Herald* (March 20, 2012). Retrieved from http://badgerherald.com/news/2012/03/20/wisconsin_claims_hig.php.

Kemble, R. Secret meeting on controversial charter school in Madison. *Progressive Magazine* (September 8, 2011). Retrieved from www.progressive.org/charter_school_madison_wi.html.

Keranen, L. "Mapping misconduct: Demarcating legitimate science from 'fraud' in the B-06 lumpectomy controversy." *Argumentation & Advocacy* 42(2) (2005), 94–113.

Kharis, R. For many, teenage Instagram photo of confederate flags speaks to larger problems. WUNC 91.5 (May 8, 2015). Retrieved from http://wunc.org/post/many-teenage-instagram-photo-confederate-flags-speaks-larger-problems#stream/o.

Kinder, D. & Sanders, L. *Divided by Color* (Chicago: University of Chicago Press, 1996).

Kovach, B. & Rosenstiel, T. *The Elements of Journalism: What Newspeople Should Know and the Public Should Expect* (New York: Three Rivers Press, 2014).

Kperogi, F. A. "Cooperation with the corporation? CNN & the hegemonic cooptation of citizen journalism through iReport.com." *New Media & Society* 13(2)(2011), 314–329.

Krause, M. "Reporting and the transformations of the journalistic field: US news media, 1890–2000." *Media, Culture & Society* 33(1)(2011), 89–104. Retrieved from https://doi.org/10.1177/0163443710385502.

Kujak, M. Experts debate ways to reduce city achievement gap. *The Badger Herald* (May 7, 2012). Retrieved from http://badgerherald.com/news/2012/05/07/experts_debate_ways_.php.

Ladwig, J. G. "For Whom This Reform?: Outlining educational policy as a social field." *British Journal of Sociology of Education*, 15(3) (1994), 341–363. Retrieved from https://doi.org/10.1080/0142569940150303.

Lamont, M. *Money, Morals, and Manners: The Culture of the French and American Upper-Middle Class* (Chicago: University of Chicago Press, 1992).

Lamont, M. & Molnar, V. "The study of boundaries in the social sciences." *Annual Review of Sociology* 28(2002), 167–195.

Lareau, A. "Social class differences in family-school relationships: The importance of cultural capital." *Sociology of Education* 60(2)(1987), 73–85.

Lareau, A. *Unequal Childhoods: Class, Race, and Family Life* (Berkeley, Calif.: University of California Press, 2011).

LaRocque, M., Kleiman, I., & Darling, S. M. "Parental involvement: The missing link in school achievement." *Preventing School Failure*, 55(3)(2011), 115–122. Retrieved from https://doi.org/10.1080/10459880903472876.

LeBlanc, J. W., Sylvie, G., Hollifield, C. A., Lacy, S., & Broadrick, A. S. *Media Management: A Casebook Approach* (New York: Routledge, 2014).

Lenard, P. T. "Rebuilding trust in an era of widening wealth inequality." *Journal of Social Philosophy*, 41(2010), 73–91.

Lewis, S. C. "The tension between professional control and open participation: Journalism and its boundaries." *Information, Communication & Society* 15(6) (2012), 836–866.

Lewis, S. C., Holton, A. E., & Coddington, M. "Reciprocal journalism." *Journalism Practice* 8(2)(2014, 229–241. Retrieved from https://doi.org/10.1080/17512786.2013.859840.

Lule, J. *Daily News, Eternal Stories: The Mythological Role of Journalism* (New York: The Guilford Press, 2001).

MacMillan, K. "Narratives of social disruption: Education news in the British tabloid press." *Studies in the Politics of Education* 23(1)(2002), 27–38.

Madison365 staff. BEST OF 2015: Harsh Truth – The White Wing Media. Madison365 (December 30, 2015). Retrieved from http://madison365.com/index.php/2015/12/30/best-of-2015-harsh-truth-the-white-wing-media/.

Mansbridge, J. Using power/fighting power: The polity in S. Benhabib (ed.), *Democracy and difference: Contesting the Boundaries of the Political* (Princeton, N.J.: Princeton University Press, 1996), pp. 46–66.

Mansbridge, J. "Should blacks represent blacks and women represent women? A Contingent 'Yes'." *The Journal of Politics* 61(3)(1999), 628–657. Retrieved from https://doi.org/10.2307/2647821.

Marchetti, D. Subfields of specialized journalism in R. Benson & E. Neveu (eds.), *Bourdieu and the Journalistic Field* (Cambridge: Polity, 2005), 64–82.

Martin, J. L. "What is field theory?" *American Journal of Sociology* 109(1)(2003), 1–49. Retrieved from https://doi.org/10.1086/375201.

Martindale, C. "Coverage of Black Americans in four major newspapers, 1950–1989." *Newspaper Research Journal* 11(3)(1990), 96–112.

Marvin, C. *When Old Technologies Were New: Thinking About Electric Communication in the Late Nineteenth Century* (New York: Oxford University Press, 1990).

Matheson, D. "Weblogs and the epistemology of news: Some trends in online journalism." *New Media & Society* 6(4)(2004), 443–468.

Maton, K. "Languages of legitimation: The structuring significance for intellectual fields of strategic knowledge claims." *British Journal of Sociology of Education* 21(2) (2000), 147–167.

Maton, K. Habitus in M. Grenfell (ed.), *Pierre Bourdieu: Key Concepts* (Durham, UK: Acumen, 2008), 49–65.

Mayer, R. C., David, J. H., & Schoorman, F. D. "An integrative model of organizational trust." *Academy of Management Review* 20(1995), 709–734.

Meares, M. & Islam-Zwart, K. "The Real Story": Blogs as a Mechanism for Employee Voice (2006). Presented at the International Communication Association Annual Meeting, Dresden, Germany.

Meisenhelder, T. "Toward a field theory of class, gender, and race." *Race, Gender & Class* 7(2)(2000), 76–95.

Mendelberg, T. & Oleske, J. "Race and public deliberation." *Political Communication* 17(2000), 169–191.

Meyrowitz, J. *No Sense of Place: The Impact of Electronic Media on Social Behavior* (New York: Oxford University Press, 1986).

Mindich, D. *Just the Facts: How "Objectivity" Came to Define American Journalism* (New York: NYU Press, 2000).

Mirel, J. "Old educational ideas, new American schools: Progressivism and the rhetoric of educational revolution." *Paedagogica Historica* 39(4)(2003), 477.

Molotch, H. & Lester, M. "News as purposive behavior: On the strategic use of routine events, accidents and scandals." *American Sociological Review* 9 (1974), 107.

Moore, R. Capital in M. Grenfell (ed.), *Pierre Bourdieu: Key Concepts* (Durham, UK: Polity, 2008), 101–117.

Mumford, L. & Winner, L. *Technics and Civilization* (Chicago; London: University of Chicago Press, 2010).

Nelson, E. & Winn, L. T. Race to Equity: A project to reduce racial disparities in Dane County. [Report] Wisconsin Council on Children and Families (2013). Retrieved from http://racetoequity.net/.

Odum, E. "The new ecology." *BioScience* 17(7) (1964), 14–16.

Oldenburg, R. *The Great Good Place: Cafes, Coffee Shops, Bookstores, Bars, Hair Salons, and Other Hangouts at the Heart of a Community* (New York; Berkeley, Calif.: Marlowe & Company, 1999).

Ong, W. J. & Hartley, J. *Orality and Literacy: 30th Anniversary Edition* (London; New York: Routledge, 2012).

Örnebring, H. "Anything you can do, I can do better? Professional journalists on citizen journalism in six European countries." *International Communication Gazette* 75(1) (2013), 35–53.

Page, B. *Who Deliberates?: Mass Media in Modern Democracy* (Chicago: University of Chicago Press, 1996).

Papacharissi, Z. *Affective Publics: Sentiment, Technology, and Politics* (Oxford University Press, 2014).

Petrocik, J. "Issue ownership in presidential elections." *American Journal of Political Science* 54 (1996), 825–850.

Pfister, D. S. *Networked Media, Networked Rhetoric: Attention and Deliberation in the Early Blogosphere* (University Park, Pa.: Penn State University Press, 2014).

Postman, N. The Reformed English Curriculum in A. Eurich (ed.), *High School 1980: The Shape of the Future in American Secondary Education.* New York: Pittman Publishing (1970). Retrieved from www.media-ecology.org/media_e cology/.

Postman, N. "The humanism of media ecology." *Proceedings of the Media Ecology Association* 1(2000), 10–16.

Powell, J. A. *Racing to Justice: Transforming Our Conceptions of Self and Other to Build an Inclusive Society* (Bloomington: Indiana University Press (2012).

Powell, T. Why young journalists of color leave the news industry. All Digitocracy (August 11, 2015). Retrieved from http://alldigitocracy.org/why-young-journal ists-of-color-leave-the-news-industry/.

Powell, W. W. Expanding the scope of institutional analysis in W. W. Powell & P. J. DiMaggio (eds.), *The New Institutionalism in Organizational Analysis* (Chicago: University of Chicago Press, 1991), 183–203.

Powers, M. "Forms of power on/through the Web." *Journalism Studies* 10(2) (2009), 272–276.

Putnam, R. D. *Bowling Alone: The Collapse and Revival of American Community* (New York: Touchstone Books by Simon & Schuster, 2001).

Quandt, T. Understanding a new phenomenon: The significance of participatory journalism in J. B. Singer, A. Hermida, D. Domingo, et al. (eds.), *Participatory Journalism: Guarding open gates at online newspapers* (Malden, Mass.: Wiley-Blackwell, 2011), 155–176.

Reese, S. D. "The news paradigm and the Ideology of objectivity: A socialist at the Wall Street Journal." *Critical Studies in Mass Communication* 7 (1990), 390–409.

Reid-Brinkley, S. R. "Ghetto kids gone good: Race, representation, and authority in the scripting of inner-city youths in the Urban Debate League." *Argumentation & Advocacy* 49(2)(2012), 77–99.

Rickert, C. Chris Rickert: Maybe it's time to stop tiptoeing around race. *Wisconsin State Journal* (September 8, 2011). Retrieved from http://host.madison.com/news/local/chris_rickert/chris-rickert-maybe-it-s-time-to-stop-tiptoeing-around/article_d5bf3770-d99d-11e0-a10f-001cc4c002e0.html.

Rickert, C. Don't let failed prep school end dialogue. *Wisconsin State Journal* (June 5, 2012). Retrieved from http://host.madison.com/news/local/chris_rickert/chris-rickert-don-t-let-failed-prep-school-end-dialogue/article_91f2249e-aea4-11e1-8095-0019bb2963f4.html.

Robinson, S. "The cyber-newsroom: A case study of the journalistic paradigm in a news narrative's journey from a newspaper to cyberspace." *Mass Communication and Society* 12(4)(2009), 403–422. Retrieved from https://doi.org/10.1080/15205430802513234.

Robinson, S. "Convergence crises: News work and news space in the digitally transforming newsroom." *Journal of Communication* 61(6)(2011a), 1122–1141. Retrieved from https://doi.org/10.1111/j.1460-2466.2011.01603.x.

Robinson, S. "Journalism as process: The labor implications of participatory content in news organization." *Journalism & Communication Monographs* 13(3)(2011b), 138–210.

Robinson, S. "Legitimation Strategies in Journalism: Public Storytelling about Racial Disparities." *Journalism Studies* (2015), 978–996.

Robinson, S. Redrawing borders from within: Commenting on news stories as boundary work in M. Carlson & S. C. Lewis (eds.), *Boundaries of Journalism* (New York: Routledge, 2015).

Robinson, S. Why is this progressive college town so racist? *The Progressive Magazine* (May 13, 2016). Retrieved from www.progressive.org/news/2016/05/188723/why-progressive-college-town-so-racist.

Robinson, S. & Culver, K. B. When white reporters cover race: The news media, objectivity & community (dis-)trust. *Journalism* (2016). Retrieved from http://journals.sagepub.com/doi/abs/10.1177/1464884916663599?journalCode=joua.

Robinson, S. & DeShano, C. "'Anyone can know': Citizen journalism and the interpretive community of the mainstream press." *Journalism* 12(8)(2011a), 963–982. Retrieved from https://doi.org/10.1177/1464884911415973.

Robinson, S. & DeShano, C. "Citizen journalists and their third places." *Journalism Studies* 12(5)(2011b), 642–657. Retrieved from https://doi.org/10.1080/1461670X.2011.557559.

Rousseau, D. M., Sitkin, S. B., Burt, R. S., & Camerer, C. "Introduction to Special Topic Forum: Not so different after all: A cross-discipline view of trust." *The Academy of Management Review* 23(3)(1998), 393–404.

Ruff, A. Ruff Talk: History, not "conspiracy": Kaleem Caire's connections (January 27, 2012). Retrieved from http://allenruff.blogspot.com/2012/01/history-not-conspiracy-kaleem-caires.html.

Savidge, N. No charges against officer. *Wisconsin State Journal* (May 13, 2015). Retrieved from http://host.madison.com/wsj/news/local/crime_and_courts/madison-police-officer-matt-kenny-cleared-in-shooting-of-tony/article_428b0cf9-da97-5951-9936-2f699547ba3f.html.

Samkange, W. "Decentralization of education: Participation and involvement of parents in school governance: An attempt to explain limited-involvement using Bourdieu's theory of social practice." *International Journal of Social Sciences & Education* 3(4)(2013), 1156–1169.

Schneider, M. *Does Culture Have Inertia?* (Newsletter No. 15), Sociology of Culture Section of the American Sociological Association (2001), p. 3.

Schneider, P. Grass Roots: Madison Prep founders won't say much about private financing plan. *The Capital Times* (January 8, 2012a). Retrieved from http://host.madison.com/ct/news/local/grassroots/grass-roots-madison-prep-founders-won-t-say-much-about/article_13becb72-3965-11e1-b72f-0019bb2963f4.html.

Schneider, P. Grass Roots: Race talk fuels tension in Madison Prep debate. *The Capital Times* (January 12, 2012b). Retrieved from http://host.madison.com/news/local/grassroots/grass-roots-race-talk-fuels-tension-in-madison-prep-debate/article_3b5e43fc-3ccf-11e1-b398-0019bb2963f4.html.

Schneider, P. Grass Roots: Dan Nerad wants you to help bridge the achievement gap. *The Capital Times* (February 7, 2012c). Retrieved from http://host.madison.com/ct/news/local/grassroots/grass-roots-dan-nerad-wants-you-to-help-bridge-the/article_6f177c46-51cd-11e1-8aec-0019bb2963f4.html.

Schneider, P. Grass Roots: Will Dan Nerad's retirement help his plan to close the achievement gap? *The Capital Times* (March 27, 2012d). Retrieved from http://host.madison.com/ct/news/local/grassroots/grass-roots-will-dan-nerad-s-retirement-help-his-plan/article_ab29112a-7790-11e1-8a6a-001871e3ce6c.html.

Schneier, C. Tests find readings key area for achievement gaps. *The Badger Herald* (March 28, 2012). Retrieved from http://badgerherald.com/news/2012/03/28/tests_find_readings_.php.

Schudson, M. & Anderson, C. W. "Objectivity, professionalism, and truth seeking in journalism." *Handbook of Journalism Studies* (2008), 88–101.

Schultz, I. "The journalistic gut feeling." *Journalism Practice* 1(2)(2007), 190–207. Retrieved from https://doi.org/10.1080/17512780701275507.

Schwalbe, M., Holden, D., Schrock, D., et al. "Generic processes in the reproduction of inequality: An interactionist analysis." *Social Forces* 79(2) (2000), 419–452. Retrieved from https://doi.org/10.1093/sf/79.2.419.

Scolari, C. A. "Media ecology: Exploring the metaphor to expand the theory." *Communication Theory* 22(2012), 204–225.

Serrin, W. Labor and the mainstream press: The vanishing labor beat in S. Pizzigati & F. J. Solowey (eds.), *The New Labor Press: Journalism for a Changing Union Movement* (Ithaca, N.Y.: Cornell University Press, 1992), pp. 9–18.

Shah, H. & Thornton, M. *Newspaper Coverage of Interethnic Conflict: Competing Visions of America* (Thousand Oaks, Calif.: Sage, 2004).

Shirky, C. *Here Comes Everybody: The Power of Organizing Without Organizations* (New York: Penguin Books, 2009).

Shoemaker, P. J. & Reese, S. D. *Mediating the Message: Theories of Influences on Mass Media Content* (White Plains, N.Y.: Longman, 1996).

Shoichet, C. & Mullen, J. Tony Robinson case: No charges for officer. CNN.com (May 12, 2015). Retrieved from www.cnn.com/2015/05/12/us/tony-robinson-madison-killing-investigation/index.html.

Silverstone, R. *Why Study the Media?* (London; Thousand Oaks, Calif.: Sage Publications, 1999).

Singer, J. B. Out of bounds: Professional norms as boundary markers in M. Carlson & S. C. Lewis (eds.), *Boundaries of Journalism: Professionalism, Practices, and Participation* (New York: Routledge, 2015), 21–36.

Snyder, J. A. Progressive education in black and white: Rereading Carter G. Woodson's Miseducation of the Negro. *History of Education Quarterly*, 55 (3)(2015), 273–293. Retrieved from https://doi.org/10.1111/hoeq.12122.

Somers, M. Reclaiming the epistemological "Other": Narrative and the social constitution of identity in C. Calhoun (ed.), *Social Theory and the Politics of Identity* (Cambridge, Mass.: Blackwell, 1994), 37–99.

Soukup, C. "Computer-mediated communication as a virtual third place: Building Oldenburg's great good places on the world wide web." *New Media & Society* 8(3)(2006), 421–440. Retrieved from https://doi.org/10.1177/1461444806061953.

Sparrow, B. H. *Uncertain Guardians: The News Media as a Political Institution* (Baltimore: The Johns Hopkins University Press, 1999).

Squires, C. *African Americans and the Media* (Cambridge, U.K.; Malden, MA: Polity, 2009).

Squires, C. R. & Jackson, S. J. "Reducing race: News themes in the 2008 primaries." *The International Journal of Press/Politics* 15(4)(2010), 375–400. Retrieved from https://doi.org/10.1177/1940161210372962.

Stack, M. "Constructing 'common sense' policies for schools: The role of the journalists." *International Journal of Leadership in Education* 10(3)(2007), 247–264.

Staff. MMSD gathers input on preliminary plan to close the achievement gap. *The Madison Times* (March 14, 2012). Retrieved from www.themadisontimes.com/news_details.php?news_id=1833.

Stanton-Salazar, R. D. "A Social Capital Framework for the Study of Institutional Agents and Their Role in the Empowerment of Low-Status Students and Youth." *Youth & Society*, 43(3)(2011), 1066–1109. Retrieved from https://doi.org/10.1177/0044118X10382877.

Sullivan, Z. Family of Tony Robinson urge calm with decision on charges for officer imminent. *The Guardian* (May 11, 2015). Retrieved from www.theguardian.com/us-news/2015/may/11/family-tony-robinson-calm-decision-charges-police.

Tajfel, H. & Turner, J. The social identity theory of intergroup behavior in S. Worchel (ec.) (Chicago: Nelson-Hall, 1985), 7–24.

Tapscott, D. & Williams, A. D. *Wikinomics: How Mass Collaboration Changes Everything* (New York: Portfolio, 2010).

Taylor, C. Multiculturalism and the Politics of Recognition in A. Gutmann (ed.), *Multiculturalism* (Princeton, N.J.: Princeton University Press, 1992), pp. 25–74.

Troller, S. Chalkboard: Madison Prep gets closer but big questions remain. *The Capital Times* (October 7, 2011). Retrieved from http://host.madison.com/ct /news/local/education/blog/chalkboard-madison-prep-gets-closer-but-big-ques tions-remain/article_bc33f60a-f06e-11e0-a62f-001cc4c03286.html.

Troller, S. Chalkboard: Will Madison School Board pull the plug on Madison Prep's planning grant? *The Capital Times* (September 8, 2012). Retrieved from http://host.madison.com/ct/news/local/education/blog/chalkboard-will-madi son-school-board-pull-the-plug-on-madison/article_f4a1284e-9012-574e-a91 1-aedb9d7ed708.html.

Tuchman, G. "Objectivity as strategic ritual: An examination of newsmen's notions of objectivity." *American Journal of Sociology* 77(4)(1972), 660–679.

Turkle, S. *Alone Together: Why We Expect More from Technology and Less from Each Other* (New York: Basic Books, 2012).

Usher, N. *Making News at The New York Times* (Ann Arbor: University of Michigan Press, 2014).

van Dijk, T. A. *Racism and the Press* (London: Routledge, 1991).

van Dijk, T. A. *Discourse and Context: A Socio-Cognitive Approach* (New York: Cambridge University Press, 2008).

van Leeuwen, T. "Legitimation in discourse and communication." *Discourse & Communication* 1(1)(2007), 91–112. Retrieved from https://doi.org/10 .1177/1750481307071986.

Wahl-Jorgensen, K. Resisting epistemologies of user-generated content? Cooptation, segregation and the boundaries of journalism in M. Carlson & S. C. Lewis (eds.), *Boundaries of Journalism: Professionalism, Practices, and Participation* (New York: Routledge, 2015), 169–185 .

Walsh, K. C. *Talking about Race: Community Dialogues and the Politics of Difference* (Chicago: University of Chicago Press, 2007).

Ward, S. J. A. Inventing objectivity: New philosophical foundations in C. Meyers (ed.), *Journalism Ethics: A Philosophical Approach* (New York: Oxford University Press, 2010), 137–164.

Warnick, B. "Parental authority over education and the right to invite." *Harvard Educational Review* 84(1)(2014), 53–71.

Williams, A. "A call for change: Narrowing the achievement gap between white and minority students." *Clearing House* 84(2)(2011), 65–71. Retrieved from https://doi .org/10.1080/00098655.2010.511308.

Williams, M. S. *Voice, Trust, and Memory: Marginalized Groups and the Failings of Liberal Representation* (Princeton, N.J.: Princeton University Press, 1998).

Winner, L. "Do artifacts have politics?" *Daedalus* 109(1)(1980), 121–136.

Winner, L. *The Whale and the Reactor: A Search for Limits in an Age of High Technology* (Chicago: University of Chicago Press, 1988).

Woods, K. M. Talking across difference in Maria Len-Rios and Earnest Perry (eds.) *Cross-Cultural Journalism: Communicating Strategically About Diversity* (New York: Routledge, 2016), 19–36.

Xenos, M. "New mediated deliberation: Blog and press coverage of the Alito nomination." *Journal of Computer-Mediated Communication* 13(2008), 485–503.

Xu, W. W., & Feng, M. "Talking to the broadcasters on Twitter: Networked gatekeeping in Twitter conversations with journalists." *Journal of Broadcasting & Electronic Media* 58(3)(2014), 420–437. Retrieved from https://doi.org/10.1080/08838151.2014.935853.

Young, I. M. Communication and the other: Beyond deliberative democracy in S. Benhabib, *Democracy and Difference: Contesting the Boundaries of the Political* (Princeton, N.J.: Princeton University Press, 1996), 120–136.

Young, I. M. *Inclusion and Democracy* (Oxford: Oxford University Press, 2000).

Zelizer, B. *Covering the Body: The Kennedy Assassination, the Media, and the Shaping of Collective Memory* (Chicago: University of Chicago Press, 1993a).

Zelizer, B. "Journalists as interpretive communities." *Critical Studies in Mass Communication* 10 (1993b), 219–237.

Index

Other Books in the Series (*continued from page ii*)